PENGUIN BOOKS

CALL IT GRACE

Serene Jones is the president of the historic Union Theological Seminary in the City of New York. The first woman to head the 180-year-old institution, Jones occupies the Johnston Family Chair for Religion and Democracy. She is the past president of the American Academy of Religion. Jones came to Union after seventeen years at Yale University, where she was the Titus Street Professor of Theology at the Divinity School, and the chair of Women's, Gender, and Sexuality Studies at Yale University. Jones is the author of several books, including *Trauma and Grace*. She is a child of the Oklahoma plains, a daughter of a university president and a single mother, a sister, a cancer survivor, a theologian, a minister, a news commentator, a public intellectual, and a devoted teacher.

* * *

Praise for Serene Jones and *Call It Grace*

"A moving, personal reflection on the alchemy of race, gender, class, and theology in rural America and beyond written by one of the leading progressive theologians in the United States, Serene Jones."
—Michelle Alexander, author of *The New Jim Crow*

"I once listed my dear, spectacular friend Serene Jones as my 'spiritual adviser,' and she is that and so much more. Our impassioned conversations across the last six years, and through travel and adventures together and apart, have shaped [my] writing in a thousand ways and flow all the way through it." —Krista Tippett, author of *Becoming Wise* and *On Being*

"'Theology' is one of those words that sends people in another direction these days, but this book is a beautifully written reminder of what it might mean in reality. For a tired, divided, angry world, this volume is a great blessing." —Bill McKibben, author of *Falter*

"Compelling as well as wise, the theology this book embodies arises from a life fully lived. Serene Jones is a wonderful storyteller whose wisdom is earned—which makes what she has to say both powerful and inspiring."
—Betty Sue Flowers, book editor and series consultant, *Joseph Campbell and the Power of Myth*

"Serene Jones demonstrates the vitality of faith in a dangerous and uncertain world. She writes with passion about her joys as well as her sorrows. A book both inspirational and practical."
—Bill Bradley, former U.S. senator and author of *We Can All Do Better*

"Serene Jones, the first woman to head the Union Theological Seminary, is one of the most visible faces of the religious left. . . . *Call It Grace* discusses her Oklahoma background, her intellectual influences, and how concepts such as original sin and forgiveness fit into her vision of Christianity. That vision, at heart, encompasses the values of many progressives, even those who are nonbelievers. As she writes, the four 'foundations' of her theology are 'the necessity of our interconnecting breath, the importance of struggling for justice, the beauty of mercy, and the ultimate power of love.'"
—*The New Yorker*

"Jones offers a deeply personal reflection on her spiritual journey and what it means to connect with the divine. . . . Moving, illuminating."
—*Lion's Roar*

"Jones is a plainspoken, talented teacher and this moving memoir illustrates her deeply reflective ethics and eloquently captures Jones's response to her life's trials."
—*Publishers Weekly*

"[Jones's] engaging stories illustrate complex theological and philosophical ideas, presenting a vision of hope for the future. This book makes a strong case for the progressive power of theology that will be appreciated by socially engaged readers."
—*Library Journal* (starred review)

CALL

IT

GRACE

Finding Meaning in a Fractured World

Serene Jones

PENGUIN BOOKS

PENGUIN BOOKS
An imprint of Penguin Random House LLC
penguinrandomhouse.com

First published in the United States of America by Viking,
an imprint of Penguin Random House LLC, 2019
Published in Penguin Books 2020

Excerpt from "This Land Is Your Land," words and music by Woody Guthrie.
WGP/TRO-© Copyright 1956, 1958, 1970, 1972 (copyrights renewed) Woody Guthrie
Publications, Inc. and Ludlow Music, Inc., New York, New York. Administered by
Ludlow Music, Inc.

ISBN 9780735223653 (paperback)

THE LIBRARY OF CONGRESS HAS CATALOGED THE HARDCOVER EDITION
AS FOLLOWS:
Names: Jones, Serene, 1959– author.
Title: Call it grace : finding meaning in a fractured world / Serene Jones.
Description: New York : Viking Books, 2019. | Includes bibliographical references. |
Identifiers: LCCN 2018055506 (print) | LCCN 2019006925 (ebook) |
ISBN 9780735223660 (ebook) | ISBN 9780735223646 (hardcover)
Subjects: LCSH: Grace (Theology) | Theology.
Classification: LCC BT761.3 (ebook) | LCC BT761.3 .J66 2019 (print) |
DDC 234—dc23
LC record available at https://lccn.loc.gov/2018055506

Printed in the United States of America
10 9 8 7 6 5 4 3 2 1

Set in Adobe Caslon Pro
Designed by Daniel Lagin

For my father, Joe R. Jones,
and
for my beloved Jones family

CONTENTS

STATION III

Hatred and Forgiveness

STATION IV

Redeeming Life and Death

What Is True

When people have asked me what kind of book I am writing, I have been tempted to name the four things that provide the foundation of my theology: the necessity of our interconnecting breath, the importance of struggling for justice, the beauty of mercy, and the ultimate power of love. I know, however, if I put it this way, most of them would politely change the topic to something more gripping, like a new favorite television series or the most recent political scandal. I'd probably do the same if someone told me this is what his or her book is about.

If I told them, instead, that this book is about the horrific lynching of a young woman and her son in my grandpa's hometown, or my mother's secret life, or a mystical experience I had in India, or the bombing of the Alfred P. Murrah Federal Building by Timothy McVeigh and my concurrent tumultuous divorce, their interest would likely instantly spark. Dramatic topics like these have the power to grab ahold of us, make us want to hear the full story, provoke our desire to learn something we hadn't known or thought about before.

The most interesting thing to me about our innately human draw toward stories is the deeper truths they reveal about our conflicted human nature and our quest for meaning. In my own life, the most astonishing moments come when grace—that imponderable gift of

God—breaks through the surface of life and shines its light on all that is. There is no bigger, more dramatic story than this. When the inner workings of our lives are laid bare before us and we see ourselves for who we really are, and in a flash, it all makes mysterious, transcendent sense—that's a truly amazing moment. It deserves our attention and is worthy of our questions.

Truth be told, everyone has dramatic stories to tell, if one dares to look closely at one's life: the tales of the horrible sins one's family has hidden, the shameful things one has done and regretted, the incomprehensible tragedies that knock out one's breath, the loves that have lasted and the loves that have failed. No question about it, the human drama is endlessly intriguing, disturbing, and quirky. Mine is not unusual in this regard.

But here's the rub. We can tell these stories till the day is done and then wake up tomorrow and tell more of them. That's not a challenge for us. The challenge is using our stories to explore the questions: So what? What do these stories tell us about ourselves and the purpose of our lives? What do our endless dramas reveal about our nature? What do they reveal about the possibility, the necessity, the reality of the divine? So what do they show about the future of our lives together? The fate of our planet? The intractable fact of suffering? The insistent corruptions of power? The sins we inherit? The glories we have yet to claim?

So what?

So what if there's God or not?

If there is, what does God have to do with me? With us?

Look at your life and dare to ask, "So what?" If you can take this one small step, it sparks the divine imagination into theological storytelling, and there begins the theological quest. Living this way inevitably helps us find our theological anchors by which to live with our eyes set on the divine even while—especially while—our feet tread this earth.

A CANTEEN, A CAMP SONG

Theology is a place and a story. Theology is the place and the story you think of when you ask yourself about the meaning of your life, of the world, and the possibility of God.

For me that place sits, windswept but defiant, on a plain in Oklahoma, a spot of red, dry earth in the middle of a farm on the outskirts of the small town of Billings. It has a population of one—a spirit, mine, who has dwelled there as far back as my imagination reaches. I go there again and again, to this dusty piece of land, to remember what is true— and to find God. I go there to find my story—my theology. I go there to be born again; to be made whole; to unite what I was, what I am, and what I will become.

One hot, hot summer day in 1910, "a devil's day," as I've heard it told, my six-year-old grandmother-to-be, Idabel, sat in that spot on a blanket beneath a horse-drawn wagon. She was thin, her skin sunburned beneath her small, white cotton dress. The horse's hooves kept shifting in front of her; the horse couldn't stand the heat. She knew the sun was torturing the creature. Her mother and father, two of the original Sooners who had migrated to that barren land from rural Pennsylvania in search of income and property, were working the arid sod with a mule-drawn plow. My grandmother was watching them work, the terrible sun surely making her realize even as a child that nature can be as cruel as it is beautiful.

And then, as she told it to me with such consistency and precision so many times, she reached out and wrapped her hands around the metal water jug hanging from the underbelly of the wagon. It felt cool to her, so gorgeously refreshing that she brought it closer to her and hugged the jug with her whole body. She forgot the impulse of thirst entirely and clung to the coolness of the metal jug. Every time, at the end of the story, she would tell me that she felt like she was touching God, that she was hugging God and would never ever again want to let go.

She gave me this beautiful story. She told me it so many times that I feel like I lived through it myself—I am she, she is I, and we are one. For her—and now for me—God is coolness in the midst of the blazing heat; God is smooth metal pressing against your body; God is water that you don't so much drink as embrace. My best definition of theology is this story. In fact, I've realized over the years that this story gives me a theology deeper and richer and more accurate than any fancy European theologian from centuries past, despite his or her brilliance, ever could.

That place has for much of my life been my version of Rome, of Jerusalem, of Mecca, of Salt Lake City, of Tibet. It is the holiest of places, the place out of which my ideas and beliefs and understanding have grown, the place where suffering and joy and fear and faith are so interwoven and inextricable that I at last understand what it means—and what it takes—to accept life for what it really is, to let my body wrap tightly around the cooling love of God.

THEOLOGY, NOT RELIGION

My theology is also rooted in another place and story, almost seventy years later and a few hours down the road from the field with the wagon under which my grandmother sat. It was a summer night in July 1974, and I was sitting cross-legged at my family's local church campground not far from Guthrie, Oklahoma. It was a dry, cragged piece of earth beside a receding lake under infinite stars hanging over what seemed infinite prairie. There was a campfire, and the air was filled with smoke and the urgency and anxiety of teenage hormones—and the sound of a guitar.

Every summer as a kid I went to this Disciples of Christ campground, but this summer—the summer of my first taste of sex and fire and music—I was fifteen and raging with life. The hot fire was what I wanted to touch—not cool, holy water—and it was right in front of me, too. All around me, a yearning for more of—well—everything. Especially things forbidden.

The song of that summer—for us and for many people our age across the country in 1974—was that wistful, aching song "One Tin Soldier." Somehow it captured the sadness and hope that hovered over the whole nation.

But we hadn't gotten to that sing-along yet—the night was still young.

In this theological memory, we were singing along to Woody Guthrie's "This Land Is Your Land." Looking into the fire's flames, I recalled that my grandfather Dick Jones, the terrible man who would marry my jug-hugging grandmother one day, grew up next door to the Guthries. "My mother wouldn't let me play with that poor white trash, those Guthrie kids," I used to hear him say, as if he were rich, white, and clean.

So we were singing the song his dirty neighbor had written, verses that I had sung a hundred times at school and at church, words my daughter still sings today:

This land is your land, this land is my land
From California to the New York island;
From the Redwood Forest to the Gulf Stream waters
This land was made for you and me.

And so we sang well-known words for three more verses. Then we came to two jarring verses at the end that completely confounded me. We fell silent as the guitar player's lone voice sang:

As I went walking I saw a sign there
And on the sign it said "No Trespassing."

But on the other side it didn't say nothing,
That side was made for you and me.

In the shadow of the steeple I saw my people,
By the relief office I seen my people;
As they stood there hungry, I stood there asking
Is this land made for you and me?

I had never sung or heard those verses before.

The campfire blazed on and my momentary confusion subsided, the fire and Bob Dylan's "Blowin' in the Wind" easing it. But later that night I asked the scruffy-bearded singer about those extra verses. He told me with barely concealed contempt, as if I were guilty of not knowing the obvious, "This country only wants us to hear the pretty verses. Happy songs. But Woody Guthrie wrote about real life, which isn't so nice. We want to lop off the hard stuff."

I felt ignorant. And deceived. And angry. And yet somehow at fault. Why had I been unknowingly singing this shortened version all these years? What were the adults afraid of? What about those two stanzas was threatening and bad? What had made my hometown ministers want to hide them from us?

I often go back in my mind to this place and story not because it's particularly dramatic or mind shattering, but because over time it has become for me a metaphor for the America in which I have lived for sixty years and for the uniquely American theology that I practice. The religion I was officially taught was sunny, hopeful, and helpful. The version of American history I was officially taught was similarly bright and instructive. But, as my father taught me, official American religion, just like accepted American history, lops off the uncomfortable verses about our lives; about poverty, suffering, cold-hearted exclusion, and raw hatred. Official histories and religions also often lop off the sin and the despair. As Woody Guthrie so rightly knew, those verses are a core part of our identity as citizens—and as believers. He viewed Christianity, in his own words, as an "every day fight" and a faith that "had to be lived" on a daily basis. And singing the hard verses—and praying them—is the only way to live what is true and to believe in what can truly sustain us.

Finding your core stories and then reflecting on their greater significance is theology—not religion. Many people, I find, confuse this simple practice of theology with "religion" but the two are quite different. Religion refers to the official organizations, institutions, rituals, rules, and codified belief systems that human beings create over time in order to contain and manage the power of faith. The biggest concerns of religion are usually order, control, obedience, and maintaining the boundaries of the system itself. Theology, in contrast, tries to rise above religion's rules and structures in order to ask the perennially big questions about the meaning of all life, of the cosmos, of the full verses of the truth about God—or at least as much as we can grasp or as much as grasps us. This book is about theology, not religion.

The word "theology" simply means "speech or words about God." In my experience, most people, at some point in their lives, ask themselves about the ultimate purpose of their existence: Why am I here? Is there a bigger point to it all? Is there a god?

Every time these questions are asked, theology is happening. Most often, these questions surface when we are faced with the loss of a loved one, or experience great tragedy, or are forced to face our own inevitable death. These questions arise, too, when we experience something utterly miraculous, like the birth of a child, or when we behold something that exceeds our normal ways of thinking, like a powerful work of art or an extraordinary sunset. Sometimes they also come amid everyday life when we quietly pause and wonder about the mere, odd fact that we are alive. Whatever the occasion for such thoughts might be, theology names both the questions asked and the search for answers, including those answers that never come.

For me, those questions and answers can be traced back to a canteen and a camp song—an experience of grace and a lesson in lies. Give some thought to what those core stories and places might be for you. And remember that theology, as a universal human endeavor, is not the special province of a few trained thinkers. It's something we all do, whether we are formed by a faith tradition or not, whether we come up with helpful answers or not, whether we finally believe in God or not. Theology simply names the human search for what is ultimately true. For me, that search for meaning brought me to an answer called *grace*.

GRACE: SIX CORE BELIEFS

People often ask me, as a theologian, if I believe in God. It is an odd question to ask an ordained minister who heads Union Theological Seminary, a famous, almost two-hundred-year-old school in New York City devoted to educating religious leaders to help people with their ultimate questions. A theologian like me has to believe in God—and even have a pretty clear vision and definition of God, right?

Well, it depends. If by God you mean an entity that hovers somewhere above us, watching all we do and constantly judging if we are doing right or wrong, then no. If you mean God as a being, like we are beings, or as any kind of an object, or even an essence, as we understand those terms, then also no. But if you mean believing the universe is ultimately loved by a divine reality that is greater and more wonderful than we can begin to imagine, and that in this reality we find our ultimate destiny, the purpose of our existence, then yes.

Based on this view of theology, I can summarize the theology that unfolds in this book in six parts.

1. *God is mystery.* For many theologians throughout the history of the Christian tradition, God has been an intellectual problem to be solved through complex sentences filling large tomes of prose. They've lost sense of the idea that mystery is, by definition, unsolvable. A true mystery is something you never figure out because its mystery lies in the fact that it can never be fully known. So by saying God is a mystery, I am indeed recognizing that I don't know entirely what or who God "is." I admit it; I don't know and I never will. Plain and simple. As a believer, I am relatively dogmaless, if by dogma one means crisp fact-statements about God and an unwavering certainty you are right. I have neither in my belief about the divine. And yet—this is the interesting part—I actually do believe in God, strongly. I believe infinitely and with certainty that the mystery we cannot know is loving; indeed, it is Love, and that in this Love we find our true existence. If that's my dogma, then so be it.

2. *This infinite mystery is our creator, sustainer, and ultimately, our consummator; our beginning, our middle, and our end.* Divine love is the source of the universe and of the dinosaurs, the planets, the elements, and the air, the force that sparked us into existence and baffles us all while we exist, the current of love and joy and beauty that runs through the human experience. God is fertile, fecund, and eternally generative. Believing in God the creator, sustainer, and consummator also means, in turn, that I understand the world as God's ever-sustained creation and us as God's creatures. Existence, in its entirety, from beginning to end, is dependent upon and always connected to and inspired by the source from which it flows, God. To be clear, this doesn't mean I think the world was literally created in six days or that God is up there

somewhere carefully calculating the character of every person who springs to life and what he or she does. It's simpler (and more complex) than that. All life flows into being out of one source, Divine Love, and it is forever deeply related and responsive to that love. That love defines, holds, and promises to be present to the lives that God calls into being. That eternally present love is, most simply stated, my definition of *grace*.

3. *Jesus stands as the truest and most vivid and profound human manifestation of that life force.* For me, raised as a Christian, this is central to my belief. I am frankly skeptical that Jesus was, strictly speaking, the biological Son of God—it's too hard to fathom what that would mean if taken literally. I do believe, however, that in Jesus, Divine Love was fully present in a way that ordinary human beings rarely, if ever, experience and embody. He was completely full of God. Some traditional theologians would call me blasphemous for putting it this way. I call it part of the mystery. I try—and always fail—every day to live like Jesus, to follow him; every day Jesus makes Divine Love in the world present to me; and I know Jesus's story brings me closer to God than any story I have ever been told or any experience I have ever had. Indeed, I see the world through that story's eyes. It is also true that, for me, stories about Abraham, Moses, Muhammad, Buddha, and others often echo these same Jesus-truths I hold. In fact, these other stories sometimes do a better job of making clear aspects of Ultimate Love than the Jesus story. And I'm confident that Jesus would not mind me saying this one bit, for the point of Jesus's life, death, and resurrection is to manifest love's fullness, not to make sure no one else ever talks about it or reveals this truth.

4. *God does not stay at a distance from us but constantly seeks to trans-form our lives by asking us to awaken to the divine presence.* God is a mysterious, creative, sustaining life force. Like my grandma's cool jug, God is there all the time. The challenge for us is to open our eyes, ears, hands, minds, and hearts to receive the truth of God's real, *persistent presence,* God's grace. When we open our-selves to it, we are changed by it. The way we perceive the world shifts, like a radically refocused camera lens, and we experience life differently. You see everything around you as suffused with God's love. You see God's grace everywhere, saturating all exis-tence. This process of awakening to what is already true, but you haven't previously seen it, is called *conversion*—a word that liter-ally means "to see anew." Sometimes it happens quickly, like a bolt of lightning that suddenly strikes, brightening our horizon and exposing us to new realities that were right in front of us. Other times, it is a slow unfolding process, like watching an art-ist slowly scratch out lines and add color and form to a painting whose depth and brilliance grow more amazing with each new stroke of paint, making what is true about life ever more vi-brant and meaningful. Most of the time, this awakening is a combination of both—lightning bolts and an artist's work—and it continues this way until the end of our days, ever clearer, never complete, always mysterious.

5. *When you catch glimpses of this truth, you become painfully aware of how asleep you've been and how most of us spend our lives acting as if that brilliant love of God does not exist, oblivious to it, even disdain-ful of it. The traditional Christian words describing this contrasting reality are "sin" and "evil."* Sin simply refers to all aspects of life where the reality of grace is not manifest and evil flourishes. It's

what happens when we've got the wrong story about reality in our heads. If we do not recognize grace, we latch onto lies about who we are. These lies are manifest in an endless variety of god-less dispositions: hatred, violence, greed, injustice, pride, despair, isolation, self-loathing, unbridled arrogance, a hardened heart, a cold soul. When these lies are aggregated over time, they get compressed into social systems and cultural patterns that look to us as if they are true, when in truth they are not. They are evil and profoundly destructive. This is what it means to be *godless*— to not be awakened to the light of God's love. It describes grace-asleep people as well as whole grace-asleep societies. Defined this way, religious people can be just as godless, if not more so, than nonreligious ones. Indeed, religions have generated some of the biggest, not-grace-filled, evil lies about human life and about God that the world has seen. And many people who appear to be godless because they don't believe in God are nonetheless quite grace-filled in the loving lives they lead. This is part of the mystery.

6. *The transformations that happen to you when you wake up to grace from sin are overwhelming and real.* Your life is radically changed. You want to love yourself and others in a way that reflects the reality that God loves both you and them, completely and eternally. This doesn't mean, however, that the path back to sin miraculously shuts down. The power of sin and social evil are as strong as the false stories and lies that are pressed into our bodies and minds from the moment we are born. You never escape them entirely, and you're kidding yourself if you think you can. When you awaken to grace, you see sin, you struggle against it, but you recognize that it is endemic to the world you live in, the world that lives inside you. One needs to develop a kind of double vision

about one's self and about human beings in general. On the one hand, we are blessed by the grace of God; on the other, we are still caught in sin's grip and left wrestling with its evil lies. This double vision is captured well in the great theological phrase: We are both saints and sinners, all.

This constant tension between sin and grace in our lived experience doesn't mean, however, that they are equal partners in determining our destiny. Because grace is of God, it ultimately wins. We are forgiven by God, whatever horrors we commit or are done to us, however unmeritorious our deeds and broken our lives, because that's who God is. Grace is free; we don't earn it nor are we required to deserve it. That's what makes grace *grace*. It comes unbidden to us all.

STATIONS

This is the sort of theology that runs through my life and through this book; it is built upon the insights and teachings of some of the world's greatest theological minds. John Calvin is the one who exerts the most influence on my own theology, his legacy passed along to me through generations of Joneses. There are also theologians who had enormous impact on my early theological awakening: Søren Kierkegaard, Reinhold Niebuhr, Karl Barth, and my own theologian-father, Joe Jones. And then there are the theologians who matured and deepened my understanding of grace as I grew older and my world expanded: Luce Irigaray, James Baldwin, Howard Thurman, James Cone, Teresa of Ávila, Gustavo Gutiérrez, and Katie Cannon. It's a great loss to our society that many of these theologians are no longer read or taken seriously. Their teachings make sense of so many of the troubles we face; to not read them is to close off access to the very truths that might save us. Time and again, they have saved me.

It never fails to surprise me, however, how many people in America today either look at this theology with elitist distaste or find it intellectually irrelevant. My ardently secular friends ask me for more evidence for all my Divine Love talk, thinking my assertions mere extensions of a liberal Christian fantasy life. Wishy-washy, they'd say. My liberal theological scholar-friends who have devoted their lives to parsing the intricacies of accessible God-talk find it intellectually weak and too experiential. Academic lightweight, I hear them whisper. Some of my evangelical Christian friends and family members quickly judge me a theological abomination, a heretical blender of Eastern and Western traditions.

But one of the many benefits of my theological grounding in Oklahoma is that I try to remain open to these questions and criticisms—as open as the wide plains of my childhood. Granted, I pretty much know what I believe when it comes to divine mystery and love and all the things I don't and never will know. But I also believe that theology is not just a personal endeavor; it is about truths that pertain to the whole of reality. With truths that big, conversation and openness are not just good, they're a theological necessity.

I came to this theology by way of key events in my life that I write about in this book. I came to it through suffering and joy, through doubt and clarity, through hatred and love, and through, most of all, my interactions with other people. I see the power, love, and goodness of our Creator in natural beauty, in food, in art, in music. I also see it painfully revealed through its contrast to the mighty evils that assail our world: genocide, racism, virulent misogyny, violence, devastating poverty, destruction of the earth, corruption, despair, moral vacuity, and the triumph of unbridled greed. But I most see this power, love, and goodness when I feel grace from others, when I am graced by kindness, humor, creativity, striving, compassion. But even these experiences don't capture the fullness of God; they point toward it, not as an object or essence, but as inexhaustible, mysterious divine reality.

The book is divided into four stations that roughly correspond to four stages in my personal theological journey. The word "station" comes from the rather old-fashioned image of "stations in life"; it is a series of places and times that shape our minds and souls in distinctive and intense ways. They are our great awakening moments or our conversion times. Stations also echoes the "stations of the cross," which are used in the Christian tradition to mark stops along the path of Christ's journey to the Cross. As with Christ's stations, I pause at each of my own stations to reflect on the universal theological significance of each place and time.

The first station in this book, called "Sin and Grace," describes the theological story that I inherited from the "old-time religion" that ran through the lives of my forebears in Oklahoma, and through the theology of John Calvin, the old-school theologian who most influenced them—and still to this day influences me. The second station, "Destiny and Freedom," explores the key lessons about grace I learned in the 1960s and 1970s from my mother and father and from my teenage awakening to the injustices of life and the contradictions of theology. The third station, "Hatred and Forgiveness," traces my theological life from age twenty to forty-five, as I evolved through studies in India in 1984, through my family's close proximity to the bombing of the Alfred P. Murrah Federal Building in Oklahoma City in 1995 and the execution of Timothy McVeigh in 2001, and through the separation that led to my divorce in 2002. The fourth station, "Redeeming Life and Death," chronicles events from 1996 to the present that led me to rethink the essence of faith. These include my daughter's and my own near-death experiences, my years as president of Union Theological Seminary, and my struggle with legacies bequeathed to me by both my parents in their later years.

While these stations do follow the rough timeline of milestones in my theological life, they are not presented as a full-fledged memoir, nor do they pretend to track the story of a belief system evolving in a straight line. There is no unbending path to truth when it comes to ultimate questions and perennial wisdom, and my own life's winding road is no exception.

As I share stories about these moments of awakening in each station, it is important to remember that my theology came not only through my grandma's faith but through my own and others' experiences of terror and suffering; not only through my father's intellect but through my mother's unrealized yearnings; not only through the incandescent joy of motherhood but through the incomprehensible pain of divorce and the shock of death; not only through the thrilling freedom of feminism but through the horror-ridden truth of white supremacy and pervasive classism. The inevitable path to grace is through sin. That I know is true, too.

I came to this definition after roughly six decades on this earth, about forty years of which have been as a theologian. So I was a theologian long before I was able to articulate what I actually believed. I still live the stories that keep helping me discover the profundity of the mystery; I keep taking the leap of faith over the abyss, each time more confident that I will land on the other side, and each time less fearful of what lies below.

This theology of grace isn't just personal, however; it's also profoundly political and social. I believe this moment in our history is a unique one for embarking on the search for a new, more grace-filled American spirituality—really for a new (and ancient) American God who can heal and succor and inspire us in such a faithless time. I sense that there is a growing American longing for this theology. As a minister, teacher, friend, and administrator, I interact with people from all walks of life. Most are searching, longing, and yet so many of us are in despair. No one believes in anything; some try, but fail, to believe in that foolish thing called "the self." Nihilism, hopelessness, and moral emptiness reign, on both the right and left sides of the political spectrum. We have grown godless. Especially, but not only, inside our faith communities. The ideas of mystery, grace, love, sin, and forgiveness need to be made available to people in an accessible way and need to become part of the public discourse again. With these concepts we can imagine a different future with a different public language. I believe a theology of grace can help us achieve the kind of honesty and openness—toward ourselves and toward others—required to banish the presiding despair and, as a culture, walk toward grace and global well-being.

STATION I

Sin and Grace

CHAPTER 1

Prairie Theology

The grace of God, which dwells in my house, will not leave it desolate.

JOHN CALVIN,
INSTITUTES OF THE CHRISTIAN RELIGION, 1559

A large painting of an Oklahoma landscape hangs in my New York living room, as it has hung in each home I've lived in since I left the American plains in 1981. It depicts a solitary oil rig surrounded by scattered pieces of drilling equipment and work trailers. The rig stands tall against an empty field of wheat and a shockingly blue sky. More than once I've realized that it captures something basic about my theology. It shows the immensity and gracefulness of my home place but also captures its paradoxes, crude and uncertain. A human creation, the rig contrasts sharply with the nature that surrounds it, especially the huge cloudless sky that fills most of the painting. John Randolph, a well-known Oklahoma artist, gave this painting to my parents years ago, when we lived in the small town of Enid, in the heart of Garfield County, previously known as the Cherokee Strip, a part of what the federal government called the Oklahoma Territory.

The reddish yellow of the prairie and the bright blue sky are so strong that people who aren't from Oklahoma often miss the fact that there's an oil rig in the picture, its unseen pipelines driven deep into the dirt below. No one from Oklahoma misses it, though. Oklahomans who visit my apartment immediately imagine what is going on underground. There's no doubt in their minds but that the large metal figure is busy pumping out black sludge that translates into money. Lots of it. Nowadays, my Oklahoman houseguests can't help but think about the earthquakes caused by these rigs, too. One friend, who told me she sometimes feels several small earthquakes a day in her home there, said that the moment she looked at the painting she saw the landscape fracturing into pieces.

A study in what is seen and unseen, the picture is uniquely American: a richly colored story of land, sky, machines, and people and their struggles to find place, power, and wealth. For some, it mattered little how cruel the cost of their struggle would be. For others, mere survival was their only goal, never fame or fortune. Just life. For most, the struggle fell somewhere between the two, their complex lives captured well by the painting's contradictions.

It also summons, for me, theology, albeit theology told in a uniquely American way. I call it prairie theology.

I was taught this "prairie" version of American theology from the time I could walk. The church where I learned it is not well known today, although during its nineteenth-century glory days it was celebrated as the cutting-edge rebel of American Protestantism. Eventually called the Christian Church (Disciples of Christ), the church started as a social movement designed to unite all Christians through the creation of a nationwide fellowship that transcended the many disparate doctrines and denominational divides that had long cluttered the Protestant landscape. My great-grandparents joined the movement when it first swept across the plains into the Oklahoma Territory in the late 1800s. They liked its simplicity; the pithy slogan "No creed but Christ, no book but the Bible" summed it all up for them.

These early Disciples didn't like hierarchies, which meant that clergy were given no pride of place and minimal performative staging on Sunday mornings. Regular people, not special priests, presided over communion services, which consisted of grape juice and bread shared around a spare wooden table every time people gathered. The Disciples were uncomfortable with anything that smelled even slightly like church decorum; they insisted that just like Jesus, God did not care about creeds or liturgies or incense, or for that matter, about social position or racial rank. In God's eyes, everyone was equal.

This dogged insistence on equality was applied to salvation as well: everyone—even bad guys—was equally saved. They were un-abashed *universalists*. No salvation ladder hung over our heads, waiting for the most strenuously virtuous of us to grab it and lead the way up to heaven. Salvation wasn't a contest. It consisted of the bare fact that as in life, after we die, God loves us. All of us. There was nothing more to add. The salvation playing field was as flat as an Oklahoma wheat field. Little did I realize how radical this would sound when compared with the punishment/reward theology that still dominates so many American churches.

This meant that threats and promises about heaven and hell, that great Protestant pastime, rarely appeared in family conversations or at church. Much heavier emphasis was put on our belief in a God who loved, and who forgave everyone's sins. Because we so ardently cham-pioned forgiveness, it was impossible to imagine why a forgiving God would decide to punish some and save others. Saints and sinners, we were all in the same boat when it came to the ultimate truth about our lives: We were all justified by God's grace alone, which was good news.

As for sin, my church steered away from the commonplace American obsession with sexual morality, instead focusing on social injustice and its moral roots in pride and greed. It was as much about public morals as private ones. The challenge of living faithfully, then, was not about being perfect but rather being honest enough to catch yourself when "unloving" feelings or actions reared their nasty heads in your day-to-day interactions. When you saw greed and arrogance running wild in your heart or in the streets, they had to be called out. Our Sunday school lesson books did not include the usual list of personal prohibitions but rather gentle advice on how to better "love your neighbor as yourself." We also learned to keep our eyes on the local political stage for similar attitudes toward others so that, as good Christians, we could live together as equals in a just society, like the early disciples.

"No question about it. Jesus teaches the greatest sin of all is racism!" my elderly white Sunday school teacher, Mrs. Walker, explained to our all-white junior-high youth group one morning as we sat in the overheated trailer that served as our Sunday-morning classroom.

"So," she said, "don't let the fact that you are white lead you to think you are special or better." She looked at our barely nodding heads, wrongly assuming no further discussion was needed. It was so typically Disciples-like, to make bold assertions about theology and social justice together and to believe it would make obvious sense to everyone.

That Sunday, Reverend Larry preached that "the sin of greed is the greatest of all" as he then moved on to talk about how the early disciples had shared everything, "giving to each according to their need.

"I know it's not popular to say so these days, but Jesus's early disciples were"—he leaned forward to confidentially share with the congregation at the end of the sermon—". . . COMMUNISTS." My kid brain had no idea what "communist" meant. But I got the bigger point. We were supposed to share what we had. For me, that meant giving twenty cents of my weekly dollar allowance to the church as my tithe against poverty.

This all made good sense to the movement's early followers, most of them poor and uneducated, many of them social outcasts of one form or another. The theology of these downtrodden believers reminded them always that even though each and every one of them was a sinner, in God's hands they were all forgiven and graced. This sense of all-encompassing love had to make the brutal prairie life—so full of failure, hunger, violence, and hardship—more bearable and explicable. We so often, I later came to realize, find the version of theology that our life needs.

Not surprisingly, this theology provided fertile ground for the populist and socialist sentiments that flourished in Oklahoma's early days. "If God thinks we are all the same, then why shouldn't our politicians, too?" was the logic that bound church and state together. In fact, so strong was this bond that in 1914 (just seven years after Oklahoma's official formation) 175 registered socialists were elected to state and local offices, making it the most socialist state in the history of the union. Religious language dominated their campaign messages—"Jesus is a socialist!" was their favored rallying cry. One of Oklahoma's most famous socialists, Woody Guthrie, captured this well when he said, "All my songs blow out of Christ." While such a bond between faith and socialist principles is hardly imaginable in today's public life, the state's founding spirit was economically democratic precisely because it was theologically democratic.

In my own childhood experience with this prairie faith and its politics, the equation that "what you believed about God" equals "what you believed about society" was as self-evident as the hard sun above us. If Jesus cares about poor people, so should we. If the prophet Amos loathed greed, then we should make sure resources were shared among us. If Jesus told us to love neighbors and enemies as ourselves, then we should try mightily to do so. And so it went. The God that hovered over this well-ordered world of right and wrong was populist—a God of the people, a friend to the sick and the lost, a lover of the hardscrabbled and downtrodden. And Jesus was right there with us, walking alongside us, giving wise advice on how to live a good life.

Later in my life, as I studied theology and learned to look more honestly at my own family's prairie faith, I began to see that it was more complicated than it had seemed to my childhood eyes and ears. I realized there were more gaps in this belief system than immediately appeared, especially when it came to questions about what awaits us at death, how to endure unrelieved suffering, how such populist sentiments could sometimes produce horrendous action, and how to find the strength when your moral convictions are widely rejected. But to the younger me, it was simple. God is love. Jesus is the friend who shows us how to live. So go out and love and try to live like Jesus. If you fail, try harder. But don't worry, for God loves and forgives you regardless. And remember always, at the end of the whirlwind of life, all of us are graced. It helped hold the anxiety and harshness of life on the plains at bay—even for a child a mere generation removed from the most brutal aspects of plains life.

SODBUSTERS

My people were farmers or, as they were dismissively called by city people, "sodbusters." No one embodied what it meant to be a sodbuster better than my paternal grandma, Idabel Augusta Seitz Jones. Her story is classic Oklahoma. Her father, Charles Seitz, was a stern, hardworking farmer who had failed in various endeavors "back east." So when he heard the federal government was giving away free land south of Kansas, he headed west to claim his share. Leaving behind his fiancée, my great-grandmother Effie Gunn, he camped for several weeks on the Kansas border, waiting till September 16, 1893, when the now famous gunshot signaled the start of the free-for-all scramble called the Oklahoma Land Run. There were seven of these runs over a period of about fifteen years, as large tracts of land were slowly sectioned off, some areas originally promised to tribal members who survived the awful Trail of Tears, and before that, most of it home to the displaced Kiowa, Cheyenne, Arapaho, Osage, and Comanche tribes.

"My father was the most handsome man in the camp," Idabel would regularly tell me as she sat in her upholstered chair in her dark living room. "He used the money he made from selling his farm to buy the fastest horse in the county. Can't remember that horse's name. But when that shot was fired at dawn to officially start the run, everyone knew that my father, climbing bareback onto that white stallion—he had sold the saddle for food on the way—would be out front. You should have seen him ride. He rode like a banshee, that man," she said. "Sweating as hard as the horse.

"My father had already scoped out the plots we wanted near Billings," she told me. "Prime land because it had a creek. He got there first, grabbed the flags with the plot numbers, and was at the land registry office in Enid by late afternoon, claiming their new God-given homestead. He then returned east to marry Effie and bring her back to their new home. They packed a small wagon with dishes and pots, a steel plow, and family Bibles." Looking at those Bibles, my grandma, to her dying day, insisted that those plots were God-given, "our divine calling" to turn its rock-hard red soil into wheat fields.

There was never any mention made of the native Osage people who had long roamed those particular plains. To the Seitz family, it was barren and free, as it was to the more than fifty thousand people who claimed two million acres of prairie on the first land run alone. Like many homesteaders' heirs, we still have the Billings farm in our family; it now supports vast fields of wheat and a few oil wells, the latter something Effie and Charles would have never imagined. Together, the oil wells bring in a trickle of money, but the few extra dollars flowing from that black sludge would have been a fortune to them. For us, it's a reminder that we are not innocent bystanders in the industry that made the state and is now destroying it through fracking. We are part of the problem.

Before the oil, though, the work of turning prairie into arable soil was backbreaking and soul tearing. They called it "sodbusting" because of the hard-hitting, pounding labor it took to crack the ground's concretelike surface open. "People thought only ignorant poor people would be foolish enough to waste their life busting soil," my grandma said. "But we were proud of our work. And we never made a fuss about anything. Just wanted folks to leave us alone. We lived far from town. We didn't have guns—they were too expensive. And if a family like ours made a scene—getting drunk, gambling, fighting, hiring strangers as farmhands—it never ended well. People would sometimes just disappear. Killed probably, by greedy neighbors or cattlemen passing through. We knew not to ask questions. Just stay quiet and tell ourselves they must have just gone back east, the work was too hard."

Quietly, her father eventually worked himself to death. But before he died, he saw golden waves of grain rise up out of his fields. "God's bounty," my grandma called it. That bounty allowed Idabel, her two brothers, Roy and Adam, and two sisters, Carolyn and Effie, to fulfill their mother's dream of going south to college in Norman, Oklahoma, where the territorial legislature had established its first non-land-grant university in 1890, now known as the University of Oklahoma, or, to us then, simply and fondly as OU. That trip to Norman was more than just going away to college. It meant leaving behind their sodbuster childhood, in search of higher things. Idabel never noted how groundbreaking it was for girls in that age to go to college. I have to believe that the example of ordained women ministers in the Disciples of Christ blazed the trail for such a remarkable anomaly. Also, that hard prairie world rendered gender roles mostly irrelevant. She, in a way, was never afforded the luxury—or the burden—of being a "girl."

OU was from its founding a "liberal arts college" where students learned more than the agrarian technology taught at land-grant schools. They discovered the world beyond the prairie and aspired to professions like law and medicine. My grandma studied biology and physical education and played varsity basketball and volleyball. A picture of her in full athletic garb hangs in my hallway. A muscular, stocky, straight-backed young woman, she bore her Dutch heritage proudly. "They called me mannish," she told me once as she pulled out of her closet the disintegrating creamy-white silk dress she'd sewn for her wedding. "Guess that's why I love expensive clothes. They show I'm a lady."

She eventually passed down these clothes to me, bearing labels like Dior and Chanel. I still have them stored in the basement in a box I open once in a while, just to smell her, to see the outlines of her body. For me, they symbolize her strength of will, her dogged determination to always move forward. She also handed down other things to me, especially when it came to theology.

She was fiercely proud of her children's and grandchildren's successes, particularly the businesspeople and the lawyers, and even those who became clergy, like my father, my sister Verity, and me. She never thought we were blood bound to stay in Oklahoma or to follow her path of getting married and devoting our lives to children and husbands.

When I asked her what she thought of my plans to get married, in my twenties, she bluntly asked, "Why do you want to do that?" She said that unlike her, I didn't need to get married in order to survive.

When I told her I'd been offered a job teaching at a major university back east, she smiled and whispered, "You should climb to the top of the pinnacle and sit on it." I couldn't help but think of Jesus on that high pinnacle being offered the world by the Devil. She laughed when I quipped back, "It might hurt sitting up there on that point."

"You'll be fine," she said, winking, reminding me of our Disciples' mantra that God washes everything out in the laundry at the end.

In all these ways, she embodied that odd theological paradox that marks Disciples culture so deeply. On the one hand, she believed in hard work and the success it would bring. Tightly gripping a version of rugged individualism, she saw us as sodbusters, breaking through whatever hard soil we encountered and pulling our fortune out of the dirt. At the same time, she knew we couldn't succeed alone. Our families, our neighbors, our friends—like the woman who saved her mother's life when she was giving birth—were part of the collective that carried us. And, even more, God was constantly there, making a way out of no way, never leaving us alone, pulling for us, promising us nurture, just as God had been in the wagon's shade with her so many years before.

OUTLAWS

Idabel's sodbuster faith couldn't have been more different from the theology that grew out of her husband's, my grandpa "Dick" Sterling Brown Jones's, experience of early Oklahoma. Several hours southeast of Billings, Dick's parents, R. B. Jones and Dollie McMahan Jones, and her McMahan family settled in the bustling town of Okemah, the first stop on the new railroad barreling through the state. As Dick Jones told us, his mother and her brothers, along with the entire McMahan crew, came in 1902 on one of the first trains to arrive there from Tennessee. He was always honest, even proud, about the fact that the whole lot of them were strong-willed Irishmen and that they arrived in Okemah because they were running from the law. As the story he told me goes, his great-uncle had shot a man after losing a poker game and then stolen the dead man's horse, the latter a more serious crime than the former. A horse was the most expensive possession anyone owned. The welfare of a whole family network depended on it; stealing one was tantamount to destabilizing an entire community. When my great-uncle stole that horse, his entire family—aunts, uncles, and cousins— had to get out of town fast. Their story is not unusual; many people who had broken laws and even committed murder back east fled to the lawless land of the Oklahoma Territory. They remained proud of their lawlessness, too, even though many of them, like my grandpa, eventually became lawmen themselves. The line between criminals and law keepers was as fuzzy as a horizon line in a dust storm.

My grandpa talked even less than Idabel, whom he met when he left Okemah to go to college in Norman, too. He studied law, and by the time he was thirty, he was well known across the state as a brilliant litigator, his almost photographic memory a steel trap quick to snap closed on anyone who challenged him. Early on he was appointed as a circuit judge, and then, after practicing law for several decades, he was elected to the Oklahoma State Court of Criminal Appeals. He made money easily, although he never thought himself a wealthy man. But when I'd ask my grandma about the origins of the fine pieces of furniture that later filled their home in Oklahoma City, she'd tell me about Dick Jones's business model and share stories of the troubled families he'd bartered with who traded their personal property for his legal services. The house was filled with the beautiful bounty of these tragedies. Even today I own an antique oak bed I inherited from her, its intricately carved and caned headboard handwoven by a woman in Pink, Oklahoma, whom Dick Jones helped divorce her abusive husband. We never thought of these objects as the spoils of war but rather as supposed gifts for improving otherwise desperate lives.

This blurred line between law and outlaw ran through everything my grandpa did. He loved to recount the times he chased Oklahoma's legendary bank robbers across the plains during the Depression years of the 1930s. He knew Ma Barker. He also joined a police team that followed the muddied—and bloodied—trail of Bonnie and Clyde and their Barrow gang as they rambled across Oklahoma, robbing banks and killing people, in 1933.

The best of his outlaw stories, though, were about Pretty Boy Floyd from Akins, Oklahoma. As he was the most romanticized outlaw hero of the Depression era, we grew up singing Woody Guthrie's famous protest ballad about Floyd's exploits. Guthrie's song tells us that Floyd would burn a pile of the bank's land-title notes before stealing the bank's cash, allowing local farmers to reclaim the land that had been taken through foreclosures.

My grandpa explained that, unlike the Barrow gang, Floyd was just a regular man—like himself, he would always add—who ended up on the wrong side of the law because he was poor and unlucky.

One hot summer evening sometime in the late eighties, I was with Grandpa at his home, and we were watching, as usual, a history program on PBS. My grandpa loved history, absorbing its details like whiskey to calm his constantly churning mind. That night, we found a show on the "age of outlaws." It ended by recounting how local lawmen and the FBI had finally killed Pretty Boy Floyd in a gun fight on Sprucevale Road near East Liverpool, Ohio, in 1934. The narrator explained how Floyd, then Public Enemy No. 1, started shooting at officers who returned fire and took him down.

Upon hearing this account, my grandpa jumped out of his rocker and started yelling at the television.

"That's a lie," he shouted. "It's a goddamn lie. I was there. I saw it. They shot him in the back, in that field. He wasn't even armed. He was trying to surrender when a gunshot nipped him in the arm, and when he fell, that damn FBI man walked right up to him, as Floyd tried to get up, and unloaded all his bullets, point-blank, into Floyd's back. There wasn't anything good about it. They could have taken him alive but instead they flat-out murdered him. Bastards. Those FBI men were bastards."

The house still held the day's heat even though he had installed ceiling fans in every room. He started to sweat so much that I worried he might collapse.

"You were there?" I asked, astonished. This scene had never been included in our childhood tales. "You were in that field?"

"Yes, I was, and don't you believe a word of how they told it." He walked over, turned off the TV, and stomped up to bed. The next day I tried to pry more out of him, but I never got any response. But the more I thought about it, the more Grandpa's paradoxical nature became clear. By all accounts, he was a fair-minded, by-the-book judge. That said, by his own account, he was always aware of the law's potential for abuse and corruption. Be it on the cross of Jesus's or in the field of Floyd's execution, the law could turn bad as fast as the twisted wills of those who wielded it—including his.

FEAR OF GOD

If my grandma Idabel's straitlaced family's theology fell more on the grace side of the sin-grace tension, my grandpa Dick's family definitely reveled in the sin side. Both families were members of the Disciples of Christ and radical universalists. But for my grandpa, the reality of human sin was a stronger presence than for his wife, who talked mostly of gratitude, hard work, and God's love. When my grandpa talked about God, in stark contrast, it sounded like he feared God more than he loved God. He certainly wasn't alone in thinking that way back then.

Theoretically, though, his church's theology rejected any notion of a judging, all-powerful God, as all good Disciples did. Nonetheless, he still trembled at the thought that they might be wrong. Deep down, the judge feared that he might be judged, his sins too great to be forgiven. He never bothered to share with us his personal account of those supposedly unforgivable horrors. But more than once, he asked us to say a prayer for his soul, sinner that he was. Ironically, his own life's work centered on imposing sentences on the supposedly lawless, an often arbitrary, even reckless task. In the same way his gavel would bang after he passed judgment, so, too, did he fear that God's gavel might slam down on his own small, reckless life with a death sentence he couldn't escape.

Another glaring difference between the theologies of Idabel and Dick was how they related to Jesus. When my grandma talked about him, she spoke of his miracles, his love for children and care for the sick. For my grandpa, those sweet Jesus stories held no interest. For him, the cross was the only part of the story that truly mattered.

"Jesus was hanged as a criminal, nailed to a cross between two common, dirty criminals," he told me one Easter. In his mind, the criminal Jesus was everyman, everywoman, and wrapped in his story was the story of all our past and present crimes. Especially his.

The leaders who sentenced Jesus to death, he would add, were just as bad. "Never trust judges like the Pharisees and the Romans. Then, as now, they make up rules to meet their needs."

Funny, but after his diatribes about the crimes committed by everyone involved in Jesus's crucifixion, he never went on to talk about how, with the resurrection, God frees Jesus from death at the hands of bad judges. For Dick Jones, the story of the cross told it all. His version of the cross story also held fast to the Disciples notions of equality—we were all equally condemned as sinners, along with Jesus. It even elevated the criminal to near saintly status despite their sins. But it is notable that my grandpa never sought comfort in the redemption part of that tale. Racked by guilt, the source of which he never named and for which he never asked forgiveness, he was left tortured and harshly judged by his theology.

It wasn't as if he had no joy in his life, though. Unlike my grandma, it didn't come solely from the church. His sense of divine presence in the world came to him from a completely different source—nature. Every spare moment he had, when he wasn't lawyering, was filled with fishing and hunting and wandering in the woods around a dirty old shack he owned on a lake east of Oklahoma City near Okemah. We were only occasionally allowed to go there, because it was his special place. There, he felt like he belonged. No judging God looked down upon him. He felt at one with the sounds and feel of the natural life around him: the scrubby trees, the tall, weedy grasses, the mysterious murky water of the lake, the fish that hid in its depths, the soft flutter of the rising covey of quail he always listened for—these were his divine companions.

He attributed his love of nature to Redman Brown Jones, his father. As my grandpa often reminded us, the "Redman" part was an ironic claim to his native identity. R.B., as he was called, was the grandson of Mary Brown, a proud Cherokee matriarch with a large tract of land she had farmed outside of Cherokee, North Carolina. I have a picture of her— stern-faced, slight but stout, her hair pulled back low and tight in a braid, she stands next to her husband, his head wrapped in the Cherokee turban. We were never told anything about him, but her bravery was legendary.

The Trail of Tears, as it's called today, names one of the most violent, genocidal actions taken by the U.S. government in history. After the passage of Andrew Jackson's Indian Removal Act in 1830, federal authorities forced thousands of tribal people from their lands in the southeastern states. With the stroke of a pen, the titles to vast stretches of land occupied by native people for centuries were simply "extinguished," to use Jackson's favored word. The last and largest removals, the Cherokee Removal of 1838, was prompted by the discovery of gold in Georgia and the rush for Indian land by white settlers that followed. The process was brutal. It began with the burning of registered land titles; then entailed the use of brute force to drag native people out of their homes and businesses; and culminated in the government decision to march the Cherokee at gunpoint through a deadly summer heat and a cruelly cold winter, only to leave them on a useless piece of dirt out west called Indian Territory. In Cherokee, the death march was named *nu na hi du na tlo hi lu i* (the trail where they cried). Along the way, disease, hunger, exhaustion, and murder took the lives of more than four thousand, almost a quarter of the seventeen thousand Cherokee prisoners. My grandpa told us some of our ancestors died on the death march, but their names remain, to this day, a mystery—so total was their annihilation.

Dick Jones still growled out Mary Brown's name, though. As he told us on one of the rare occasions when he went into detail, she refused to leave when U.S. troops arrived at her door. The rest of her family was forced to join the march, but Mary never left her land. As to what became of her after the troops left, nothing is known. I like to think she lived there long beyond her years; that her spirit still does. She certainly lived on in Dick Jones's memory and habits. His speech was sprinkled with Cherokee words not even he knew the full meaning of. There were also the haunting chants he would hum at night in his rocker, fragments of a past that lingered within him, wistful and soft.

It has long struck me that the family tree that traces my Oklahoma kin looks more like a scrappy, short-rooted scrub oak than the deep-rooted hardwoods we typically imagine when we think of ancestral lines. Unlike a thick-branched maple or a towering pine, our scrubby family branches grew low to the ground, sprawling outward in untamed twists of fate and lineage. In the wilds of an unsettled land, Dollie McMahan, a woman born to a Tennessee-Irish family, found herself in Okemah, Oklahoma, married to Redman Brown Jones, a man born to Cherokee survivors of a genocidal march. Out of the odd sprawl of their union came my grandpa, Dick, a judge who condemned criminals all the while fearing his own destiny lay among the unforgiven. In time, he, too, spread our gnarled branches further by wedding my grandma, Idabel, the staunchly upright daughter of homesteaders. Unlike him, she found God's love, not judgment, in a wagon-shaded jug, with rock-hard earth stretching out around her as far as the eye could see. Like most life forms that dared to plant themselves on those plains, it's a miracle that any of them survived. Not only that, they grew strong enough for generations of Joneses to spread out around them. Still scrubby and tangled, yes. And still startlingly alive.

CHAPTER 2

Buried Treasure

Oh! this old-time religion,
This old-time religion,
This old-time religion,
It is good enough for me.
Makes me love everybody,
Makes me love everybody,
Makes me love everybody,
And it's good enough for me.

FISK JUBILEE SINGERS, 1872

Here, she wanted you to have these. They're yours now," my aunt Carolyn explained to me as she handed me a box filled with Grandma Idabel's beloved books. There weren't many, only a dozen or so dried-up leather volumes, most of them family Bibles. Scanning the pile, I gently lifted out just one. The one she'd treasured the most. John Calvin's 1559 version of the *Institutes of the Christian Religion*. Fine red dust long settled on its pages coated my fingers. It smelled like Billings, Oklahoma.

It was June 1994, and my family had buried my grandma the day before in the family plot in the old cemetery just outside Okemah.

Grandma had first shown me the book over a decade before, in the early 1980s, but back then she had not allowed me to even touch it.

"My father, Charles, who never went to college, mind you, carried this book all the way from back east," she told me as she pulled it out from her bedside table one afternoon. "He treasured it like a Bible. Lit a candle to read it at night, especially when he was worrying over things, a long dry spell or grasshoppers that sometimes infested our summer wheat. He told me reading it calmed him down and gave pleasant order to his thoughts when troubles threatened to overwhelm him."

When she first told me this story, I had been surprised to learn that my great-grandfather—the one on the white stallion—had read theology, especially something that looked as dense and weighty as the book she held in both hands. She explained that Charles's father and his father before him had done the same, and so had others in his family, as far back as he could remember. For all of them, she said, Calvin's *Institutes* was the basic textbook where they learned what they believed and remembered who they were.

"I don't mean they didn't read the Bible, too," she added, as if by talking about the *Institutes* this way, she had somehow left Jesus behind. "Of course we did. But my father told me that Calvin was more plainspoken than scripture. More practical."

"Have you read it, too?" I asked, my curiosity about Calvin growing greater by the minute.

"Heavens, no, child. I've never even opened the book. I prefer the women's devotionals from church. But still, I love having it close to me. I knew that the ministers and elders who taught us had read it, like my father had, and I trusted what they said."

"But, Grandma, if it's this important, why have I never heard anyone at my church talk about Calvin or this *Institutes* book? Not even my dad talks about it, and you know how he loves talking theology." It struck me as odd that here I was, the daughter of a minister and theologian, hearing about this supposedly precious book of theology for the first time and not from him but from my grandma, a woman who mostly told sweet Jesus stories when she talked about God.

She leaned forward, as if sharing a secret.

"This, my dear," she said, tapping her finger on the book now resting on her lap, "is old-time religion. The strong kind. Medicine for what ails you. Not that newfangled gibberish they teach in church today." She paused. "But let's keep that last part just between you and me, all right?"

She stood up and carefully returned the book she never read but loved to have on her bedside table. "I think it's time for a Coke, don't you?"

By the time my grandma died ten years later, I had left Oklahoma for Yale Divinity School to enroll full-time in theological studies, and in the process, I had imbibed fully of that "medicine for what ails you." In fact, when my aunt handed me the box with my grandma's copy of the *Institutes* in it, I had already read my newer two-volume version from cover to cover at least half a dozen times. Today, the inherited copy sits inside a glassed-in bookshelf in the corner of my bedroom, a worn witness to her history, to mine, and, in many ways, to America's. On my own bedside table sits my working copy, its dog-eared pages and pencil-scribbled margins a testament to its continued influence on my life and thought.

Maybe it was because of some quirky love-of-Calvin gene passed on to me from Idabel, and Charles and their kin. Maybe it was because my beloved grandma had so intriguingly prepped me for it. Whatever the reason, from the moment I started reading the *Institutes*, I was as consumed by it as her father had been. Little did my grandma know that the afternoon in her bedroom had initiated a theological journey that would bring me face-to-face, so to speak, with the historical figure who would influence my theology more than any other. Like generations of women and men before me, that old-time religion of Calvin's held me fast in its grip from the moment I entered its orbit.

What exactly was so compelling about it? The theologian Karl Barth once said of his first journey into Calvin's *Institutes*, it was as if he found himself wandering through "a primeval forest." To that I would add, "And was awestruck by its wonders and sheer majesty." The beauty of its theological vision is all-consuming, its language captivating.

But for me its appeal was more than just the beauty of its words. When I first read Calvin's *Institutes*, I experienced—and still do to this day—the strange sensation of falling backward in time, breaking through the surface of my modern belief system and plunging downward into an ancient subterranean cavern filled with images and stories that flow like underground streams through everything I know about God, myself, and the world. It is an uncanny experience—opening a book and falling into a world of ideas that you immediately recognize as living inside you, but before that moment you were completely unaware of their presence in your life. And those familiar but unexplored ideas were "the strong kind"—big, basic ideas about good and evil, life and death, hatred and love, God and humanity, and the meaning of life itself. In Calvin, I quite literally hit the bedrock of my theology— and the universe.

CALVIN AND THE AMERICAN STORY

Reading Calvin helped me to understand more fully the worldview that allowed my family to survive all those years on the plains. Our family's prairie-style Disciples faith was, I learned, saturated with images and concepts that Calvin had first articulated almost five hundred years earlier. It also revealed more about the deep theological currents that run not just through Disciples thought but through almost every kind of Protestantism practiced in the United States today. Presbyterians, Congregationalists, Reformed Christians, and Evangelical communities are the groups that most openly acknowledge their debt to Calvin. But the founding theology of all varieties of Episcopalians, Methodists, and Baptists also emerged from leaders who eagerly drank from those same Calvinist waters. Indeed, it is impossible to understand even the most basic things about Christianity in America without plumbing the depths of the theological book where much of it originated.

There is more to Calvin's influence than his directly religious legacy reveals, however. Reading his *Institutes* helped me to understand, more than any political science textbook or historical study ever had, the deep theological undercurrents that flow through the very heart of American culture, even in its most secular forms. Although it is rarely named as such, Calvin's theology shaped core features of our distinctive American identity, especially the subterranean world of American impulses and assumptions that exists within our collective American unconscious. You hear echoes of Calvin's core ideas in the patriotic songs we sing, the Pledge of Allegiance we ritually chant, and the Constitution that forms our foundation; and still today, you hear it in the varied speeches and slogans that pepper American political campaigns, on both sides of the aisle, as well as in the chants and slogans of those who protest our policies, pressing us beyond the limits of the system we have. Across the spectrum, Calvin's thought undergirds the most fundamental tale we tell ourselves about who we are and where we should be going.

By making these claims about the importance of Calvin in understanding almost everything Protestant and many things American, I do not mean to imply that other religious traditions and a vast array of cultures and histories have not played key roles in shaping America's past and present. Our nation's theological undercurrents are rich, diverse, and constantly changing. I also do not want to suggest that the

influence of Calvinists has always been positive. Nor do I believe that
our Calvin-anchored American tale has only one version. To the contrary, our takes on the basic Calvinist tale are as wildly diverse as we
are. Still, running through them all are core ideas and an anchoring
story line.

The world, as Calvin describes it, is a light-filled place where God's
glory shines so brightly that no part of the human condition is left hidden in shadows or closeted away. Divine glory illumines all. Whatever
may be your condition or state, Calvin shows that the divine is there,
in your exact spot, sharing your plight and lifting you upward toward
glory. The sheer force of Calvin's eloquence takes you to that elevated
divine place and makes you feel it. It becomes real. Palpable. Visceral.
And standing in the brilliance of that light, you are neither diminished
nor shamed but rather fully and completely known, both your flaws and
your greatness revealed and claimed. It's an all-consuming experience
of life unfolding, in its entirety, in the presence of God's love. Call it
grace. Put in more secular terms, it imbues a pervasive sense that as a
collective people, we are completely known and guided by an ultimate
"good" that is both greater than we are and yet personally close to us.

As to what that "unfolding life" consists of, Calvin begins the Institutes by describing the grave plight of the people he was originally
writing to. In 1559, that audience consisted primarily of French evan-
gelicals who were being persecuted by the king of France because of
their religious beliefs. But as Calvin describes it, that audience could
be almost any community or person who experiences life as a difficult
struggle against earthly forces that threaten them. The central human
protagonist—which is every single human being at the end of the day—is
an underdog, the little guy or gal, the besieged in all of us. You could
be a sodbusting Sooner, a terrorized Cherokee, a fleeing horse thief, a
disillusioned lawman, an unlucky fisherman, a lonely plains woman,
or even an all-powerful judge plagued by hidden fears. According to

Calvin's story about humanity, almost no one falls outside this broad description. To be human is to be downtrodden and struggling against the odds, whatever those odds might be.

Speaking to the downtrodden, Calvin then acknowledges that the task of simply staying alive under such conditions, much less thriving amid them, is hard. At times, it is seemingly impossible. But he encourages you to move forward nevertheless. Resist whatever impedes your journey, overcome whatever adversity assails you, survive the onslaught of life's evils. And do so knowing God is with you all along the way, encouraging you, pulling for you, giving you the strength you need to keep on going, even when you stumble and fall. This divine imperative to strenuously press forward in the face of life's hardships is constant. In fact, it's the most basic feature of Calvin's story of humanity's quest. The call to move forward, the goad to reach toward ever-greater things, the desire to advance—again, it is hard to miss the resonance between this core image and that deep American cultural will that, against all odds, strains toward progress.

HUMAN NATURE

This is not the whole of the story, though. Calvin was a keen observer of human nature, of that gulf between our interior nature and exterior behavior. He tells us: If you want to move forward, first and foremost, you must understand yourself—which inevitably involves understanding the God who put you here. To aid our understanding, he lays out a complex picture of human nature, a nature that is always intertwined with divine nature. The picture constitutes the real essence of Calvin's thought and reveals the part of his theology that lingers most persistently in our culture.

His is a multilayered portrait of humanity, drawn heavily from the writings of the Catholic Saint Augustine and, before him, the letters of Paul in the New Testament and the stories about David in the Hebrew Bible. Each layer is superimposed upon the next, creating a picture that is more like a holographic image than a static photograph. We are many things all at the same time.

The first layer is beautiful. Calvin believed that we are remarkable creatures, capable of great love and stunning feats of intellect and invention. We see beauty around us and create art that captures the largeness of our imaginations. The vast mysteries of the world are there for us to discover, as we should always seek to do, and the scope of our ability to build just and good societies is endless. We are marvelously made: resilient, smart, creative, good-willed. All of us—every living being and every inch of universe—shine with the glory of the God who created it all.

The second layer of his portrait, however, shows that we are also the opposite of this. We are fragile and fearful creatures. Composed of mere flesh and bones, we are easily felled by natural and human forces, the coverings of our mortal lives too thin to protect us. We are also strangely drawn toward things that are not good for us, evil things. For reasons we never quite grasp, we refuse our marvelous nature and turn our energies toward harmful endeavors of endless variety. Just as we cannot help but be wondrous—it's our nature—so, too, we cannot help but turn away from the good and reach toward destruction.

The word for this is the old-fashioned term "sin," and for Calvin, humanity's sin is "original"—as in "original sin." "Original" means that it is a core part of us, not something we can just shrug off. It is an endemic and inevitable feature of our lives, originating ceaselessly in the mystery of our freedom, "spewing forth ever new flames of depravity." For him, sin names not only the bad things people do; it describes, too, the destruction that can happen to us because of others' actions. He also didn't see sin exclusively as the product of individuals. Sin lives in the social systems and structures that we collectively create: exploitative economic systems, unjust and biased legal systems, culturally habituated racial hatreds, deeply imbedded restrictions on gender and sexual expression, and so forth. On and on goes the list of our collective sin.

The most egregious sin is humanity's will to be powerful in a way only God is—to control our own destiny, to assert our prideful will and allow greed and our unquenchable thirst for power to dominate our minds and compel our actions. Everyone wrestles with these desires, Calvin insists, and if you think you don't, then look in the mirror more closely. The flip side of the sin of pride is our equally strong propensity to simply give up, become passive, and throw away our glorious, God-given potential when faced with such evils. This is sin as well, albeit the sin of weakness, of concession and not willful assertion. Like pride, this capacity exists in everyone.

The examples Calvin gives of both dimensions of sin—their classical names are "hubris" and "concupiscence"—are so cutting and accurate that he could have pulled them straight from today's headlines: our unfettered hunger for more and more money, more and more power, and more and more control over the lives of others, and along with these, our easily triggered use of violence to get what we want. We also see it in the mass use of drugs, alcohol, and other addictions that pull us under, as well as in the pervasive sense of despair that befalls us when we simply put our heads down and give up, the odds against us too mighty to resist.

The existential depth and breadth of Calvin's understanding of sin is stunning and, to me, rings more true than ever. It is a terrible loss to our culture that such a rich account has been so disregarded or even ridiculed. When people hear "Calvin," the instinctual response is to see him as the guy obsessed with shame who thinks we are bad through and through. Nothing could be further from the truth. Yes, he did believe we all have within us the capacity to thwart the thriving of others and of ourselves.

But it's not just a personal capacity; it's broadly social—something we spend far too little time reflecting on or acting against. It is also crucial to remember that Calvin's portrait of human nature has super-imposed over this sinful account a portrait of our positive capacity—our brilliance and our capacity to love. This side of our nature is just as powerful, if not more so, than the sin side. And herein lies the most important feature of his account of human nature: his insistence that we are at the same time both magnificent and sinful, both saint and sinner, both graced and fallen, and that neither side of us ever disappears. That is what makes our human quest for progress such a vexing and difficult quest. The war inside us rages as fiercely as the warring world around us. It is enormously helpful, he believes, if we have enough self-awareness to see this. If we do not, we are hampered from the start, confused, reckless, and incapable of taking responsibility for who we are and what we could become. Our tumultuous world becomes the mere reflection of our unknowing selves. In such a state, the "progress" we pretend we are making is a lie as distorted as the lies we agree to tell about who we really are.

To aid the growth of our self-awareness, Calvin adds a few more layers to his portrait of humanity. He believed that within each of us, there was "a seed of divinity" that intuitively sparks in us an awareness of the divine. We get an inkling of this when we behold the vastness of the heavens or stand awed before the exquisite complexity of planetary interconnectedness. It feels sacred to us, even when we're mired in the negative. We also become aware of divinity when we do harmful things—or have them done to us—and our conscience strikes us with a terrible intuitive knowledge that these things are wrong. While we do not always recognize this seed for what it is, it's always there, opening us toward the divine, even in our dreams.

And therein lies the most important aid we are given in our human quest for God.

From the beginning of time, Calvin tells us, people have looked at their lives and wondered if they might be part of a greater reality that holds it all together, the marvelous and the broken. For Calvin, as a Christian theologian, this sparking knowledge of divine reality points us toward the Bible and toward Jesus, who manifests God. But he also insists that even without the Bible, nature itself gives us the same testimony to God's good intentions for us. The Bible just says more plainly what the world itself shows. Not only is there a God but this God also cares about us, wants us to live good and beautiful lives, and promises to help us. The fact that nature itself bears witness to this reality is key to understanding how a secular version of Calvin's tale of humanity is possible. If you don't see it in Jesus, then the world itself—its natural laws, its insistent progress, its place in our conscience—narrates the same story for you. Again, it is hard not to hear the voices of America's deistic, nature-loving founders, much less many of today's nontheistic, humanist American leaders echoing in Calvin's tale: "Conscience is our guide."

Interestingly, Calvin doesn't try to prove the existence of the God who implants this seed, either by logical reasoning or by painting an abstract picture of an otherworldly divine reality. For him, the divine is not a thing we can analyze like an insect pinned on a specimen tray. Instead, God becomes known to us only through the work of God's "hands and feet" as they bestow upon us divine gifts that, if accepted, give us the strength needed to carry the weight of life's journey. These gifts are not those of a godlike puppeteer orchestrating our lives from on high. Rather, they are gifts of insight and practice that allow us, through our own free will, to live within the sin-grace tensions—never perfectly, mind you, but with a semblance of joy, especially when things are hard.

For Calvin, the rarest and most important gift that God bestows is the sheer, wondrous awareness of our existence in this complex, expansive universe. And when we pause long enough to appreciate this, he believed, we experience the gift of gratitude. For him, gratitude wasn't a passing moment when we offer a quick "thank you" to God. Rather, gratitude is a state of being in which we realize with bone-deep, all-encompassing awe that we could not exist—and yet we do, as does the world. With this realization comes awareness of our utter contingency—and the contingency of everything.

It could not be . . . but it is; it is . . . but it could not be.

God is the word we use to describe the continuing source of this miracle. For Calvin, this doesn't mean that God is a clockmaker who millions of years ago set the world ticking or a magical lord who in seven days whipped us up out of nothing. The miracle is much more profound than that. Imagine all that is, and was, and ever will be, including time itself and everything that may exist beyond time—this entire reality, Calvin tells us, is not a given. It is a gift. The most supreme and loving gift of all. And once you see this, every cell in your being and each thought in your mind is flooded with gratitude.

You then begin to realize that in some mysterious, ultimate way you belong to God. And this is comforting, especially when you feel stripped bare by your plight, alone and naked. God is there. There is also the spontaneous gift that comes to you as a deep desire to be a good, loving person, just as God has been good and loving to you. And there is the gift of prayer. For Calvin, the purpose of prayer is not to get God to give you wealth, fix your mistakes, or heal your mother's cancer. It is a simple but constant practice of consciously lifting up our messy, mixed-up, hard-hearted lives before God, and in doing so, knowing that God is present.

As for the promise and threat of heaven and hell—something generations of Christians have used as a goad to live better lives—Calvin's

view is complicated, and more nuanced than meets the eye. He believed, based on scripture, that "in principle," either divine blessedness
or eternal damnation could await us when we die. That said, he rightly
worried about the human tendency to use heaven's reward and hell's
torture as our primary motivation for behaving well. It is not a good or
satisfying way to live. We should want to do good because we are grateful for the blessing of life itself, not because we are terrified of punishment or are competing to win the ultimate prize of heaven. To counter
this tendency, Calvin insisted that we treat everyone, including ourselves, as if we are *all* destined for eternal blessedness. For all we know,
it may well be the case that hell is a place where no one lives. Moreover,
given the limits of what we know, the social consequences of believing
everyone is saved are much better than those that follow from a view
where we divide the world into the damned and the treasured. So,
practically speaking, believing in universal salvation is our best bet.

As to the mechanics of this eternal salvation, Calvin urged us not
to occupy our minds with its details because, finally, its beauty is something we are unable even to minimally grasp. It remains a mystery to
us. But even in its mystery, there are at least two consoling things to
be said about what awaits us when we die. First, just as God loves us
and is with us in this life, so, too, God loves us and is with us in and
beyond death. God's loving presence is eternal. That's what heaven is.
Second, God created each of us as particular people with our own histories and identities, and these very particular, individual lives are the
lives that God loves. When we die, God doesn't stop loving us. That
love of our particular selves and histories continues eternally.

Trying to firmly grasp what this actually means, however, is a fool's
errand. It exceeds what we can know, and trying to know more than we
can distracts us from the here and now, where all of our energies should
be focused. Is this enough for us to know about life beyond death? If
fear of dying is the only connection you have to God, then probably

not. You'll want more assurance, even if it's false. But if the whole of your existence is illumined with grace, this understanding of eternal life makes a kind of perfect, peaceful sense. And what more could one want than the beautiful "everything" you have already received, the form of the sheer gift of existence itself.

Calvin courses through my life. In fact, many of the theologians I depend on to survive are avowed Calvinists: Kierkegaard, Niebuhr, and Barth. And most of those who aren't avowed Calvinists come pretty close to sharing his bedrock worldview, albeit in constantly shifting form. It may seem odd to build my American theology around the thought and meditations of a long-dead white European male like Calvin, whose experience of the world was so different from the diverse lives that comprise America. But, frankly, theology is pretty odd to begin with, existing on a plane beyond the superficial and focusing on the single, unifying story—the human one. Theology tries—but often fails—to rise above all the muck of history, racism, sexism, violence, and trauma. Theology seeks to grasp us fully and gracefully.

Calvin is my theological base, and I unabashedly read the vast array of theologians who succor me through the lens of his bedrock theology. Many Calvinists will disagree with the particular way I read Calvin, and that's just fine. The point of Calvin's theology—and this book—is not to once and for all win a debate over correct interpretations of Calvin, or the Bible, or even the whole of Christianity. The real point is to talk about grace in ways that illumine our lives and point us toward well-being. That is the only proof of correctness that ultimately matters.

My grandma Idabel, I believe, never lost the sense of that divine glory and God's constant presence. It buoyed her, as it did her parents, and gave her an abiding sense of comfort and purpose. She also managed to hold sin and grace together in her head. Her hard plains life— and life with Dick Jones—kept her aware of the many sins that thwart

us. At her funeral we sang a hymn I often heard her hum: "I Greet Thee
Who My Sure Redeemer Art." A song long associated with Calvinism,
the fourth verse captures that presence best:

Thou hast the true and perfect gentleness,
no harshness hast thou and no bitterness:
O grant to us the grace we find in thee,
that we may dwell in perfect unity.

As for Dick Jones, he never seemed to get the grace part. He stayed
stuck in the sin part, the muck of his own fears and brokenness dragging him down. Knowledge of grace never got the upper hand. At his
funeral four years later, in 1998, it was hard to find beautiful words
to say about him. Smart and industrious, yes. Committed to the law,
yes. But loving and grateful, not really. Not toward himself or others.
He seemed to fear God's judgment against him too much to let God's
love inside.

At his funeral, the best words the preacher could find to say about
him were to remind us, in good Calvin fashion, that God's grace wins
no matter what, no matter how unwilling its recipient. And for my
grandpa, that probably meant that he was now at one with the fish with
whom he spent the happiest times of his life, the lake water cool, the
bondage of sin no longer restraining him.

CHAPTER 3

Original Sin(s)

Beauty without grace is the hook without the bait.

RALPH WALDO EMERSON

On my fifteenth birthday Dick Jones treated me to a singular privilege rarely granted to any of his twelve grandchildren—he took me fishing with his closest fishing buddy, Melvin Porter. I felt, even then, that I was undergoing a sort of initiation into many things—adulthood, fishing, nature, even the rite of grown-up friendship.

Dick and Melvin were quite a pair, equally matched in their devotion to fishing, their knowledge of the law, and their sharp—and often wicked—humor. I couldn't believe my luck. I loved fishing, and that alone was enough to wake me up at 4 a.m. with anxiousness. But I also had a free ticket to what was sure to be the funniest, most interesting entertainment in town, the Dick and Melvin "banter while casting" show.

Mr. Porter, as I then referred to him, was better known across Oklahoma as Senator Porter, who in 1964 was the first African American elected to the state senate, where he served for twenty-two years. Originally from Okmulgee, he was in the first class of African Americans to graduate from Vanderbilt Law School and was widely heralded as the major force behind Oklahoma's passage of the Anti-Discrimination

Act, the state's equivalent of the Civil Rights Act. Accounts of him leading protests and sit-ins for civil rights were legendary. He and my grandpa first met during their early days in Oklahoma courtrooms and campaigns and discovered in each other not just a love of fishing, but an ardent commitment to going fishing *every day*, if only for an hour or two. Five times a week was an acceptable compromise, if other things like court or the senate got in the way. On Saturdays, like my birthday trip, they would be on the water the whole day—from dark to dark, not dawn to dusk.

As we stepped into their rowboat, I could see the sun's first light sneaking over the tall grasses and scrub brush surrounding their favorite fishing hole about an hour south of my grandparents' home in Oklahoma City. To the special handful of folks who fished it, it was mostly known as "the lake." I never learned its formal name.

I grabbed my pole as I stepped into the boat.

"Wait a minute, young lady," Dick Jones abruptly said. "You may get in a cast or two, but your job today is to row us around. Grab those oars."

My grandpa wasn't discriminating against me because it was my first time fishing with the two of them or because I was a girl. Any child or grandchild who found themselves in a boat with him had to paddle in order to earn their right to be there. I knew that even when my own grown father went fishing with my grandpa, he was given this task if there was no one younger around to take it.

I awkwardly strained at the oars as Mr. Porter pushed us off.

"Let's head toward the east shore first," the senator directed me as he sat down to tie his first lure of the day.

"Melvin, that lure is not going to catch you squat," Dick said.

"You don't know anything about fishing, Dick," Melvin replied. "I believe you caught exactly nothing the last five times we've come."

"At least when I catch them, they're bigger than the perch you keep popping out. Not even one bite of meat on 'em. Girl, you need to watch how a real angler fishes today." My grandpa looked at me as he bit the end of his line with his teeth to tighten the hook's knot.

"At least you fish better than that old Senator Jimmy Bob legislates," Melvin said, jumping headlong into local politics, their favored topic.

"Yeah," Grandpa concurred. "That man jumps over the fence of the law like a farmer jumping over the rail to catch a loose bull. He doesn't know a thing about even basic statutes."

They were referring to a state senator from Garfield County who tried to pass a law making it illegal for city planners to put Yankee-style one-way streets anywhere in the state.

"It's outright un-American of him, that knucklehead," Melvin agreed, turning the conversation to what it meant to be American, not missing the irony of calling ultra-right-wing Jimmy Bob "un-American."

"Un-American, hell, he wouldn't know the Constitution if it bit him in the ass," Dick said as I tried to focus on my rowing and not laugh.

"Speaking of asses, how's the men's Bible class going?" Melvin asked, moving the conversation to another favored topic—the Bible study my grandpa taught each week at the Pennsylvania Avenue Christian Church (Disciples of Christ) where he and my grandma belonged as long as I could remember.

I was barely moving the boat, the weight of both men and our gear quickly becoming too much for my thin arms. But Dick Jones paid no heed to our pace or my struggles.

"This week we talked about Jesus raising Lazarus from the dead," he said. You could tell my grandpa was itching to share more.

He suddenly tapped me on the shoulder, and I knew I had reached his preferred casting spot. My biceps burned and my upper back ached, but I knew there would be no sympathy.

He paused as he made his first cast toward the center of the lake where a large bass had just slapped its tail on the surface, the ripples moving toward us.

"Well, I have a question about that Lazarus passage that I've never been clear on," Melvin said dryly. "Did Lazarus stink like a rotted dog when he walked out after a couple of days in that dank tomb?"

"Of course he stunk," Dick Jones said as he cast. "People were snorting and backing up like horses in heat, trying to get away from him." My grandpa acted like he had personal experience of dead bodies being raised.

"Well, that's not how I see it," Melvin began. "If you believe the Lord heals all wounds, wouldn't he have healed Lazarus's stink when he brought him back from the dead?"

He made a perfect cast in the opposite direction, landing it inches from the shore in the shade of a calm pool sure to be filled with fish.

"Jesus, Melvin, how can you think such a thing? If Lazarus didn't stink to high heaven, how would people believe that he had actually been dead?" Dick said back.

They both suddenly sent up howls of laughter, slapping their legs and rocking the boat so hard that water splashed over the sides. I got the can to bail the water out without being quite sure what was so funny. I was also relieved that my grandpa was avoiding his standard fare of dirty jokes about women and that he most likely wouldn't let loose his standard fare of racist jokes with Mr. Porter around.

And so the day went, until the sun had set and they pulled the boat up onto the shore. My grandpa pulled out a small flask, took a sip, and then handed it to Melvin, who took a swig as they rested, perching on the back gate of Mr. Porter's pickup. Suddenly remembering I was there, my grandpa lifted the flask toward me, as if to toast. "Hair from the dog that bit ya. But not for you, young lady. Not for you."

Twenty minutes later we were headed home after a successful day of fishing. We never caught a thing, but at the end of it, they had covered almost every subject I could imagine that related to religion, local politics, and the meaning of being American. When they weren't asking me to row, mostly they acted as if I wasn't there, which was fine with me.

CALVIN AND LAW ON THE LAKE

Days like this showed the degree to which mine was a Calvin-saturated childhood. It was there like the air we breathed, so present that we never paused to actually notice its presence. Dick Jones was many things: a lawman, an upholder of order and right-mindedness, a stickler for detail, a student of scripture, a humorist, an outdoorsman and lover of not just fishing but all sports that got one outside or onto a basketball court. His mind never stopped churning. He was a brilliant litigator and judge, a well-spoken teacher, a strategist, a coach, a politician, an Okie through and through. But most thoroughly and succinctly, he was Calvin's underdog, a little guy from questionable origins, striving against all odds toward progress and success, hoping with each cast of his life that he'd catch the big fish that most of the time eluded him. And true to Calvin, his raunchy, disrespectful parts lived side by side with his law-loving, proper-judge parts, both sin and grace alive inside him. He embodied a phrase that explains much of this country's history, politics, and culture: American Calvinist.

When I think of what America meant to me in my youth, and of what American religion means to me still, I think of Dick Jones and Mr. Porter sitting together in the boat that day, laughing at the silliness of the world around them, ribbing each other, taking pride in their love of their country and their deep commitment to not just upholding her laws but improving them. Their friendship has also stayed with me all these years. Both of them were so-called self-made men who came from nothing and through their sharpness of mind and dogged wills rose to positions of power. Both openly fought against corruption and loved to read the Bible. I knew that the "nothing" out of which they came was so vastly different given their races, but they were bonded in the sense that they had grabbed ahold of the American dream by sheer force of will and spent their lives wrestling with its promises and limits.

I can't help but believe they discussed topics pertaining to race, at least at a high level. My grandpa publicly supported Senator Porter's Anti-Discrimination Act, passed by the Oklahoma legislature in the mid-1960s. As for what they felt deep down inside about racism, my guess is that it would have hurt them both too much to hear the other talk honestly about what divided them the most. And if they had had conversations like that, they would have had to stop fishing together. That was a treasure too rare to risk.

It's hard to imagine a more perfect picture of America at its Calvinist best—especially knowing what the story lopped off: the sexism, the racism, and all the other topics you couldn't talk about. In Calvin's great book *Commentary on Psalms*, he uses one of my favorite theological phrases to describe the range of topics covered in the Psalms, from the good to the downright awful aspects of human nature. As Calvin said, the Psalms give us "an anatomy of all parts of the soul." The Psalms are just that for Calvin, and Dick Jones's life has come to symbolize for me an anatomical study of the complicated, profane, and often frightening puzzle of the human soul.

SINS OF THE FATHERS

The day after our fishing trip, my grandpa walked into the dining room at home and watched in quiet supervision as I helped my grandmother assemble each of the twenty-odd place settings on the long table. Dick Jones was a small man, but over the years he had somehow become larger in my imagination. The fishing trip the day before had only increased my sense of his largeness, although I now felt newly special to him, having spent a whole day on the lake as the chosen granddaughter.

At first, I thought he was looking at a place setting where something had to be askew. Was the napkin poorly folded? Did I put a knife to the right of a fork? He walked closer, smiled at me, then brushed up against me as he passed me on his way into the kitchen. He went out of his way to brush up against me. He rubbed against me, his loins (a euphemism we actually used to say and hear in Oklahoma not too long ago) pressing against my back. My fifteen-year-old brain finally grasped what my formerly childhood brain could not: that he had rubbed against me on purpose.

The giddiness of yesterday's fishing trip blew up in an instant, leaving my arms and legs, sore from rowing, frozen, and my heart hurt and confused. He hadn't done this the day before around Mr. Porter. I kicked myself on the inside for letting myself be tricked into thinking he was just a funny old fisherman. The years I'd spent in that household had shown me his other side, and it had just returned with a vengeance. The really bad parts of Calvin's "anatomy of all parts of the soul" were being revealed in all their gory glory.

"Grandpa," my little sister Kindy said after we prayed at the table. She tugged at the too-tight ponytail she'd been complaining about since breakfast. "Can you tell us a joke?"

Kindy could be such a fool. Given the mood Dick Jones was in—and the absence of Mr. Porter—I knew that what had started out as a seemingly simple request was now going to mutate into a nightmare. The whole day was about to be ruined. If he used the "n" word, as he usually did in his at-home jokes, there'd be a fight with my dad. A big one. My dad would start yelling and then storm out while my grandpa laughed, saying it over and over again, our visit ending in an explosion.

All twelve of us grandchildren, ranging in age from around five to eighteen, were about to be graced with Dick Jones's jokes.

"Did I tell you about the boat old Elroy bought last week?" he said. "Wasn't good for much, so he named it Betty, after his wife. When Judge Johansen asked how Betty was doing, meaning how was she doing since her blood sugar got so high, Elroy got all confused and started talking to the judge about the boat instead of his wife."

My father and grandma tried to shush him, which only spurred him on.

"Elroy told the judge she was sturdier than he thought she'd be at her age. Her seams were tight and she was holding water well."

My cousin Reb coughed. My mom sat there, quietly wringing her hands. My dad shook his head, a forced grin turning into an uncomfortable frown.

"Said even though Betty had seen a lot of use over the years, he thought she'd make it through another season or two. Get some good last years out of her, with just a little care." We could all imagine the judge's face, its shock and its pleasure.

"Then Elroy asked the judge if he wanted to come over for a ride, try her out himself and see what he thought." My grandpa then started laughing so hard the last lines came out in spurts. "Told him . . . she could easily hold one man . . . even two . . . but he was afraid that three might . . . split her in half. He was willing to try, though. See what she's . . . made of." He finished, his eyes closed, a look of sheer joy on his face. "Can you imagine it?" His shoulders shook with laughter.

My vivid childhood imagination saw her there, down by a lake a lot like the one I'd been at only yesterday, an old woman with three men wrapped around her.

My grandma again tried to quiet him but ended up leaving the table; my mom began clearing dinner dishes for dessert even though no one had finished eating. But no one tried to stop him. Dick Jones had the little moment of mastery that he craved.

Then, so appropriately, I felt a menstruation cramp. Right there, right then, as Dick Jones was whipping out his list of sexist jokes. Another cramp started, this one in my back. I knew what it was right away. I had started my period only the year before and was still regularly shocked by its emphatic monthly announcements. I grasped the horrific irony of the moment and then said a prayer thanking God that it hadn't started at the lake.

Everything started to hurt, including my head and feet. Fiddling with my fork, I couldn't look at my cousin Reb, the college-age old boy whom I worshipped. I didn't want him to see me being uncool. But the violence of the story kept sinking into me, descending further and further into my belly, deep into my bones, into my blood, and burying itself between my legs. That small place, down there inside of me, the place from where blood came, mocked me with the hard truth: I wasn't now and never would be a fisher "man" the likes of Dick and Melvin. I would always be more like the "woman" in their jokes than they would ever be.

"That's enough, Dad," my father finally said, wiping chicken grease from his mouth.

Enough of what? Enough of men? Enough of blood? Enough of sex? Enough of laughing?

Enough of lunch?

My grandpa shook his head and went back to his stewed tomatoes.

I put a small bite of potatoes in my mouth and looked up slowly. It stuck in my throat like wet newspaper, fighting for space with the food that was trying to come up. I kicked my sister Kindy under the table.

Reb leaned back in his chair, chuckling softly. He looked at me, nodding like we shared an understanding about how insane this whole

Jones family scene was—and always would be as long as Dick Jones presided.

I leaned back in my chair, arms hanging loose on the sides, trying on the pose of a comfortable man. Kindy looked at me, waiting for something to happen.

And so I tried on the words to go with the pose. Manlike words that would make my cramps disappear like a bad dream. And earn me a proud seat back in the boat, not a shameful place, victimized on the shoreline.

I tried to speak with bravado. "Tell another one, Grandpa." I said. "Tell us about Mrs. Collier, the one with the big jugs."

After I said it, I couldn't believe what had come out of my mouth; it was as if some evil spirit were inside my brain. Yes, I wanted to be special, to earn his approval like I had the day before. But did I really? What I had just asked for was sure to be gross and awful when he told it. I was torn between my pride and my desire to belong, on the one side, and my own bleeding body and my fear of his virulent, abusive relation to women, on the other. There it was, the thing we talked about in Sunday school when the good things we want to do we don't do and instead we do the bad things even when we don't really want to. Like a demon inside us compelling us to act against our inner goodness.

I didn't realize it as completely then, but I was experiencing the full force of what Calvin called *original sin*, that persistent and all-too-human pull toward our own destruction. At the table that Sunday, it was the sin I'd inherited from Dick Jones that pushed me to ask for another joke. I had some of him in me; I was appalled by the perversity of it—mostly by my role as a participant. And as a victim. It was perhaps the first time I was fully cognizant of the tension between the saint and the sinner within me, warring for pride of place. It was, upon later reflection, my first illustrative Calvinist moment as an actor in life's complex churn between our better and worse selves.

As long as I could remember, my grandpa would choose a cousin to look at when he told his stories. It was a matter of dubious honor to be picked, sort of like being a short-season TV star. When we were young, he had dispensed these rewards broadly. Everyone had airtime, everyone got a turn in the prized seat, and everyone got a chance to be jealous. But it got more complicated as we grew. When he'd grace the boys with his look, they'd spend the next hour strutting around and talking too loudly, like him, telling us what to do and such.

But when the girls got the gaze, we had to go sit on his bony lap or cuddle up next to him and "spoon," as he called it, like "Grandpa's girls." To the adults in the room, the scene was supposed to be cute and old-fashioned. To me, it meant closing my eyes, crossing my legs, and pretending like I didn't feel his breath on my neck or the pinches of his wandering hands. It also meant praying like heck that Grandma would call me into the kitchen to dry her dishes, a dreaded task suddenly turned salvific.

As we grew older, Dick Jones would grow even less inhibited. During one particularly horrible dinner, he told one of my cousins in front of everyone that her cherry was ripe for the picking, his own fingers plucking at the air. One afternoon, he'd slapped another cousin on the butt for no reason and then left his hand there way too long, making her cry.

And it got worse. When my sister was in college, he tried to grab her breasts with both hands and kiss her, tongue and all. Other girl cousins whispered tales of similarly gross attacks. Then my grandma started having problems getting women to come help her with the cleaning. They'd tell her my grandpa was trouble—it usually happened when she went out shopping and left him alone with them. They would regularly march off without pay.

This was the flip side of the outlaw pride we took in ourselves—men like Dick Jones took our renegade culture as a mandate to bash through the boundaries around other people's bodies and lives, particularly when it came to women, especially his women. In the privacy of his home, the bridle of the law had no restraining power.

Later I would realize that Dick Jones was acting out his rage on us. I never knew the causes of that rage, but I am sure a mix of explanations is rooted in his family history and his childhood. I wish I understood more. But what I do know was that he was also acting out the most primal and ancient mode of violence, for sexual violence against women and girls is as old as hunting and gathering. Dick Jones's inheritance of original sin was twofold, its wellspring in his personal history and his gender's assumed right of sexual dominance.

Years later, in college and then in seminary, I would discover an endless stream of words for my grandpa's sins: patriarchy, sexism, predatory masculinity, sexual abuse, and the word that still turns my stomach and catches in my throat, incest. But at the time my sisters and cousins were caught in his grip, it never occurred to me to say, "Hey, Grandma, Grandpa is abusing us." The same held for church. Those liberal Sunday school teachers who taught lessons about every imaginable social injustice—poverty, war, racism, capitalism—never included the fact that the men we lived with, some in our own church, were sticking their tongues in their granddaughters' ears and sneaking hands up their shaking legs. Silence was as American as church for us.

The same with our progressive pastors. All of them vehemently rejected "women's submission to men," telling us over and over again from the pulpit that women were equal to men. But no preacher ever talked about how unequal it felt to be cornered in a dark hallway, afraid to even flinch when a grown man's hot breath brushes your neck, while unaware grown women gossiped about piecrust in the kitchen downstairs. Like Woody Guthrie's lopped-off verses, this part of the Jones girls' story never made it into our Okie family's lore or our supposedly grace-laden theology. We were left on our own to figure out why.

AMERICA'S ORIGINAL SIN

But it wasn't just biblically proportioned measures of sexual abuse he meted out—that wasn't all that was lopped off in the official Dick Jones public presentation. When he was at home, Dick Jones spewed out racist tirades of biblical proportions, too. That day in the dining room, his sexist jokes were mere prologue to the terrible jokes that followed about black people. And it wasn't just at the table; he used racist language like it was part of regular, everyday normal speech, not something lewd or sneaky like his "dirty jokes."

As a child, it confused me to no end that one day he could be in the boat with his best fishing buddy, Melvin, and the next day be at home dishing out racist rants like they were Sunday dessert. I knew from an early age that his views of African Americans were not just wrong but shameful and dangerous. My parents talked openly about it and deep down his virulent racism scared me. I didn't get how his fishing-boat self could live right next to his hateful racist self. It seemed like he was two people in one. I was too young, of course, to see how normal he was as an American Calvinist in all his good and evil. Many of his pals "had black friends" and yet still believed that black people were fundamentally inferior—the butt of jokes—not regular Americans, like their upstanding white selves.

His white self, of course, was part fiction, given his Cherokee heritage. I always thought of him as my Native American grandpa, not the "white man" his jokes seemed to suggest he was. When I asked my father about the odd character of my grandpa's whiteness, he explained that when Oklahoma's Jim Crow laws were passed in 1910, Dick's parents, one Cherokee, Redman Jones, the other Irish, Dolly McMahon, signed legal papers stating that they were both "pure" white, because the new laws stated that only white people could own property in their "white" part of Okemah. With the stroke of a pen, they officially became white people in America. It seemed to me that inside the grandpa I knew, that lie had become truth, at least when it came to who he was with respect to black people. He wasn't like them. He was white, not black. When it came to racial identity in America, that was the distinction, among all others, that mattered the most.

My grandpa never once talked about his constructed whiteness, but it is hard to imagine that he didn't feel conflicted, knowing he was part Native American but because his father could pass for white, his family profited from hiding that part of his father—and himself—away.

There was more to his racism than his jokes and name calling, but it took my young mind longer to see that. My grandparents employed an African American woman, Arlene, who "helped around the house," as my grandmother put it, never using the word "maid." When I was little, I never thought to ask questions about why she was there; she just was, a part of the adult world that my sisters, cousins, and I tried to avoid as much as we could. But it made me uncomfortable. My immediate family never had "help" in our home, and African Americans who visited our house were students, professors, neighbors, and activist colleagues.

Arlene always wore a white dress and tattered shoes that set her apart from the rest of the adults in their house—and the fact she was African American in a house that no black people, except Senator Porter, ever visited. Arlene and my grandmother cleaned, cooked, washed, and ironed together. Every afternoon, they sat next to each other on the old upholstered rockers in the living room to watch *General Hospital* and *Days of Our Lives*. My grandfather did not talk much to my grandmother, but when it came to Arlene, this absence of speech was total. He didn't even make eye contact—it was as if she didn't exist.

In the late fifties, my grandparents had moved to Forest Park, a predominantly black and Native neighborhood on the outskirts of Oklahoma City that still, today, feels like country. My grandma had wanted a garden to tend; my grandpa needed a big pen for his bird dogs. Both Arlene and my grandmother refused to feed those dogs—I think they hated them. Not even the kids would go near the pen; they were mean and almost feral.

One Christmas Eve, as she was taking off the tablecloth, I asked Arlene, "Why aren't you home for Christmas?" I was around eight years old and had never given much thought to Arlene's life beyond my grandparents' home before that moment.

She looked angry and was about to speak when she caught herself. She shook her head and walked back to the laundry room.

I followed her back there, so when her son came to the back door to pick her up a few minutes later, I cheerily said, "Merry Christmas. Hi, I'm Serene. Are you going to have Christmas tonight, too?"

In the background, I could hear my grandfather ranting about Martin Luther King Jr. again, as he always did when he had an audience.

"Come on, Mom. Let's go," her son said kindly to her as he reached to help her untie her apron, ignoring me completely.

Before that evening, my own sense of privilege had made me unaware of the whole setup—Arlene's poverty and invisibility, Dick Jones's regular and unabashed use of racist and sexist language in front of her; his disgust at her presence or, even more, her existence. Before, it had seemed so common that it faded into the generally disgusting noises that his mouth seemed to produce. But now suddenly all of it shocked me. And I felt shame that night when I went to bed. Instead of wondering what Santa Claus would bring, I wondered what wrath God would deliver on my family for all our sins against Arlene and her son, and especially for Dick Jones's rage-filled racism. More practically, I worried that my dad and Dick Jones would soon come to blows over these endless rants.

When I got to college at OU in 1977, I finally felt liberated to investigate the racism all around me. For years I kept hearing about what had happened just north of Okemah in Tulsa in the twenties. But even then it was impossible for me to find a good history book in the library that told the facts. My high school teachers had said nothing about it, and the Internet obviously didn't yet exist.

I first heard the real story in a one-on-one reading course I took on Jewish history in Oklahoma from a rabbi in Norman who, in addition to teaching Jewish studies, served as the campus's Jewish chaplain. As it turns out, for a few of his students like me, he was the source of all kinds of information about Oklahoma's past that Christian white people didn't want to talk about it.

In May of 1921, a group of black Tulsans had raced to the local jail to try to prevent what they anticipated would be an effort to lynch a black suspect accused of raping a white woman. Words were exchanged, pushes and punches ensued, and then shots were fired. At the time, Tulsa had the wealthiest African American population of almost any city in the country. It had been dubbed the "Black Wall Street." The music scene rivaled Chicago and New York. There had never been slavery, at least officially, in Tulsa or anywhere in Oklahoma. It hadn't even become a state until 1907. Though the truth was that many African Americans had arrived as the enslaved human property of the wealthier members of the displaced Native American tribes—they had been brought on the Trail of Tears death march and kept as slaves in Indian Territory. When emancipation came after the Civil War, these formerly enslaved communities were given parcels of land that soon became Oklahoma's famous "All-Black Counties."

At its height, this eastern edge of Oklahoma was home to more than one hundred small, thriving black towns. The promise of free land seemed inviting to African Americans who wanted to get out of the South and start life afresh in uncharted land just beyond the Arkansas border. Whole families and entire black communities from Tennessee, Georgia, South Carolina, Mississippi, Louisiana, and Florida migrated west to join this growing African American world.

These black towns were devastated, however, when the newly established state passed those Jim Crow Laws in 1910. Like the Okemah Joneses, white settlers around many of the independent black towns were hungry for land. Along with them came newly formed chapters of the Ku Klux Klan preaching the need to run blacks off the land so that it could belong to its rightful owners, white people. Before statehood, the Oklahoma and Indian Territories had recorded a small number of lynchings, mostly of white cattle rustlers and horse thieves. After 1907, the number of African American lynchings surged, bringing the official count to fifty by 1930, though the real number was most likely five times as high.

In Tulsa, our rabbi professor told us, the riot that grew out of the battle in front of the jail turned into an American holocaust. I will never forget his use of that word. I was sitting in his classroom, a sophomore still missing home, and I heard a Jewish man use a word I had thought could only be applied to the sins of the Nazis. Hundreds of African Americans were murdered during the course of those few days, many dying in their burning homes. Airplanes dropped turpentine bombs on the African American part of town. A huge swath of Tulsa burned to the ground. More than three thousand black homes were destroyed, whole neighborhoods left ruined. And within a month, most of Tulsa's black population had fled the state. And I, age nineteen and an Oklahoma girl through and through, had just learned about this history for the first time.

I grew enraged at Dick Jones like never before. In my anger, I imagined Okemah burning, his own family's house going up in flames. If this had happened to his white family—which, of course, it never would have—the details would have been etched deep into the bark of our tree of family stories. But because it happened to black people, that particular branch of history was lopped off. Inside myself, I railed at him for this, my imagination aflame. How could he have never discussed this event, not even once, in our presence?

This was my Oklahoma and this was my grandpa. I had grown up in the shadow of a mass cleansing, and no one, certainly not Dick Jones, had ever mentioned it. How could I make sense of this as my social conscience kept developing in college? How could I make sense of this as a faithful person, as my faith gained nuance and depth? How could I, I kept asking all through college, have attended hundreds of Disciples of Christ services and events and never once heard anyone pray for the people of Tulsa whose homes were burned to the ground? What was my church in the face of this silence? Where was my supposedly liberal faith in the face of a horror so close to home? What other lopped-off stories, what other horrors enacted by white people, was I missing?

THEOLOGICAL SHOCK

Many years later and by then a trained theologian, I had received tenure at Yale Divinity School and, as senior academics are tasked with doing, was chairing a search committee for a professorship in our theology department. The position, an associate professorship in African American religious thought, was very competitive, and I was feeling the looming burden of having to reject so many superb candidates. That day, we were sitting in a classroom, the other committee members in the student seats and the candidate up front doing his presentation. He was using slides to supplement his lecture, and I remember hearing the click before the slide that triggered this particular moment of theological shock.

Click, and then boom: There was a slide showing a close-up section from postcard picture of a young African American woman hanging from a bridge, lynched, her long cotton dress covered in dark stains, her leather lace-up boots turned inward. Her head lay unnaturally sideways, the rope tight against her distorted neck. Her eyes were closed. Underneath it, the hand-scrawled tag read: Laura Nelson, Okemah, Okla., 1911.

Dick Jones was six in 1911.

In 1911, Okemah was nothing more than a handful of streets that connected the tightly bonded group of white people who lived there.

The moment I saw the postcard in that classroom with its creaking wood floors, that feeling of fury stormed back into my bones, and I knew with near certainty that my young grandfather had to be standing there in the crowd watching this young woman's brutal murder. I had seen many photos of Dick Jones at that age, for he insisted on showing us photos of himself from the different intervals of his "glory days" almost every time my parents took my sisters and me to visit him.

For a terrifying moment, I spotted his young face in the crowd standing just beyond the postcard's edge even though I knew I was imagining it. I felt sick, flushed. It was the closest I have ever come to truly feeling the blood, despicable, lying Jones blood, coursing through my veins. My family's past, my own made-up white privilege, my grandfather's deep-seated racism, and the shameless, sickening violence of the young woman's lynching—all this shame literally caused me to curl over in my seat, at the front of the room, beside the lecturer. I was going to have to lead the questioning part of the presentation, and part of me wanted to confess all my family's white supremacist sins right then and there. Another part wanted to just stay curled up in a little ball, willing away the reality of my own close proximity to racism and a suddenly very present, very real lynching.

I pulled myself together—something I know guilty-feeling white people are very good at, especially when it comes to dealing with racism in ways that cut too close for comfort—and led the round of questions with a flushed face but a steady voice. I didn't even mention the slide to the presenter afterward, afraid I would sound too stoic or start crying, neither one a good option. I went home that night and felt the urge to take a shower—on the inside of me. I wanted to wash Dick Jones's blood and history right out of my being. As if I could! I also felt the blood of Laura Nelson on my own hands, covering me all over. I tried to imagine her terror, her fury, her cries for help, her own family's rage and fear. As if I could. I knew it was a fear that as a white person I had never felt or had any right to claim knowledge of. But I also knew that I couldn't afford to blot out her fear, making her once again into an unknowable object of violence, not a person, a woman, a human being like myself.

Lynchings, I knew from my own studies, were such sickeningly public spectacles that white people would come from miles away, picnic lunches packed alongside blankets and games for a day in the sun with friends, watching a body swing in the breeze. It is hard to believe that my grandfather's family could not have resisted such a festive gathering. Knowing his violent family history, I couldn't be sure that his father and uncles hadn't themselves, self-righteous and drunk, actually been part of the lynching mob. I couldn't get out of my mind images of her being raped before she was hanged—as I knew it was part of the torture meted out to lynched women. Even though I had no postcard evidence of this, the fact that it was realistically imaginable was enough to make me sick.

I had grown up thinking that lynching was done by other white people to other black people. Now there was, right in front of my eyes, a real woman named Laura Nelson who had been publicly shamed and brutally annihilated by real white people in Okemah.

My people? Yes, my Okie people.

Later that day, as I walked to my office on the Yale campus, I could feel my grandpa's hands on my once-teenage body again—those blocky, coarse fingers grabbing me in a way that was still impressed upon my skin. With me, he came close to those places he shouldn't have, skirting them by the width of a knuckle or fingertip, and I sometimes still shudder at random moments when I feel his hands on my side or my hip, looming so close to spots he felt he owned.

That night in my study at home I pulled off the bookshelf the autobiography my grandpa had written—yes, he self-published a book about himself—and searched for the mere mention of the word "lynching." I realized then the true definition of the word "whitewashing." Even in his own official history book, he hadn't mentioned the Tulsa burning, let alone the mob murder on the bridge.

The most abhorrent part of it all for me was that my grandma, the woman I had grown up idealizing and adoring, had lived with this man, been in bed with him, cooked thousands of meals for him, consoled him, and surely cursed him. She had also protected him, I painfully saw, and held his secrets. She had participated in the lopping off of his official history, of the theological truth about his life and soul.

I felt Calvin's theology in my bones. He described the theological meaning of this ongoing sin better than anyone since. He strongly rejected the old-fashioned view that original sin referred only to Adam's original sin of having sex with Eve—the fact that it proved all of us were conceived through the sinful sex and thus bore its guilt. For Calvin, original sin was active, alive, and constantly churning in the lives of everyone, today and every day. This sin is passed down to us from our parents and their parents before them, not through their literal seed, but through the seeds of the sins they, too, inherited. The seeds of harmful economic and racist cultural systems that all of us are born into and that taint everything we do. To complicate matters more, Calvin held that even though we do not choose to be born, let alone to be born into sinful social systems, we are still wholly and completely responsible for its effects in our lives. Indeed, we are guilty because of it; and for this reason, the weight of repentance for all our sins falls heavily upon our personal and collective shoulders. Along with inheriting my grandpa's love of fishing, I now had to face my inheritance of Laura Nelson's brutal murder.

For the first time in my life, I understood why Calvin referred to our collective state of sin as "total depravity." It captures the utterly depraved nature of humanity's most horrific sins. Lynching was total in its depravity. For Calvin, the word "total" signaled that when this level of corruption—like the disgrace of white supremacy—gets ahold of people, evil can become so routinized and normalized that people can no longer see that it is horrifying. Its hold on us is "total." We can't see beyond it.

In the United States, our nation's sin of chattel slavery, of the culture of white supremacy it created, and of the Jim Crow systems it engendered and continues still, is the political and social equivalent of Calvin's version of original sin and total depravity. The whole system is America's original sin, as it is often referred to. And so were my grandfather's sins—both the sins of his parents and the sins he freely enacted. Although more than a hundred years separated me from that murderous event that Dick Jones likely attended, I still bore responsibility for it, and for finding remedies for those harms, both individually and collectively.

Why do I bear responsibility for the horrible things that happened before I was born? How could it be my fault? I hear these questions often asked today, and in response Calvin's understanding of the human inheritance of original sin is the best answer I can find. It stops people like me from trying to hold the past at arm's length, glibly claiming we aren't like that anymore. The notion of inheriting sin makes the bond between the past and the present much tighter. So tight, in fact, that we are forced to look directly at the full scope of what has been passed down to us, especially those aspects of our lives that we take for granted or those good things we think we've earned.

It forces me to reckon with the fact that I was raised with that virulent racism inside me and all around me. It forces me to reject the lopping off of my theological and family truths. I inherited it, literally. It lived in the lies I was raised on, the lopped-off truths I was never told, and the privileges of whiteness that I was never forced to see but benefited from every step along the way. I inherited it insofar as that white privilege earned my grandpa a level of social power and money that he was able to pass down to my own father, allowing him to go to Yale. That same inheritance then allowed me, an heir to a racist heritage, to step into the family business with a generation of money and confidence behind me, telling me every step of the way that I belonged there. My ever-increasing inheritance, still today, is a result of others' massive losses.

Calvin's understanding of original sin also kept me from reducing white supremacy to my own personal or familial problem, as if it were something that could be fixed through individual enlightenment and a single person's virtuous actions. He reminds us that endemic sin is much bigger than just individual intentions. In fact, it thrives even more strongly in social collectives than it does in single people. It lives in the policies people enact, the attitudes we enforce, the beliefs we propagate. It lives in the pride and arrogance that allows "whites" to feel entitled to special treatments that "blacks" do not have, as if their white specialness is natural. It lives in economic structures that assure wealth for some, deprivation for others. It thrives in collapsing school systems, lack of health care, job loss, and inadequate housing. It dwells, too, in the recesses of our unconscious minds and biases, as sin we never even know we have. And sadly, original sin, in its social form, takes root in spiritual and religious communities that collectively support worldviews that breed hatred, not love.

That is for me the most startling revelation about original sin. It finds welcome shelter in churches; it always has. For this version of sin, Calvin meted out especially harsh words: idolatry, heresy, and total depravity. Those words ring true for Christians and their churches that supported chattel slavery, the most brutal, massive, organized system of extractive labor and human torture practiced in modern human history. It wasn't there for just a decade or two. It wasn't a short-lived war.

Slavery was the religious sin of this country for three hundred years. And in too many churches today, it's alive and growing stronger, not weaker.

Furious and exhausted, I finally threw Dick Jones's little book of lies across the room. I heard the words from the book of Exodus banging off the walls of my brain: "The sins of the parents will be visited upon their children, and their children's children, onto the third and to the fourth generation." Dick Jones's sins were on my skin, inside my body, in my room, in the world outside my house, at my university, on the streets of my town, my beloved home state, and my country.

Upstairs, I crawled into bed and pulled my covers up tight around me, trying to protect myself, I suppose, from the ghost of Dick Jones. But his sexual abuse of all of us Jones girls and his racism were the ghosts, not him, and they would never go away. I was a victim, a child whose body had been violated by my own grandfather's hands. But I was also the inheritor of a racism that came from a family of victimizers, lynchers, and vile white supremacists. And Dick Jones, the child of an oppressed Native people, was also surely the victim of America's most egregious of sins, genocide. And yet he turned around and inflicted those sins on others, not just once but for an entire lifetime.

But Calvin also showed me, thankfully, how these layers upon layers of inherited sins do not constitute the final truth about our lives. He believed, as do I, that if we open our eyes to grace, another path is possible. James Baldwin says it even better in *The Fire Next Time*. He writes: "Love takes off the masks that we fear we cannot live without and know we cannot live within. I use the word 'love' here not merely in the personal sense but as a state of being, or a state of grace—not in the infantile American sense of being made happy but in the tough and universal sense of quest and daring and growth."

I don't throw these statements about a "state of grace" out lightly, as if I am simply looking for a nice ending to America's original sin's horror story. I actually believe it, like I believe the sun will rise tomorrow. I, we, this nation, our world, humanity cannot afford the luxury of naming sin—of reveling in the mire of our collective brokenness—without also naming grace. Given that huge pile of inherited sins we all bear, the act of asserting grace in its midst is incredibly hard; everything around us strains against such a wild assertion. The facts don't point toward it. Nor does an honest look at history. Or a truly honest look inside our conflicted interior lives. So where does it come from, this assertion of grace, this willful belief that we are capable of better things? That God's love ultimately reigns?

For me, believing in grace is a spiritual, theological matter, albeit an utterly earthly one. I've heard that graced love spoken of in stories of old. I feel it tug at my heart when I hear their witness. And I've seen it, alive and breathing, in the good that manages to wiggle its way into the world in spite of the horrors raging around us. In my grandma's cool jug, in the joy shared by two old men fishing, in the ringing songs of freedom fighters who dare to march against the tide of sin, in the startling truth telling of James Baldwin and John Calvin, in the dust-reddened pages of Idabel's beloved book, in the persistent, scrub-brushed spread of a family of sinners, and in the simple but surprising reality that we are here, alive, if only for a moment—and we could not be.

My spiritual belief in grace also grows out of a deeply practical choice I've made. If we stop believing love is real and worth striving for, then surely there is no hope for us. We cannot afford to give hatred that victory; the cost is too high. It would betray the beautiful parts of our humanity and toss away as trash too many bodies, too many thwarted futures. In the face of such evil, I choose not to give in. Something in me—call it a divine spark—simply cannot concede. Which doesn't mean I've got all the answers; it only means I've chosen to accept that grace dwells side by side with sin. Even when—indeed, especially when—the odds are against it.

Embedded in this acceptance of grace is also my abiding belief that love has already won the battle. Ultimately. But in us, the struggle is still in motion, our tough quest incessant, and the outcome . . . well, it will only be as good as we believe it can be. This is, more or less, what is true about America. Grace is always there. Grace is more original than sin. And it is time—indeed, way past time—for us to wake up.

STATION II

Destiny and Freedom

CHAPTER 4

Kierkegaard on the Playground

> The greatest danger, that of losing one's own self, may pass
> off as quietly as if it were nothing; every other loss, that of
> an arm, a leg, five dollars, a wife, etc., is sure to be noticed.
>
> SØREN KIERKEGAARD, *THE SICKNESS UNTO DEATH*, 1848

W here are you?"

My mother stood on the back porch, her hand shading her eyes as she scanned the tangled shrubs surrounding our suburban backyard in Richardson, Texas.

"I'm coming, Mom," I shouted to her as I scrambled out of my hidden scrub-oak tepee, panting as I ran toward her. I was nine years old and had spent the morning lost in the outdoor wonderland of our yard, imagining myself caught in a high-stakes battle to ward off the U.S. Army that had encircled my small Apache camp. Like many other children at the time, I was oblivious to the genocidal history my game mimicked as play, another example of those normalized depravities that marked white culture.

"There you are, sweetie. I thought I'd lost you," she said when I finally jumped onto the porch. Her words sounded loving, but there was no warmth in them.

It was a constant refrain of hers, saying she thought she'd lost me. I remembered Reverend Larry telling us just last Sunday the story about Jesus and the woman who was happy when she found her lost coin. Why couldn't my mother sound even a little bit happy she'd found me?

She reached over to yank a feather out of my tangled curly hair, the headdress I had spent days constructing just riffraff to her. Her hair, in contrast, was long and tar black; it never tangled but always fell straight and thick over her shoulders and down her back. When Reverend Larry had said that my mother was the most beautiful woman he'd ever seen, I had wondered why I couldn't learn to sit still or wear dresses and have perfect hair like her.

"I hate these panties." I pulled away from her, reaching behind me to tug at my shorts.

"Stop that. It's not ladylike," she said. It was another of her constant refrains.

Underwear was a sore point between Mom and me. I wanted nothing to do with the flowery panties she bought for my sisters and me. I was not a girly girl. I wanted my guns, swords, and arrows.

"Come on. Your little game will be still here when we get back," she answered, now looking around for my eight-year-old sister, Kindy.

"It's not a little game, Mom." I defiantly pulled at my shorts again. "I was trying to save people's lives."

I knew it was a game, but it was still big. To me.

"You have such a big imagination for such a little girl," she answered back with a heavy sigh that made me feel as if my flourishing fantasy life was somehow an incomprehensible burden to her.

The whole interaction—her looking for me and me running toward her only to find her seemingly disappointed by my arrival—happened all the time, inside and outside the house. Each time she found me, I was never the prize she expected. It turned my stomach into knots, knowing I could never give her what she was looking for.

As a child, every time we went through this routine, I hoped the ending would change: she'd be happy, I'd feel proud. This particular day felt no different. Little did I know that she was looking for her "self," lost or shattered years before in her own childhood. And she was looking not where she could ever possibly find it—in theological spaces and nooks—but in the material world. She was doomed to be perpetually looking because she was forever looking in the wrong place.

LOSING YOUR SELF

"I have an idea," she said, pointing to my flip-flops piled in the porch corner and then to my feet, all skinned-up toes and bug-bitten ankles. "Put them on." It sounded ominous.

Kindy came out the back door and sat down beside me.

"I have to go to the grocery store so you and your dad will have something to eat." Mom never hid the fact that she dreaded shopping and cooking and all the other housewife-mom chores that filled her days. She did it *for* us, because we needed to eat, not because she enjoyed it. "What if I dropped the two of you off at Floyd Park while I shop? Just for an hour or two. Let you stay by yourself."

"What about Verity?" I asked, confused at first by her offer to let us play unconstrained by parental oversight. Verity, the youngest of us three Jones girls, was being looked after by our next-door neighbor, my mom told me, relief in her voice.

Verity was barely two years old and a constant drag on my mother's energy, something she never failed to point out, especially when she felt exasperated by her two older daughters' constant bickering. To Kindy and me, Verity was just the opposite—a magical, beautiful toylike creature we could never get enough of, her babble and wobbly walk a constant source of fascination for our burgeoning preadolescent brains. But she wasn't yet much good at crawling through shrubs and building tepees. Knowing I wouldn't have to look after her at the park sent the electric shock of the full freedom my mother was offering us through my body.

I'd been dreaming of this moment since I was old enough to memorize my address and phone number and rehearse it for that imagined policeman who might find me wandering through town alone as I snapped photographs of all the strange faces and buildings that enchanted me.

Floyd Park was a ten-acre place of mystery for me. And it was surely baking in the afternoon heat that day. The muddy creek that ran through its center was a trickle by early July, and the sloping fields surrounding it sent their scorched-earth fragrance around for several miles, whenever a breeze passed through. We silently rode with Mom, still in disbelief at her offer. Was she secretly going to park somewhere and watch us? Was this a trick?

Suddenly, she pulled our Ford station wagon off the main road and stopped in an empty parking lot by the playground. Before her tires had even stopped crackling across the gravel, my door was open, my sister jumping out before me.

"Little missy, listen to me. I want you to take my watch." Mom handed it to me as she leaned across the front seat. There was, again, a sad seriousness about her, almost anger, her words heavy laden and coarse, as if their roughness might give them grip. "It's valuable, your granddaddy gave it to me, so DON'T LOSE IT. When it's three thirty, an hour and a half from now, meet me right here." Her finger pointed to our spot.

The watch felt cool in my open palm, a slender gold band too big for my bony wrist.

Closing my fingers around it, I answered her. "Okay. Don't worry,

Mom. We'll be fine." I basked in the glory of being the oldest daughter, the one now in charge, if only for an afternoon.

A pocket, I thought as the car pulled away. I needed a pocket for a job this big.

But I was completely pocketless. My red stretch shorts had none, and all I had on top was the green striped bikini top I'd pulled on when I climbed out of bed. I thought of tying the watch to the bikini's string strap and wearing it like a medal. I thought of clasping it around my ankle but then figured that, no, the sand could hurt it or I might kick it off. I thought about hiding it somewhere on the ground and getting it when she came back, but that felt too risky.

I then did the most logical thing I could—I shoved it down the front of my shorts, into my panties. My panties always felt too tight on me, the elastic torture on hot days. Seemed to me the most secure place was there.

With an awkward bulge in my pants, I started to run.

In the medium distance a new rocket ship rose out of the flat playground field around me. Its massive frame shadowed the swing sets and benches. Red on the bottom, military gray on the top, it had a slide curled around its side winding to the ground. No one was there but my sister and me, and today we were going to be astronauts. Before I even reached the rocket ship's door, I had entered a different cosmos.

Mars was under attack and our outpost threatened by the Purple Terror, a race of aliens who ate people to keep their joints oiled. My mission was to escape from the planet with a small group of survivors, a remnant of a soon-to-be-extinct humanity. With no supplies and no crew, I went to work.

Preparing for takeoff, blasting off, dodging enemy fire, yelling at my lazy little sister who wanted to pee in the middle of a particularly brutal frontal assault, bandaging the mortal wounds of my passengers while steering through asteroids, my body and mind fused, and I achieved what later I would learn, in adult psychological language, was called "flow." I was flowing all right, right through outer space.

I was poised, ready to slide down and stop a Purple Terror contingent from stealing our dwindling food supplies, when suddenly the ship's emergency alarm went off. I stopped. What, more enemy forces in the area? Could I hold them off any longer?

It sounded a second time.

Only then was I jolted back to my earth-bound surroundings. I was in the park, the vast blue sky holding the searing sun above us, and my sister was running to the car, where my mom was honking the horn. Its sharp, harsh noise another demanding "Where are you?"

Frozen at the top of the slide, my hand grabbed the smooth front of my shorts.

Not only was the watch not in my panties, I also couldn't remember when I'd stopped feeling it there. There was no trace of its cool metal feel between my legs, no hinted flash of its unseen departure down my leg, no evidence of its fall to earth. It was gone without a trace. Shame flushed through me, running up my arms, across my knotted-up belly, and ending, hot and churning, in my crotch. My stupid, stupid panties. Without even deciding to be bad, I had done the worst thing I could have imagined: I had lost my mother's watch.

Mom knew it before I told her. The rage in her voice made my arms cold, my bathing-suit top tightening around my chest as my heartbeat rocketed.

"You lost it? My watch, you lost it? My father's gold watch, it's gone. It's gone?" My blank stare and shaking legs did nothing to lessen the pounding truth. "I should have known not to trust you, you selfish child. Your stupid games matter more to you than your own mother. You are terrible, just terrible. You disgust me, you little b—" She suddenly stopped her rant.

We stood in silence, my mom and me, her eyes staring into the cloudless sky and mine at the ground. I had failed her again. This time it was big. Really big. I was terrible. Completely terrible. I had heard her call me all those words before, especially the bad ones, but I had learned early on to let them slide off my skin. This time I couldn't. The parking-lot gravel felt scorching hot under my bare feet. I'd kicked off my flip-flops somewhere by the duck an hour ago and lost them, too. I began arching my feet and curling my toes in and out.

I remember pushing down hard on a sharp rock under my big toe. I wanted to make it bleed to distract her or to show her evidence of the shame that covered me, inside and out.

"Do you have anything to say for yourself?" she demanded, like a Purple Terror general torturing a captured enemy, intent on extracting a truth.

My toes kept curling in the gravel, the concrete getting hotter all the time. My ankles were starting to sweat.

"Serene, pay attention to me." I was back in the interrogation chamber. "Try to remember what you did with it." She pushed me harder, holding back her desire, it seemed, to step on my foot and push the rock in farther. She wanted me to hurt.

"I put it in my panties, Mom." I stuttered it out, pulling on the edge of my shorts.

"Your underwear?" Shocked, she stared at my pants.

My legs began to shake harder.

She then put her hand low on her stomach, as if checking her own. "Your underwear?" she repeated, her anger growing.

"Right here." I grabbed and twisted at the place it should have been and looked at her.

Our eyes met for the briefest moment as we stood there, hands pressed against our panties.

"I'm sorry, Mom." It surprised me to hear my apology.

"That's not good enough." Her voice quivered as she looked back at me.

I stepped off the hot gravel onto a patch of crunchy brown grass, but the pain in my feet increased once its source had been removed.

Rubbing her watchless wrist, she turned and walked toward the playground.

"Come on," she said, her voice still serious but now calm. "Let's look for it. Where did you go first?"

We searched for what seemed like hours. We dug, sifted, piled and pushed, and beat away the dirt and sand from all the places I'd been—the ship, the duck, the swings, the bike rack, the banana-shaped trash can, the plastic park map, the wooden creek overlook, the rusted-up water fountain.

Around five thirty, we left. It was time to pick up Verity, my mother sighed as she told us, her searching interrupted once again by the demands of children.

Looking back at the rocket ship as we pulled away, I wished more than ever that it was real, that it could carry me away. That evening, another more distant and even more disappointed version of my mother descended upon her. She didn't speak to me for the next three days save for giving basic commands. Each night I dreamed of the rocket ship again, lifting me off to Venus or the moon—to the heavens, away from this woman who could never find what she was looking for, who could never find herself. And because she couldn't, she raged. At me.

CRIMES OF DESPERATION

Almost twenty years later, during a family fishing vacation in Colorado, I was alone with her cooking trout in the kitchen of the log cabin we had rented. I was almost thirty and she was nearing fifty. Stirring up a big bowl of cornmeal, I finally asked my mother about the watch. She seemed surprised by the detail of my memory: the park, the rocket, my flip-flops, the dried-up creek, the hot gravel under my feet, my creeping underwear, and the horrible things she'd said to me.

"Oh, honey, I don't remember any watch. That was such a long time ago. Worlds ago," she answered, adding, "My goodness, you are almost thirty years old now, aren't you? Lord, your wild mind still amazes me."

"Surely you remember something."

"I do recall the spaceship. It was 1969? Armstrong walked on the moon that July. Yes. Jungles and moonwalking fascinated you. I couldn't keep up with any of it."

She paused. "Oh, Serene, it was all so hard."

"Yes, it was, Mom." I stood there hoping for more stories to come. And they did. But not as I'd expected.

At the end, she sighed. "My choices were easier than yours, though, I suppose. My world was smaller. I was too shaped by my mother's worries to adventure into the places you did. Like your trip to Antarctica this year. It would have never crossed my mind to actually do such a thing." She still managed to tinge her words with an edge of envy, a woman deeply wronged by the mere fact of her daughter's choices.

It hit me then, like a rocket barreling down from Mars. That day when I was nine, and so many other days like it, she was not really looking for me or for the watch I'd lost. The perennially lost child she was looking for was herself. She was searching for the lives she dreamed of living, lives that escaped her desperate grasp. That's what made it "all so hard" for her. It wasn't me.

It was one of those conversion moments, when suddenly the world you thought you knew shifts before your eyes and a whole new landscape appears. I thought again of the playground and wondered if she saw me, her daughter, as what stopped her living those other lives, the child that held her down. Or was I—so free roaming and wild—a painful reminder of the freedom she wanted but failed to realize. Was I her ball and chain? Or a glimpse of what she yearned for? Or both?

I almost asked her, not really expecting an answer.

As if anticipating my question, she stopped me.

A conspiratorial smile crossed her face and, as if conferring a secret never to be spoken again, she whispered, "But you know. That day in the park. I probably left you there so I could smoke a cigarette on the way to the grocery store. Maybe I wanted to flirt with the store manager. Or . . . who knows? Who knows, sweet girl, what crimes I was planning?"

"Crimes?" I hadn't seen that coming.

I had to shift my lens on my mother yet again, as another new piece of her came into view.

"I got away with a lot, you know, because I was beautiful. People were so taken with how I looked, they never wondered what I might be like inside."

It wasn't news to me that she was stunning, but it was good to hear her admit it. Throughout my life, I'd heard men compliment her so often it made me sick.

"The spitting image of the young Elizabeth Taylor."

"Movie-star gorgeous."

"She looks just like Natalie Wood."

Even when no one was around to hear him except my sisters and me, my father called her "my beautiful wife"—to us!

As a child, I'd ponder my own "chubby" (my grandpa's word) young-girl body and would add to myself, "And so unlike her ugly daughter." The family portraits covering our living room wall always showed her standing—relaxed, elegant, demure, her perfectly shaped features and long neck framed by thick coal-black hair. In the photos I was in, I saw myself standing in front of her—dress off-kilter, eyes looking somewhere off camera, my curly hair as disheveled as hers was straight and combed.

But even more important than this admission about her own beauty was her confession that her outside and inside didn't match up. I wondered if she finally saw herself the way I had.

If asked, even as a child, I would have said she was unhappy, easily wronged, and empty on the inside. Not empty as in full of nothing; she had lots inside, especially disappointments. She was empty like a bottomless well that no amount of water could fill. If you dropped your bucket down far enough, it'd find water, deep down, but her well level never rose. No matter how much got poured into it. And the deepdown water was always churning with sadness, gnawing frustrations, and rage. Especially at me.

But crimes?

Crime was such a willful, specific word for a woman to use who couldn't ever find herself. I couldn't get my head around it.

She turned, half smiled at me, and left the kitchen. I watched her leave, so much of her newly revealed. So many questions left unanswered.

She hid her emptiness beautifully, at least to the outside world, employing a smile that warmed and a quiet presence that calmed. But everyone in the family knew there was another woman behind it. She also knew it. She wrestled her whole life with the brutal fact that her external appearance and interior life didn't match up, the one full of light, the other cavernous and shadowed. Occasionally, as her daughter craving her mother's love, I had been able to find her deep waters. Most of the time I was left grasping at empty air.

In the silence of the kitchen, I gasped again and wondered what she'd intended with that peculiar word choice. I realized I would likely never know, but it left me wondering if she perhaps had a deeper interior life—a more developed conscience and self-awareness—than I had ever suspected. What was she lopping off, too, from the presentation of the mother we had all come to know and distrust?

THE DESPAIR IN ALL OF US

I'm now familiar enough with psychological diagnostic manuals to find names for my mother's ailments, her bottomless pit, consuming regrets, occasional tenderness, and flaring cruelty. Later in her life, when she went to graduate school to become a therapist, she told me, on one of her good days, that she thought she suffered from borderline personality disorder, a diagnosis that meant different things back in the eighties when she first read about it. But for me, that term never came as close to capturing her character as the theological description of despair given by the nineteenth-century Danish theologian Søren Kierkegaard in his little book *The Sickness unto Death*. I was assigned the book in a philosophy class my sophomore year at the University of Oklahoma. Reading it in my dorm room late one night, I felt my mother breathing over my shoulder when I came to the part that summed her up.

The dorm room where I first read Kierkegaard had two built-in single beds in cheap veneered wood, a shared chest of drawers, and a tiny bathroom that my roommate and I shared with the two women next door. I lived on the twelfth floor, and as I adjusted the reading lamp to read Kierkegaard's pages even more carefully, I pulled up the white bedspread with the blue and pink flowers my mom had bought for me.

Despair, Kierkegaard wrote, is a fundamental feature of all human life. No one escapes it. But people manage it in dramatically different ways—some destructive, some healthy. He tells us that everyone, by virtue of being alive, has to confront a terrible but inescapable contradiction. On the one hand, we are *finite*; we are born, we die, we have bodies and must grapple with circumstances we don't control. These features of our lives—whatever form they take—are simply givens. They comprise our destiny, those things about us over which we have no control. Of course, the hardest truth for us to accept is the unavoidable fact that we will die. Our lives are finite because they have a definite endpoint. However death arrives, the day will come for all of us. On the other hand, we are *infinite*, insofar as we are self-aware and can imagine ourselves living other lives, doing other things, being other people. We can also imagine higher realities like God, truth, and goodness. We can even imagine—and yearn for—the possibility of living forever, immortality. We know time keeps going on earth after our death, and we imagine what it might be like to keep living, on and on. Failing that, we dream up a place called heaven onto which we project this desire, a place that promises to satisfy our quest to transcend our finitude.

Kierkegaard explains that this tension between our finitude and our capacity for imagining infinity—the tension between our given destiny and our imagined freedom—creates enormous anxiety in us. No one escapes it. It is an endemic part of our humanity. We know what we are and imagine always what we might have been or could be. From this unavoidable anxiety is born despair, especially when we face the hard truth of death. We will die, having lived only a fraction of what we imagine was possible, much of it having been determined by the fate of our particular circumstances. There's no way around it, but even so, we rage against it, always imagining, pleading for, demanding otherwise. And yet no matter how forceful or loud they may be, our demands do not change the outcome. This is why we despair. Our lives are a riddle that we can't solve, and we are tempted to collapse under the weight of this knowledge, to lose hope, to feel the whole setup is a cruel game, and worst of all, a pointless one.

Kierkegaard then provides four "character sketches" of how different people manage this internal struggle with despair and death. The first group of people—I think of them as "the flitterers"—just refuse to acknowledge it; they flit about, untroubled by it, but also not thinking much about anything. As Kierkegaard describes this type of person, "one can never forbear to smile at such a despair, who humanly speaking, although he is in despair, is so very innocent. Commonly such a despairer is infinitely comic." The second group—I think of them as "the cravers"—recognizes despair but tamps it down by attaching themselves to things like jobs, families, religion, art, or, in far too many cases, drugs or alcohol. As Kierkegaard puts it, "What we call worldliness simply consists of such people who, if one may so express it, pawn themselves to the world."

The third group recognizes the inevitability of despair for what it is—inevitable—but furiously rages against the fact that they do not control their own destiny. Consumed by their anger, they fall into lives of desperate misery—these I think of as "the ragers." Constant victims of their own failed desires, they hate themselves or, avoiding that, hate the people around them.

There is also a fourth group, those who, when confronted with their despair, are able to see themselves as part of something bigger. They recognize this something "bigger" not by more rigorously asserting themselves but by releasing their rage and losing themselves as they let themselves become part of that bigger reality. Kierkegaard calls this "bigger" "the ground from which we come" and "eternity." Some people call this bigger thing God. I call it grace. Accepting grace doesn't mean your life suddenly gets easier, but it does give you the courage, gratitude, and humility needed to live fully. It allows you to be present in life's mystery and complexity rather than railing against it. The paradoxical nature of this acceptance is that it allows you to gain yourself by losing yourself. Rather than desperately holding on to things that will never satisfy you, you let go of your frantic grasping and trust that the ground from which you come will hold you. Then, without the usual props needed to keep you going, you are more radically open and vulnerable to life as it is. Although Kierkegaard would never have named the fourth group this, I think of them as the "awakened."

As for the first three characters, Kierkegaard's depictions spare nothing, especially when it comes to the "ragers":

> Eternity asks you and every individual in these millions and millions only one thing: whether you have lived in despair or not, whether you have despaired in such a way that you did not realize that you were in despair, or in such a way that you covertly carried this sickness inside of you as your gnawing secret . . . or in such a way that you, a terror to others, raged in despair.

Those words "a terror to others" seemed to me, at the time, a harsh term to use to describe any mother. But the longer I stared at them, the more I found my mother's beautiful face looking back from the page at me, showing me what I had known from the beginning. That was her. Sarah Jones was a terror . . . to herself, to me, to others, raging in despair over the lives she never had.

MOTHERS AND DAUGHTERS

How she came to be this way remains partly a mystery to me as it was to her. She did not have much respect or love for her own mother, Peggy Horton Jones. My mom often told me—and only me, as it turns out—the story about the day she, my mother, was born. That day, at exactly that same hour, her grandmother, Sarah Elizabeth Cole Horton, died of a heart attack, back in Tennessee. From that awful day on, Sarah Elizabeth's daughter, Peggy (my grandmother), then twenty-two, talked in a baby voice, as if she were stuck in the gravity of the moment, becoming forever the young child of a dead mother. She was

baby voiced through and through. She even ate like an infant, picking
at her food like a small bird, dropping little bits in her mouth here and
there. She was frail, fragile, and absent. She flittered. Like Kierkegaard's first character.

Peggy, born Lou Lynn in 1909, and her sister, Naomi, born in
1903 (we called her Aunt Sissy), came from a sharecropper family who
worked a small farm outside of Milan, Tennessee. They spent their
early lives in the fields, carrying the harvest in bins on their shoulders,
and walked to school and the town and back. One day as they were
walking home from school they spotted smoke over the top of the
nearby hill. Running to its crest, my grandmother and aunt saw their
small wooden farmhouse on fire. Their mother, Sarah Elizabeth, had
been ironing and left the iron on a pile of clothes while it was still red-
hot from the coals. She later said that she had simply decided, midway
through, to take a nap. That she would send her entire family's meager
belongings up in flames for the sake of an afternoon rest was troubling
to the whole Horton crew.

As her daughters ran screaming and shouting for their mother,
Sarah Elizabeth awoke and drifted out of the house, unharmed and
blissfully unaware of the fire blazing around her. Their father, Samuel,
rebuilt the house and strategically planted the flittering Peggy by Sarah
Elizabeth's side, to keep her, as they said, "pinned to the ground." And
so it started. Peggy became her mother's mother. And my mother,
then, became her own mother Peggy's ground-pinning mother. It continued with me. I was tasked with pinning her down lest her despair
sweep her away with nary a thought. In response to my given "pinning
down" task, my mother both loved and needed me and, at the same
time, railed against me.

Mothers and daughters and mothers again. A bit like the original
sin that stained Dick Jones's family, my mother's inheritance directed
her behaviors and life path. Despair consumed her, albeit in its distinct

"beautiful woman" form. She inherited the sin of always being any-where other than where she actually was, defined always by the gaze of whomever beheld and adored her. The other's gaze was never perma-nent, her own life never a solid object of her own desire or love or grace. Forever captive to the opinion of others, her internal world was a con-coction of externally generated value. No wonder she raged. The roiling steam of those empty valuations must have infuriated her. No wonder, too, that she raged at me. I was the daughter who she hoped might love her completely, fulfill her, be the mother she never had, take her be-yond herself, awaken her. But I couldn't. A kid in tight red shorts, a gold watch in her panties, her mind set on extraterrestrial matters, plan-ning how she herself might escape the traps that awaited her on Mars. On Earth. At home. Sadly, my mother was smart enough to know that her life could have been otherwise. I also believe that she knew I couldn't carry her to that grace-filled, otherwise place. But knowing that I couldn't—that no one could—made her rage all the more unbearable.

Did Kierkegaard ever imagine the despair that generations of mothers could pass along to their daughters? I talk to him often in my mind, trying to explain this imposed inheritance. Wondering what he might have said about flitterers, cravers, ragers, and the awakened in female form? Its female traps? Its maternal rage? Its daughterly failures?

It is much easier, I believe, for a person to have the courage to let go of herself, when she knows she has a self, in the first place. For my mother, she couldn't grab ahold of the self she had long enough to re-lease herself from it. Like so many women of her generation and gen-erations before her, her destiny was to be a flitterer, a craver, or a rager. The social system defining women's roles—the destiny she inherited—was constructed to pin her down, to prevent her from waking up to the freedom she had. In many ways, Kierkegaard missed this reality, al-though he got the bigger picture. For most of my young life, I missed it as well.

Much later in her life, my mother would reveal to me the even greater depths of her despair, its desperate secrets, its failed graspings, its supposed crimes. It followed her all the way to her grave. In my own life, too, I've felt the creep of that despair and rage. Especially when I so strenuously wished my life could be otherwise, my family could be otherwise, my work could be otherwise, that the world around me could be otherwise, that our nation could be otherwise. Especially when I focus on my "self." It usually lasts until I realize eventually that I cannot create that otherwise world for my needy self and recognize the arrogance of presuming that I could. Of all the sins that befall us, despair is the most cunning. Kierkegaard saw this with excruciating clarity.

When I look at America, this Dane's characters leap off the page and land like colored map pins, marking the varied despairs with which we grapple. Our country sells "the self" and all the things that can improve it, satisfy it, feed it. But the self can never be satiated. Its four manifestations according to Kierkegaard are flourishing in America today.

The flitterers are easy to spot. They are the sparkly ones who find fulfillment in the superficial pleasures of our culture. The clothes. The cars. The perfect body shape. The music videos. The latest blog. The celebrity obsession. The imagined spotlight. Kierkegaard tells us they are blissfully innocent, unaware of their shallowness. Indeed, they delight in it. Then one step away from the flitterers are the cravers, millions of them, who, unlike the flitterers, know they are missing something. The well of need inside them is deep, dry, and thirsty. So they grab ahold of things that promise to fill them up, to stop the craving. So frenzied are those cravings that the world around them, the people they are connected to, recede from view, their individual scramble after personal need too consuming. Our market-driven, capitalist society depends on cravers to do this so that they might better consume its products. In fact, the market creates them; like a burning furnace of desire, it throws off endless flames of hot, unsatisfied needs so that it can profit from the quenching water it appears to offer. Cravers are addicts, and in America, our addictions are legion. The great lie that haunts addicts is the belief that their drug of choice might satisfy them, wake them up, and connect them to life. But in reality, their drugs assure that they slumber away a lifetime.

And then there are the ragers—my mother and her countless American relatives. They are awake enough to know that life has much to offer them and that they are responsible for the choices they make. They are industrious, ambitious, aspiring, goal setting, and often goodwilled. But when markets crash, jobs disappear, families fall apart, health disintegrates, bills pile up, homes are reclaimed, and in the other numerous ways that life thwarts these ambitions, all those hopes spiral down into a state of despair. And then comes rage. Billowing hot rage at the failed state of their existence. The fact that they are blessed (or cursed) with the capacity to imagine that life could actually be otherwise serves to fuel that rage and it eventually morphs into hatred. Hatred for people who have what you don't. People above you as well as people below you. Hatred at the people you believe caused your failure, scapegoats for your fury. Ragers find easy targets, ready distractions. My mother found me. White people find black and brown people, the poor, the outsiders, the immigrants. Christians aim their rage at Muslims. Liberals at right-wingers. Conservatives at liberals. In the rubble of a failing country, the historical targets available to us are as endless as the new ones we manage to conjure up. But as Kierkegaard points out, this raging despair is profoundly misdirected. Rather than rage, which is usually rooted in the fear of death, the cure lies in letting go of these useless gambits at control, stripping off the armor of hate that clothes you, and turning your attention to the freeing truth about our ultimate destiny. A destiny that holds us even in death. Love. Grace.

In his books *Fear and Trembling* and *Either/Or*, Kierkegaard describes in his own uniquely powerful way the path my mother—and so many others—could have taken. It was there for her, from the start, only inches away. But instead of stepping toward freedom, she clutched her pain tightly, afraid to release the pleasures of her beauty and her easily acquired scapegoats.

He calls the person who walks this path "the knight of faith" and "the knight of infinity," images that always bring me back to that day on the playground where, caught up in the mystery of infinite possibility, I lost not only the watch, but I managed, even then, to momentarily lose myself, to let go of the given and travel to far-off lands where my quest was to defend goodness. Letting go of everything—treasured watches and the hot metal of a playground gym—I fell into something greater. In an often-quoted passage from *Either/Or*, Kierkegaard describes this falling:

> When around one everything has become silent, solemn as a clear, starlit night, when the soul comes to be alone in the whole world, then before one there appears, not an extraordinary human being, but the eternal power itself, then the heavens seem to open . . . and the *I* chooses itself or, more correctly, receives itself. Then the personality receives the accolade of knighthood that ennobles it for an eternity.

I've tried to find a better image than "knights." Perhaps it is that of a lover. A curious lover. An openhearted, questing lover. A world-embracing lover. A lover who accepts that they—and all of us—are beloved so long as we defer to the divine and forgo the unquenchable needs of the self. Although I can hardly claim that my own life has embraced this depth of lovingness, I glimpse its possibility. My greatest regret for my mother is that she never got near it. The world, it seems, stopped her, pinned her down to motherhood and wifedom, hampered her ability to see beyond her beauty, hindered her from letting go of the self she never claimed.

Or did it?

Was this the whole of her? Kierkegaard's failed knight of resignation? A stilted lover of the divine?

After our conversation in the cabin's kitchen that day, I never forgot that odd, seemingly off-the-cuff comment she sneaked in about the crimes she was planning. Whatever she may have been referring to—at that point in my life I had no idea—her words nonetheless suggested an agency, a willful overstepping of given boundaries, an imagination that reached beyond the expected. It hinted of a mystery hidden somewhere in her depths, down there churning away at the bottom of her well.

In the instant of her strange comment, our roles flipped over.

I was calling to her, "Mom, where are you?"

She was trying to tell me, "I'm coming, sweet girl. I'm coming."

And when she finally showed up, I was the one surprised by her presence.

Mothers and daughters.

Daughters and mothers.

And mothers and daughters again.

CHAPTER 5

Barth and Niebuhr in the Bell Tower

By grace you have been saved! To be saved does not just mean
to be a little encouraged, a little comforted, a little relieved.
It means to be pulled out like a log from a burning fire.

KARL BARTH, "SERMON IN THE BASEL PRISON," 1955

When you go to church as regularly as I did as a child, you end
up daydreaming a lot to pass the time. I enjoyed the singing,
so about half of each service was pleasant and engaging. But during the
other half—when there weren't songs to sing—I grew even more intrigued. Going to church became one of the most stimulating times of
the week for my imagination. My mother would hand me colored pen-
cils and blank donation envelopes to keep me still, and I would proceed
to draw the Bible readings. Abraham's long beard; the burning bush;
Jesus on the Cross; the loaves of bread and fish; Goliath—this was my
weekly chance to sketch all the characters I heard described from the
pulpit into vibrant and occasionally ghoulish color.

By the time I was six or so, certain phrases from the service or from
a recitation or a prayer or the songs began to trigger avalanches of
fantastical landscapes and adventures in my imagination, and my mind

would quickly float out of the church hall and enter a realm of theological creativity.

The image set that perhaps most triggered my imagination and charged my fantasies was from one of my favorite hymns, "Be Thou My Vision." One of the verses was: "Thou my best thought, by day or by night. Waking or sleeping, thy presence my light."

The idea of God influencing your thoughts, making them better and brighter, captivated me. I would imagine God in my brain, directing traffic through it and plucking out the bad thoughts from the good. I literally thought I could feel God inside my head orchestrating the movement in my brain like a cop at an intersection. And God as light. I would look up from my pew and feel the light streaming in on me, beaming in on me like a spotlight and warming me, warming my insides. I intuited that these were two very different sides of God in the same lyric—the God who monitored my thoughts and the God who warmed me up, flooding me with light. But the dissonance of the images did not trouble me then. I loved them both. As I sat there in the pew, I alternated between feeling God inside my brain and feeling God's warm, bright light on my body.

Outside of church, the verse would sing itself in my ears during car rides as the sun came in through the windows, during long family Sunday lunches when my thoughts would wander, or during boring elementary-school lessons when my imagination would run wild, too. I would address my imaginary friends as "thou"; I would pretend to play the piano in accompaniment; I would see shapes of pure light outside the window and offer a secret wave at "God."

That verse was singing itself in my head as I rode in our station wagon packed with six of my friends on my eleventh birthday on July 31, 1970. My dad had taken a job teaching at Perkins School of Theology at Southern Methodist University in 1964, so we were living in Richardson, a mostly white suburb of Dallas. My parents had planned a pool party at my request, and I had, in the days prior, turned the event into an overdramatic, self-involved stage play. The car weaved through our neighborhood as we picked up friend after friend, and as each girl squeezed into the backseat, filling it with new bits of gossip and girl-speak, I felt my stardom slowly slipping away. And then the hymn started. It kept singing itself, my little girl's brain uncontrollable and my little girl's emotions in flux.

We picked up the last invitee, and she had to stretch out across our laps to fit in. None of us were wearing seat belts, of course, and my dad drove not so much like a madman as an intellectual—distracted, his eyes wandering, his mind locked on ideas and not on stop signs or pedestrians. We pulled up to the Richardson public pool and it was clear to everyone that it was closed. My dad drove closer to the entrance and got out. I could make out the handwritten sign: CLOSED FOR MAIN-TENANCE.

My dad looked up to the sky like he always did when he faced a conundrum. He wasn't praying or asking for divine intervention, but I think now that the habit of praying and the sensation of being per-plexed had somehow become one and the same for him.

He walked back to the car, hopped in, and turned the key.

"We're going to have to drive over to the Lake Highlands pool," he said as he pulled out of the parking lot.

I was stunned. Lake Highlands on my birthday? The party I had been imagining for weeks was now going to take place in Lake High-lands?

I wanted to cry, then I wanted to scream and punch the back of his seat. I remember those two emotions so vividly that I still clench my fists when thinking about the moment.

"Oh, gross!" I said. "I don't want to swim with black people!"

I remember feeling an overwhelming heat come over me, from my throat to my feet.

Lake Highlands, we all knew, was in the African American part of Dallas. The few times we had driven by it from our white suburban side of town, I remember feeling like I was looking at a world so radically different from my more familiar surroundings. Another land.

"Who said that?" my father demanded, but I could tell he knew well it had been me. He dramatically pulled the car over to the side of the road and looked back at us one by one, his fierce eyes finally locking on mine.

I was in the middle of the backseat and I wiggled my arm out of our squeezed mass of bodies and raised my hand. Then I started to tear up. "It just came out of me!" I whimpered.

My friends pulled away from me as much as they could and stared out the windows. I could tell they were relieved that I had said what they were thinking and they were startled by my father's wrath.

"You have no idea how horrible what you just said is," my dad said, his voice trembling with rage. "I can't imagine an appropriate punishment. I am going to give you a choice, young lady. We don't go to the pool and you never have another birthday party again. Or we go to the pool and you get to have parties each year. That simple."

I could feel that my friends' bodies were starting to squirm. I couldn't breathe.

"I never want to have another birthday party again," I said, staring straight into his eyes, feeling myself become emboldened the longer I went without blinking.

But I was picking a fight with the wrong guy. As a teenager and young man, my dad, much to the chagrin of Dick Jones, had already been in the thick of the civil rights movement. Later, he was the head of a campaign called LEARN, an effort to try to change the composition of our Richardson Public School Board. The goal was integration of all Dallas schools, something that did not go over well in our all-white suburban neighborhood of the 1960s. That same spring the FBI had tapped our house phone. We'd overheard my dad telling my mother his suspicion one day. I remember my sister Kindy holding the phone to my ear so that I could hear the slight clicking noise that the old-fashioned phone taps generated. I was seven years old and wasn't sure what it meant to be watched by the FBI, but my abiding sense was that my dad was somehow important. I liked that.

But now I felt like I could barely see him. The fog of shame was all around me; the lyrics of "Be Thou My Vision" abandoned me. I was so concerned that my friends would abandon me if we went to the pool. In my mind, my dad was forcing me to choose—be moral or keep my friends. I was—like so many times in my childhood—deeply ashamed. By things I didn't fully understand.

Then I grew really mad at my dad. My shock at his fierceness turned into a stomach-tightening anger. He had snapped at me like he did at Dick Jones—he was equating me with Dick Jones! I felt the horror of saying something racist and sinful and feeling like it was the absolute end of the world.

We drove back to our house. I went right to my room, closed the door, and, as was my usual course of escape, I cried. Everyone else stayed in the living room, eating all the party food my mom had put out. I could hear them playing Pin the Tail on the Donkey. They were all Kindy's friends, too. She was quite the organizer, and I could hear her orchestrating the proceedings with exaggerated friendliness to compensate for my absence. I heard Verity, now four, squealing with delight at the antics of my sister and friends. Neither my mom nor my dad came to comfort me. I told myself I would never go outside again. My parents socialized with African Americans far more than most white parents, not least because of my dad's political involvement. And I never wanted to face a black person again—they would all know what I had said. I would be so ashamed that I could not look at them, any of them, ever again.

Then my mom knocked on the door and shouted that they were ready to blow out the candles on the cake. I composed myself and walked out, refusing to look my friends in the eye for fear of sensing their fascination with my plight. My mom had promised me a red velvet cake, but as soon as I set eyes on the cake, all I saw was a concrete-colored slab.

"I'm sorry, honey, I forgot to put the red dye in!" Her words were touched with humor. "Verity had climbed onto the kitchen table and was about to jump off, and I got all distracted. Just close your eyes, honey, and pretend it's red."

That broke me. I had so desired a red velvet cake, not a gray one, that I crumbled. I ran back to my room and buried my head in my pillow. Twenty minutes later, I heard the kids leaving, the car doors closing out front. I guess I fell asleep, for the next morning my father awakened Kindy and me. I went out into the kitchen and expected another tongue-lashing, but it never came. Like so many things, no one ever mentioned the debacle again. As my mother washed dishes, my father cheerily started planning my birthday party for the next year, even though according to his harsh terms I hadn't earned it.

My confusion about racism would only grow, not least because of my parents' failure to address it in a more age-appropriate way. What I had not yet grasped was the deeper social harms embedded in my young-girl words. The centuries of violence that undergirded them. The very real damage they were still inflicting upon African Americans, not just in Richardson, but throughout the United States. Why was it that I didn't want to be in a swimming pool, my skinny white body sharing the same water with, maybe even crashing into, black bodies? That afternoon, crying into my tear-soaked pillow, I had to ask myself that question. What was so horrible about it? I knew the thought of being in that pool felt icky, but I didn't know why I felt that way.

I wasn't old enough then to realize that the knee-jerk repulsion I felt was the inheritance passed down to me from literally hundreds of years of white people propagating and benefiting from this learned reaction to black bodies: They were impure, dirty, somehow threatening, a source of revulsion, a cause for fear—all views forged in the crucible of a brutal chattel slavery system that spawned such feelings and attitudes in order to bolster and enforce it. I had absorbed—or, Calvin would say, inherited as sin—these feelings, most of them still inarticulate, from the white world I inhabited. Despite my liberal upbringing, they were pressed into my being with excoriating force. These days, we would call this kind of inheritance "unconscious bias," a term that captures well the degree to which our deepest hatreds and fears live within us, burrowed away in places that escape the restraints our conscious minds impose.

Racism and white supremacy thrive in habits our brains and bodies learn without our ever having to "think" about it. White revulsion at blackness was in the air I breathed and the water I drank and swam in in Texas and in Oklahoma in the 1960s. And it had been there for centuries. Even though my parents lectured us constantly about the sins of such views, that day of the disastrous pool party both they and I faced the horrible reality that changing one's conscious white ideas about black people didn't put a dent in the hatreds that roiled around under the surface of those liberal thoughts, exerting more force than the liberal ideals that lived in the shallow waters of my thinking mind. All of this escaped my eleven-year-old brain.

What didn't escape me, though, was the simple fact that the power my peers had over me was stronger than the conscious lessons I had learned from my parents. At eleven, I was old enough to know basic right from wrong and to realize I had choices about it. The moment I said it, I knew it was wrong, even though I didn't comprehend the depths from which it originated. My desire to be accepted and liked by my friends, to fit in, to be cool, to be the center of attention on my birthday, overrode everything else I knew. Every little white girl in that crammed-full car had the same racist feelings that I had. I could feel it. I knew it. In the face of that collective force, the pull to belong socially won the day. It has, in fact, won the day when it comes to racism in the United States since the beginning. The pressure of the crowd, the need to prove that I was truly a member of my/their white-girl tribe, to find safety in the same-mindedness of the group—these basic human instincts took ahold of me with stunning force and speed. In a split second, I chose to concede to that desire to belong, knowing it was wrong. I knew I was responsible for my concession. There was no way around it. I did it. There was no one to blame for this but me. Getting mad at my father for making me feel bad was but a meager attempt to avoid this truth.

I wouldn't have put it this way back then, even though at the time it was something I knew and felt. I hadn't chosen to inherit the embodied legacy of white supremacy, but I had chosen to please the crowd by enacting it. And I was responsible for the continued presence of white supremacy in the world. Years later, Calvin gave me the words to understand this awful reality. Caught in sin we didn't choose, we are nonetheless responsible for it.

Burning in the fires of sin, I also caught a glimpse of grace—the love that ultimately wins. My dad's hard line that day belied the softer, contemplative side that came out the next morning during breakfast, when I discovered my sins were not forgotten but were forgiven. On the other side of my terrible act, love pulled me out of shame and gave me permission to get on with the tumultuous task of growing up. That display of grace from my father might seem implausible coming from a son of Dick Jones, who never showed such compassion. In this and many ways my father wasn't Dick Jones's son but rather the son of Idabel and, before she died, my great-grandmothers, Effie and Dollie.

THE INFLUENCE OF BARTH

My father was the youngest child; by the time he was born in 1936, Dick Jones was gone a lot, traveling for his booming legal practice. My grandma loved talking with him about her roses and he would help her cook; when he was small, he followed her around the house, holding the hem of the blue denim culottes she wore as skirtlike pants. She taught him a lot about the value of community, telling him stories about how everyone pitched in to help run her childhood farm. And about kindness, God's kindness in giving to the wheat fields in Billings and now the roses in her garden all the sun and water they needed to grow, just like my father had all the love he needed from God to grow into a strong, kind young man.

All the while though, Dick Jones did his best to encourage competition between my dad and his brother, Sterling. As boys, they fought constantly; Sterling, being older, always had the upper hand. Since they played on the same basketball team when they were young, the court became the source of even more tension. Over the years, that tension would spread even to their dramatically different life choices.

Nowhere was this more evident than in their lifelong political differences. In the sixties, Sterling ended up joining the John Birch Society, a conservative antigovernment, racist advocacy group, and had regular conversations with Dick Jones about the tyrannies of the federal government and the threat of black people. In contrast, as a young adult, my dad was consumed with reading theologians like Kierkegaard, Calvin, and, most important, the famous Reinhold Niebuhr, a theologian from Union Theological Seminary who had become the public voice of moral America in the 1950s. As to why these two sons chose radically different paths, it is hard to say. It may be as random as the fact of their birth order or that Dick spent more time with Sterling while Idabel spent her days with Joe. There is no doubt more to it than that, but the deeper reasons escape me, as it most likely also escaped them.

For my grandpa, my father's reading choices, and eventually his choice to become a theologian, were a sign of some strange genetic glitch. All the men in the family were predestined for lives in business or law. Oklahoma was in the throes of yet another oil boom, and money was there to be picked up as easily as pulling grain off wheat chaff at harvest if you were clever enough. My grandpa took particular pride in his ability to claim it.

As a young lawyer, Dick Jones helped dream up the previously unimaginable legal concept that one could separate the surface of the earth from the ground underneath it and sell that unseen underneath as "mineral rights." He told us he helped refine this idea—for which he became well known through his successful defense of a mineral rights claim of the heirs of the Creek man Jackson Barnett—because he wanted to help land-rich but dirt-poor Native Americans sell their underground rights for a profit while keeping the topsoil for farming. Whatever the reason, the law eventually cleared the way for clever white men to buy up Oklahoma's vast oil fields for nothing. Tellingly, Dick Jones never sold the mineral rights to my grandma's farm in Billings. It supported several wells that went dry in the sixties but by 2004 were trickling out oil once again when oilmen like my uncles and cousins figured out how to squeeze out even more oil by pushing chemicals deep into the earth. Little did my grandpa know that his idea about mineral rights would eventually lead to fracking and that he'd inadvertently set the stage for the constant stream of earthquakes that one day would topple the chimney of his former house in Forest Park.

As if by some miracle of grace, however, the particular sins born of oil lust were never visited upon my father. He had little interest in money. His currency, from an early age, had been in ideas, especially theology. At the University of Oklahoma, he started studying with legendary philosophy professor J. Clayton Feaver, who took him from reading theology for fun to a disciplined study of not just Niebuhr but another Union Theological Seminary professor, Paul Tillich. Feaver, a beloved teacher, told my dad that he had a great philosophical mind and pointed him toward a life of scholarship, beginning with doctoral work in philosophical theology at Yale.

My father wrote his dissertation on Karl Barth's *Church Dogmatics*, a fourteen-volume work that changed the landscape of twentieth-century theology through its pounding insistence—page after page for thousands of pages—that the biggest danger for Christians was the tendency for us to make God in our own image. When my father first explained Barth to me as a young girl, he didn't jump to this point, however. He told the story of Barth's first job as a pastor, right out of seminary, in the small Swiss town of Safenvil, where he served for ten years from 1911 to 1921. That our grandparents were digging around in prairie dirt in Okemah and Billings at the same time wasn't missed by me. My dad described Safenvil as a poor town, where everyone worked long hours of hard labor and suffered the pains of their toil. I imagined another young Swiss version of Idabel, there in Switzerland, lying under a cart in the fields while her parents worked the harvest. Barth, my father told me, was shocked by the conditions there. No health care, scant education, little money for food, and even less sense that their lives mattered to anyone outside the walls of their small village. In the great halls of power, they were nothing.

Europe was tumbling headlong into World War One at the time, a war that Barth believed was invented by rich men so that they could become even richer off the war machine they were building. He was also astounded by the willingness of educated, elite Germans to sign on to Kaiser Wilhelm II's demonic war policies. When his own beloved teachers from his seminary in Germany supported the kaiser's war agenda, Barth's rage exploded, knowing that the war would lead to even further suffering in his small village. He took pen to paper and in a matter of weeks wrote what now stands as a classic in theological annals, *Der Romerbrief*, his commentary on Paul's Epistle to the Romans. So biting and forceful was his critique of German Christianity's willingness to follow the lead of rich, greedy men that it immediately gained worldwide attention.

"This little book," my father said as he held up the slim volume for me and Kindy to see, "was so powerful, so groundbreaking at the time, that it was as if Barth had stumbled into the Safenvil church tower and pulled its bell's rope, ringing it so loudly that all of Europe came running," He had borrowed that image from the annals of Barth scholarship and it captured him perfectly.

My dad also loved another image used for the book at the time. "He dropped a bomb on the playground of German theologians." Kindy and I delighted in the drama, translating it immediately into some Wild West version of the virtuous outlaws/lawmen stories we'd grown up with.

What Barth detested most was the fact that German theologians at the time were so caught up in celebrating the resurgence of German nationalism that they forgot their deeper connection to the God of love and mercy who cares for the poor and detests the arrogance of the powerful. Like Okemah had done to our own Woody Guthrie, Safenvil turned Barth into a lifelong socialist who insisted, even when no one was listening, that the universal equality of God's love, not nationalistic self-love, was the most fundamental truth of all. My father told us, over and over again, of Barth's insistence that human beings were always building idols of self-interest that they turned into gods and in doing so shut their eyes and ears to the real message of divine grace with which God blessed humanity.

I heard this so often that I eventually drew a little picture in my head that helped me understand what Barth was talking about. At the bottom of my picture, there were lots of little men in suits and uniforms, carrying bags of money and big guns, running around acting like they owned the world and, along with it, God. I could see little cartoon bubbles above their heads, filled with the word "God," and attached to it their pictures. There were so many bubbles like this, from so many men, that they formed a crowded canopy of bubbles, a protective umbrella of theological truisms that covered the whole bottom part of my mind's scene. Way above and stretching out all around these little men and their bubbles was a place called Infinity, where God lived. It included everything from the beginning of time all the way to the future yet to be lived. And there was God—he was still an old man in my mind, but a very, very big and good one—who was trying to send down to the people messages about his love and hope and grace. But in my picture, God's words kept bouncing off that huge canopy of word bubbles, never breaking through, and finally failing to stop the bloody war that was soon to break out among them.

But there on the ground, running around frantically among the puffed-up, deluded men, were two bright lights, Karl Barth and my dad, Joe Jones. They were caught in a life-and-death struggle with the bad men, weary but valiant, struggling to cut a hole in the vast umbrella so that God's love could break through and shine a light onto the world's frantic deceptions. To my young mind, the whole scene was even better than the outlaw tales of my grandpa's because in this one the stakes were cosmic and my father, a philosopher/theologian/basketball player from Oklahoma, was a hero, a soldier of truth, a fighter for God's justice.

This image of him passionately fighting for God's justice has never left me, although my view of God and the world has changed since that time. But my pride in my father remains, particularly my pride in the earnest commitment he brought to his life's work. As for his fellow theological warriors, I see them all so clearly in my mind, not just pretend pictures but real ones that hang beside his desk in his study even to this day. When my father was working on his dissertation, my mother had photocopied pictures of Kierkegaard, Barth, Schleiermacher, Tillich, and Wittgenstein and put them in little black frames from the local hardware store. These old-style European men simply looked theological—like they most certainly should be thinking about God and ethics and faith. I would come to realize, once I had found my own theological mentors, that these men told the story of my father's life, his quest as Kierkegaard's knight of faith. To be sure, they were his chosen lineage, not his actual bloodline of horse thieves, sodbusters, racists, canteen huggers, and wealthy lawyers. But for him, neither one displaced the other. Rather, the two parallel legacies threw ever-changing shadowy shapes across each other, revealing the endless depths of the truth each held for the other. To be sure they were also all Western white men, something my father never managed to get entirely beyond, an urgent challenge he would leave to me.

Some children grow up with pictures of athletes or Elvis or Kurt Cobain or Beyoncé on the wall; some children of doctors grow up around the medical world; some children of musicians grow up with sounds all around them. I grew up with ideas about God and justice floating around, and these men on the wall also set my destiny in a way. Some days I would walk in and stare into their intense eyes, squeezing my own brow tight as I tried to picture the cosmic struggles they had endured, the truths they had sought. Not surprisingly, it never occurred to me that I could live in their theological world or even stand beside them in the cosmic battle. They were brilliant men. I was just an Oklahoma girl with an extravagant fantasy life, unruly hair, and an emerging passion for cosmic truth.

SPIT IN THE FACE

One day in October 1971, an encounter with my father on a street corner in Richardson, Texas, defined my practical view of theology from that day forward. In addition to being a seminary professor, Dad was committed to his work in local politics. For me, his activist endeavors had redeemed the family name from Dick Jones, not so much publicly but internally (for our collective shame at Dick Jones—and his shame about us—grew as my immediate family's involvement in the civil rights movement increased). That year my dad was managing another school-board campaign for an African American man and a Jewish woman. That Saturday morning in October he took me with him to hand out flyers in front of Gibson's Hardware located in Richardson's small suburban shopping mall.

I stood next to him as he discussed the issues and his candidates' perspectives with passersby. It was a sunny day, hot for the fall, and I remember trying to position myself to catch his shadow.

Then, as a group of men in baseball caps approached, I suddenly felt what I thought was rain. How could this be? I looked up, squinted at the sun still alone in a cloudless sky, and saw a man spit straight into my father's face. My father's head whipsawed as if he had been punched; he kept his jaw against his shoulder for a moment, suddenly reaching for my hand; then he raised his head and watched as the men walked off. His hand still clenched mine, but I felt his body relax and saw him stand taller.

Repulsed, I wiped the spittle from my hair. My eyes started to tear up. My father let go of my hand, took out his handkerchief, and wiped his face. Then he looked down at me, smiled kindly, and dabbed my hair.

"We are all children of light and children of darkness," he said. "You and me and those men, we are children of the same God."

I did not register then that it was the title of one of Reinhold Niebuhr's best-selling books on religion and politics, *The Children of Light and the Children of Darkness: A Vindication of Democracy and a Critique of Its Traditional Defense.* I could only register shock at my father's lack of anger and my startled sense that something deep had happened. I did not say a word. I just kept holding his hand again for another half hour while he kept handing out flyers. Martin Luther King Jr.'s pacifist resistance had so influenced him, I think, that he had come to imitate the civil rights leader in moments large and small. But back then, I was simply awed by him. His studied restraint and pithy theological summation of the encounter seemed more powerful, more manlike than any reaction John Wayne would have acted out in the movies.

On the drive home in my family's station wagon, I experienced another cosmic rush in my imagination. The picture I had drawn in my mind of Karl Barth and my father suddenly looked different. Yes, my father was still a man who fought for goodness in the face of evil—his patient work of handing out flyers to people who mostly ignored him made that clear—but when those men spit at him, he didn't respond by slugging them or shouting angry words at them about their bigotry or the offense they had caused his daughter. No, he accepted their anger with what almost seemed like kindness. Kindness? What a strange way to fight for justice. And even more strangely, his words to me about all of us being children of light and darkness seemed to suggest that he saw a part of himself in those despicable men. Like he, too, was one of them. The high drama of my earlier version of theology fizzled out right then and there, diffused by his act of drawing these seemingly bad guys toward him, sharing their lot. As a political, theological act, no less. My confusion was profound.

Later that night at dinner, over my mother's hamburger casserole, I tried to tell the family what had happened, not sure whether I should act ashamed that my dad had been spit on or admit how oddly proud he had made me feel. Kindy pushed a noodle through her pursed lips, comically threatening to spit on me. Verity spit out the hamburger meat and asked for an Oreo. My mother glared at my dad, her eyes furious that I had been exposed to such a grown-up thing.

"I'm sorry you had to witness that, Serene," my dad finally responded, now using his professor voice. "I don't agree with the views of those men, but it's critically important that we never allow ourselves to believe we are fundamentally better than anyone else. Who knows what life may have given them to deal with or how they were raised."

I thought about how he was raised by Dick Jones and marveled even more at his theological poise.

"Dad, please don't start talking about Schleiermacher or one of your other guys again," Kindy blurted out, feeling another one of his theological lectures coming on. She kicked me under the table, mad that I'd brought the whole thing up and provoked what was sure to be a theological onslaught of words we barely understood.

"No lecture tonight, girls. Sometimes actions teach theology better than any theologian's words could. Just remember, the grace of God falls upon us all in equal measure." He smiled at my mother. Kindy was visibly relieved at the brevity of his pronouncement. My mom got up to get Verity a cookie, a small reward for our collective avoidance of a long dinnertime lecture.

It struck me then like never before, even though I'd always known it. The theology I was raised on wasn't just a series of grand cosmic dramas. It was a way of life. It was made up of actions, like campaigning for change and being kind to mean people. Like my Disciples Sunday school teachers had been telling me all these years, faith and love were not two different things. They were one and the same, which made us all one and the same, as children of God.

CHILDREN OF SIN, CHILDREN OF GLORY

Years later, when I finally read Niebuhr's book *The Children of Light, the Children of Darkness* for the first time, I was sitting in the old redbrick library at the University of Oklahoma. Dick Sterling Redman Jones had probably sat in the same chair, as I was a third-generation University of Oklahoma student (eight of my cousins were enrolled at the same time as I was). I loved to go there on Saturday afternoons, during OU football games, because the space was so quiet, almost hallowed. And suddenly that day I could almost feel again the spit from those men's mouths landing on us. As my own understanding of the meaning of social justice grew, I read it with different eyes, not only seeing both groups of children as one, but understanding, in disturbing ways, the profound political implications of this theology for America's future.

Writing in 1944, Niebuhr clearly saw German nationalism as an assault on the underlying values of American democracy. When he describes the "children of light," however, they came across as naive idealists who, seeing the good in human nature, insisted that goodness will conquer evil, and that as a society we were surely evolving toward a more loving world where human rights and equality were embraced by all. As a young college activist, I saw my own utopian idealism reflected in his words. At the time, I was the campus coordinator of the student caucus advocating for the passage of the ERA—the eventually failed Equal Rights Amendment that would have stated, in the Constitution, that in all things, women claimed the same rights as men. It had seemed so obvious to me that this was a true and good movement that when it failed to pass, my own innocent political excitement about the amendment was abruptly called into question. I was shocked that huge numbers of people did not see it my way, the way of Niebuhr's children of light.

In contrast, Niebuhr tells us that the children of the darkness were cannier and more worldly than their romanticizing counterparts who embraced the light. They were evil, yes, but that allowed them to have a more realistic appreciation of the role that self-interest, greed, pride, and fear played in political life. For these children, fear and selfishness would always prevail in public life—like it had with the failed ERA—because they were more pragmatic about the driving forces behind human behavior. Self-sacrifice for the sake of a greater common good might be laudable, but ultimately it would never hold sway among the masses of people for whom their own individual and communal survival and advancement would always take pride of place in politics.

The book also forced me to wrestle with hard questions about my growing commitment to a more economically just vision for America, which was supported by my Woody Guthrie theology. Would people ever choose to share the fruits of their labor with everyone, equally, without an authoritarian party forcing them to do it? Surely Dick Jones would never willingly agree to such a system. Could a democracy ever find the collective will to embrace such a radically egalitarian version of economic life? If the fruits of my Jones family legacy were true, it seemed a long shot. Especially if the cannier children were always smarter about manipulating human nature toward their own greedy agenda. I was disturbed, however, by Niebuhr's inability to grasp the depth of racism in America—and its ongoing legacy. When it came to both economic and racial justice, Niebuhr failed to enlighten me or convince me, but reading him intellectually convinced me, as had no other theologian, of the inextricable link between theology and politics.

For him, there was no such thing as "faith" that didn't intrude into "politics." If people's faith included, as it inevitably did, deeply held beliefs about human nature and the character of good and evil, then faith would always insert itself into policy decisions, which at every turn manifest those values in public form. He also gave sharpened form to my understanding of the collective, social nature of sin. More than even Calvin or Barth, Niebuhr pushed the point that while individual self-interest, pride, greed, etc., were always going to be there, the greatest threat of sin was the form these instincts took when they were aggregated into human systems of thought and politics. As long as societies existed, original sin would impress its evil desires upon our lives, often in ways we failed to notice or couldn't escape, like the white supremacy that seemed to live in the drinking water of Oke-mah or the sexually abusive air that seemed to flow through the vents in my grandparents' home.

But as my father would never fail to remind our family—and gen-erations of his theology students—the inevitability of this social ver-sion of original sin never provided an excuse for not struggling against it with every ounce of energy we had. It was our moral obligation, as people of faith, to work for justice, albeit armed with Niebuhrian prag-matism. It was also more than a moral obligation. It was a way of life, a state of being. If one believed in the ultimate truth of God's grace—its loving yes to all existence—then you couldn't help but reach toward that goodness. Your state of being—every part of your heart, mind, body, and soul, and its ancient knowledge of our connection to the earth and everything that dwells therein—yearned for it. And in that yearning, you became it.

My father believed this and tried to raise his three daughters this way. For him, the political force of faith was clear. I have never met a person who lived these commitments so thoroughly and theologically. By that I don't mean he lived better or worse than most, or that he necessarily lived a more moral life. I mean that he prepared for each human interaction—and later analyzed it—through his theology.

Every time we would go to Idabel and Dick's house, we would stop on the side of the street before pulling into the driveway, and there my dad would prepare the three of us for the likely encounters with Dick Jones's sin by quoting or summarizing some theologian's wisdom, more often than not it was Niebuhr's or King's. And whenever we would leave their house, my dad would analyze whatever catastrophic deed Dick Jones had inevitably perpetrated through some sort of theological lens.

The sin-grace tension that would form the basis of my theology later in life has its origins in Dick Jones. Sin is everywhere—in us and in our neighbors, in our institutions and in our gatherings—but so, too, is grace. And so, too, are all the other tensions in human nature that go along with them: innocent idealism and canny self-interest, utopianism and pragmatism, rage and release, despair and hope, fear and trust. To see ourselves for what we really are, he taught me, is the first and hardest theological lesson of all. Niebuhr's insistence on our dualistic nature—each and every one of us and of humanity in general—would someday become the basis for what I would call a theology of forgiveness. If we cannot know and forgive the messy sins of our neighbors and our enemies, I would come to realize because of Dad, we can never learn to forgive the messy mix of sin and grace inside our own selves.

CHAPTER 6

The Impoverished Souls

In the final analysis, poverty means death . . .
Hence the poverty of the poor is not a call to generous relief
action, but a demand that we go and build a different social
order.

GUSTAVO GUTIÉRREZ, *A THEOLOGY OF LIBERATION*, 1973

His name was Freddy. I met him at a Sonic drive-in the week after my family moved back to Oklahoma from Dallas in 1974. He had long blond hair, a charmingly crooked smile, and unstoppable blue eyes; he was the first taste I ever had of pure energy and life. You might say that because of him, not my father, I decided to pursue a career in theology. That may be the most unromantic thing ever said about a former boyfriend, but it is true. He was James Dean without trying to be James Dean. He was a natural.

Four years later, having moved east after college and settled into life in the elite liberal eastern establishment, I realized he was also these things: white trash, dirt poor, lowlife, career criminal, pothead, social failure, marginal. And I loved him, and some days I still crave watching him ride off on his motorcycle after sheepishly kissing me just before midnight as my dad peered through the curtains of the living room.

Freddy fulfilled my force-fed vision of the Oklahoma outlaw: He had spent part of his boyhood in a juvenile detention center; he was arrested for breaking and entering and grand larceny the spring of my junior year of high school; he got arrested again for stealing a stereo and was charged with grand larceny a second time the month I finished high school. And yet his criminality was part Paul Newman in *Cool Hand Luke* and part Pretty Boy Floyd—he always seemed to prey exclusively on bad people (at least according to him) and he did it with such élan, with such an enchanting wink, that he embodied what would come to be known in cinema as the antihero.

After his second arrest Freddy decided to jump probation to avoid the possibility of going to prison, and to leave the state, going to work on an oil rig off the coast of Louisiana. It was the spring of 1977 and I was getting ready for my freshman year at the University of Oklahoma, less out of passion for that particular school than to fulfill my family's legacy there. I remember an aching all over my body as he told me his plan. I had never felt such a longing and romantic sadness, and I did not know what to make of the buckling sensations. We were the same age, had been in love for two years, and I was about to lose him to another state, a distant job, and myself, to college in another town, another world.

We were an odd, rebellious match. Everyone knew it. Especially his friends and our families. To his mother, who said she adored me, I was their ticket out of Enid and on to better things. I was the daughter of the president of our small town's university. My family went to church and belonged to the country club. To my parents, however, he was a troubling, teenage "moment" they patiently prayed would pass, and quickly. A high school dropout, he never belonged to any club or team or congregation; he couldn't imagine it. But that didn't mean he wasn't smart. He was smarter and quicker than most of the high school boys who strutted around acting brilliant and worldly in football jackets and pressed jeans, and he knew it. He wore a leather jacket and put his smarts to more practical uses, coaxing a smile out of me or figuring out how to buy or steal his next meal or put gas in his Harley.

Picking up fly-by-night jobs was his other talent. Mostly he laid tar on warehouse roofs or dug sludge out of the ponds around Enid's endless spread of oil rigs. He was also kind; he loved his brother and sister, worried endlessly about his mother's drinking and whatever man happened to appear in her life, and when it came to his friends, he freely shared what little money he had, though granted, it was mostly for beer or joints. He lived in the back bedroom of his mother's broken-down house on a dirt road in the poorest part of town. The electricity was usually cut off, the kitchen a repulsive mess, but he kept his small room spotless and lit candles and incense to create an enchanting atmosphere.

He was also ambitious, in his own way. He had learned from his older brother how to play the electric guitar and was a pretty good bass player in a local band. They played a few times a year around the county; their lead guitarist, Jimmy, was stunningly talented. Between the two of them and Eddie, their speed-freak drummer, they had dreams of making it big. Rush, Jimi Hendrix, Black Sabbath—these were their hero bands, their fantasy future. At age eighteen, I willingly shared that rebellious, clichéd fantasy. In our teenage brains, anything was possible, especially with a dose of hormones charging our hopes. Intrigued by images of roadie girlfriends, I let myself believe that one day we would show everyone. He would be a rich rock star. And I would be behind the stage curtain, waiting for his impassioned after-show kisses. I imagined, too, Kindy and Verity sitting in the front row at his concert, envious of their big sister's exciting life, sorry they hadn't made risky choices like I had.

The last time I saw him was on a Friday afternoon in September. He had driven down from Enid to Norman on his Harley to say goodbye to me at college before he hit the highway east. We met in the parking lot behind a local burger joint. He didn't want to meet in the dorm parking lot. I couldn't convince him to stay over in my dorm room, either, and we didn't have money for a hotel room. He sat on his bike for the whole goodbye, all the more a rebel amidst the ivy-walled college scene. He was awkward and nervous, and after half an hour of quick kisses and stilted chatter, he rode off. There were a few hours of light left. As I watched him lean his bike to the left and wave as he rounded the corner, I wondered where he'd sleep.

During my first months of classes I could not concentrate enough to read. I would go to the library at night with my girlfriends, set up my advanced trigonometry textbook and my Introduction to Philosophy class readings around me, and sit there trying to turn the numbers and words I was seeing into coherent meanings in my head. But I could not: Freddy consumed my brain—and my stomach and my heart. I was suffering and homesick for him—but he was no longer there. I was meeting boys every day at college. It was the era in which working out in the gym was first becoming fashionable, and almost every boy who tried to impress me seemed to think that he had to do so with his gym-generated muscles. But all it took to make me scoff at their overtures was one passing image in my head of Freddy, his body glistening with sweat as he heaved greasy thick chains on an oil rig in the hot sun in the middle of the Gulf of Mexico, surrounded by shimmering water.

Then one Sunday morning in early November as I was getting dressed for church I got the call I had never explicitly expected but, even then, had imagined might one day come: Freddy had been killed on a stretch of a long Arkansas road at 2:00 a.m. that Saturday. Freddy's sister told me that he was driving back to Enid for a break. I imagined that he was driving home to surprise me, secretly planning a trip down to Norman so I could show all the boys what a real man was like. And he could show me the biggest check he'd ever received. Offshore rig work meant huge bucks.

Then came more news: Freddy had been drunk; he had crossed a lane and killed the people in the oncoming car he hit.

I was devastated. Freddy was dead. And he was, for all intents and purposes, a killer.

He was the best driver I had ever met. And he never drove drunk. Had life on the rig been that hard for him?

The shock of his death hit me hard. It actually physically brought me to my knees. My legs gave out, and I crumpled, ragdoll-like, to the floor when his sister told me what I did not want to hear. In a split second, everything that held me together—muscles, bones, sinew, skin, memories, worries, plans, love—lost their ability to hold me up. My mind short-circuited as I fainted, and all I could see was red. Blood red. Floods of red. Numbing red.

If a friend hadn't walked by the dorm phone booth I was in, I might have stayed in that crumpled-up state for hours. Even after she helped me get back to my room, that fuguelike state lingered. My capacity to listen, to read, to make even minimal sense of where I was or where I was supposed to be, disintegrated. Her words, his death, cleaved my insides in half, leaving all of me undone. For the next several days, sleep was the only solace I sought, and even then my dreams were filled with frantic searches for him, a man who now existed just inches from my touch but was horrifyingly unreachable.

And on the heels of numbing shock came overwhelming guilt. The "if's" were endless. If I had stayed in Enid with him, not gone to college, maybe he would never have left town? If I had convinced him not to jump probation and serve his time, might he have been in jail but still alive? If I had gone to visit him in Louisiana when he left the rig for his break, maybe we would have been partying in New Orleans that night? If we had married before I'd graduated from high school, maybe he'd have been with me at college? All of these were fantasies. I knew that. But being responsible for his death felt better than being powerless in the face of it, especially from the safety of my dorm room. Somehow the thing that divided us, the upward trend of my life, had to have been the source of his fall.

Neither Freddy nor any of his friends, all of whom had been my Enid posse, had gone to college. They had not even contemplated the idea of going to college. Couldn't imagine what it was, why it mattered. During our last summer together, I had begun to feel suddenly conscious of this, as if some sort of difference, not self-imposed but hovering, had arisen between us. It was that same divide that had hovered over our last goodbye. He wouldn't enter my dorm; I wouldn't ride behind him on his motorcycle to New Orleans.

There had always been a wall between us; I knew that, too. But our youthful stubbornness had refused it, covered it up with illusory futures. It was the mighty divide of class differences. Economically and culturally, the future was mine to bravely dive into headlong, always resurfacing, refreshed and ready for more, with college just the beginning; for him, the world was a headlong dive into deeper and deeper poverty and crime, never resurfacing, never advancing, finally crashing on a highway far away from home. I could see it so clearly. When we lay together on his small bed in that back room, our intertwined bodies were two different Americas, pressed together yet worlds apart. In my America, I would live a long good life. In his America, poverty meant death. That was the simple, brutal, unbearable truth.

GRIEF AND DEATH

By the time I went home for his funeral two weeks later, the shock had begun to fade as raw grief replaced it. With that grief, a strange knowing settled in. I had grown up in a household where we avoided talk of the afterlife, in good Calvin fashion, but suddenly heaven was all I could think about. Not heaven in the sense of some otherworldly, fluffy-cloud kingdom where Freddy might be happily hanging out with God. It was more visceral than that. More real but also more nebulous. To me, he wasn't gone. I could feel him, alive, close to me. Walking near me. Whispering in my ear. Waiting beyond the next corner to see me. His dead-but-alive self lingered somewhere both intimately close and yet distant. I felt the uncanny touch of a living afterlife.

So certain was this feeling that if anyone had tried to tell me there was no life beyond death, I would have slapped them silly, furious at such an insidious, evil lie. My insides shouted, "God would not throw Freddy away like a broken, useless toy carelessly tossed into a trash bin of nothingness. It was impossible." I had a profound if not also desperate certainty that God was with me. About that, I was utterly clear. My churched faith held strong on this score. I was wrapped in grace even if I didn't deserve it or didn't really seek it out. And just as clear to me was the mysterious fact that Freddy was also held in grace, still in his earthen form. Dwelling in God. Living on. Still existing. I also felt in my bones that, inexplicable as it might be, held together in the strange reality of God's love, we remained near to each other. Him near me, me near him. Both of us enfolded in love.

I don't mean to sound weird, as if I believed his ghost was literally following me around. It was deeper and truer than that. I had never been more certain of anything in my life—and now in his death. Love would not let him go. Love would not let him leave me. Or me, him. This strong sense of our divine connection didn't magically relieve the pain of his death. The grip of grief on my heart was tight. Nor did it explain why he died, as if God had planned it. Instead of that, it opened the door between the finite and the infinite and allowed us to be together, intertwined in our ultimate destiny.

It wasn't something I could talk to my parents about. I was too mad at them for never liking Freddy to give them the comfort of knowing about this uncanny experience of grace. But I needed to be near

Freddy's friends, hoping their nearness to him and to me would confirm the bond I felt. I called Jimmy, Freddy's best friend, to see where
they were hanging out after the funeral. My experience with death up to
that point had been limited to older adult relatives and included church
receptions and family gatherings. In the church world, death was a
highly organized affair. As it turned out, in Freddy's world, there was no
organized anything. His mother went to the bar. His sister and brother
went home. And his friends ended up in Jimmy's living room, the television on with the sound off. The rock band Rush was blaring from the
stereo. No one said much, just smoked and drank, which I guessed was
probably the oldest form of repast, definitely older than church.

After about an hour of sitting together, I tried to ask the question
that had been burning in me: Was there any chance that someone else
had been driving, not Freddy, and that he had moved Freddy's man-
gled body into the driver's seat? Especially when this person realized
he might save himself from a prison sentence for manslaughter? When
I finally finished sharing my meandering suspicions, they shook their
heads, looked away, said nothing. It was clear I was grasping at straws.
Freddy had been driving. It was his fault. It was then that I felt the
physical weight of the difference between us. I couldn't explain it, but
I saw it in their glances, felt it in their lack of energy, suspected it in
their languor. They did not dislike me or wish me ill; they simply no
longer wanted me around.

It had happened so fast, this rupture in our little group, our self-
fancied gang. I fought back the urge to run away, to change myself back
into someone they wanted to hang out with, if only to blissfully smoke
and drink with them. Sitting quietly, I racked my brain for clues as to
what I should do. I had purposely tried to dress as I had done before
heading off to OU, wearing jeans and a T-shirt with Frye boots and
dangly earrings and leaving my black knee-high boots and long black
suede jacket at home. I tried to monitor my vocabulary for college-isms,

for anything that sounded bookish or highfalutin. I tried to censor my conversations, eliminating any recounting of experiences in Norman. But it was all to no avail. Freddy was dead, and his friends—so romantic, so rebellious—were dead unto me.

In America, like anywhere else on the planet, if you are born poor, it dramatically increases the odds that you will die young, that life will kill you before old age does. This class of life—Freddy's class—quite simply kills you. That is the deplorable thing, not the people born into it.

I left Jimmy's around ten and went home to find my father waiting up for me, sitting in his leather chair with his pipe, reading the paper. My parents had always been worried about Freddy's troubled presence in my life; they never hid it. By troubled they meant he was pulling me into a class of life that frightened them. I had been surprised, then, to see them sitting in the back row at his funeral. I hadn't asked them to go and had avoided them afterward, not wanting to sit anywhere near them.

"Thanks for coming today, Dad," I said quickly, heading upstairs to bed.

"Wait, Serene. Your mother and I are concerned about you. We are very sad about Freddy's death. We know it must be hard on you." The fatherly concern in his voice was clear.

"Don't act like you're sad, Dad," I bit back, my anger ready to spew out. "You guys are probably relieved he's dead and out of my life. No longer a threat to your precious daughter's future, blah, blah, blah." My urge to fight intensified. "You talk about justice and loving your neighbor all the time, but how many really poor people do you know, Dad? Like friends. Like a partner. Like real people that you've given your heart to? Felt their pain? Exactly none. Zero. Zilch. You talk about the poor and poverty all the time, yes, but it's an abstraction to you. Economic justice is a theological idea. An intellectual toy. A policy issue! But Freddy wasn't a policy. He was a living person, and he is dead. Dead! Dead! Because he was poor. He never had a chance." Tears were running down my face by then. "I loved him, Dad. I really truly loved him."

He stepped up to the stairs to hug me. "I know, Serene. And he loved you."

I shrugged off his hug, as if by pushing him away I could magically catapult myself back to the other side of that class wall that had divided me from Freddy and now from his friends. A wall that college was building higher and higher, brick by brick and book by book.

I wanted to destroy something, get on his motorcycle and drive so fast into the night down a deserted road that maybe I might join him in the afterlife. I rationally knew I hadn't killed Freddy. But as my connection to his real physical presence slipped out of my reach, the cruelty of my privilege—of being alive—began to choke me.

My father let me stomp upstairs. That he didn't try to argue with me was unusual. Maybe he realized I was in a place he had never been, with my heart in my hand. I was right about his adult connections to poor people. He and my mother and our whole family lived well. I was on track to be just like him in a few short years, with my love and indignation growing fainter. I feared that precious transcendent closeness to him would fade over time, and I would eventually remember the curse of Freddy's poverty as little more than a passing childhood nightmare.

LIBERATION THEOLOGY

That wasn't how this story went, though.

When James Baldwin wrote, "Love takes off the masks that we fear we cannot live without and know we cannot live within," he was right. He was right, too, when he preached that only this love could save us. Youthful though we may have been, Freddy and I took off our masks, before we even knew we were wearing them. Love allowed them to fall away. For us to touch and listen and see each other, and for a shared longing to unfurl between us as we peered into our separate worlds. You don't ever recover from that kind of connection; its tender, cutting knowledge lingers.

When I started reading Latin American liberation theology in seminary many years later, this social movement, which began inside the Catholic Church in South America in the early sixties, gave me a new language for what I knew about class. The writing of the Peruvian priest Gustavo Gutiérrez, its most prominent theological voice, taught me several things.

He forced me to vividly see and feel—to imagine with great clarity—the truth I knew: The vast majority of the earth's population lives in death-dealing poverty, exploited and oppressed by a capitalist economic system that cares not the least for their well-being. They are mostly invisible, often extinguished, and include all races of people, even poor whites like Freddy. If divine love makes every creature an equal, then anyone who claims to know and love God must commit to stopping this.

He also insisted, as a theologian, that changing this deadly system requires a massive social uprising of those most harmed, joined by those willing to let go of the privileges that protect them. He calls this joining together, when it's grace filled, "solidarity." To be in solidarity is to be bonded with others in their plight, knowing you are not the same but committing to share in a common endeavor. That endeavor for liberation theology was creating a radically egalitarian economic order, which when translated in old-fashioned Christian language meant building God's egalitarian kingdom on earth.

As I was raised on the radically egalitarian theology of the Disciples of Christ, this immediately rang true for me. I couldn't help but think that if Woody Guthrie had written theology, it would look just like this, albeit in Okie guise. It all seemed obvious and right. Particularly its bracing insistence on economic inequality and poverty as the deadliest collective sin of our time. The collective sin that befell Freddy, cutting short his time, our time.

The part of Gutiérrez's theology I felt uneasy about—but understood completely—was his insistence that Christianity's obsession with otherworldly salvation was a massive Christian cop-out. Recalling the classic views of Karl Marx, he describes these beliefs as the opiate of the people. Dreams of heaven's perfection let us off the hook when it came to taking on the present-day hell of oppression. Fixating on heaven's afterlife rewards allowed people to accept in-life oppressions because of their false belief that in the next life, they would have the things that earthly reality denied them. It made us passive, he insisted. And bled out of people their desires to create that heavenly life on earth. If God's grace means anything at all, he said, it had to make a difference in the here and now, the land of the living where the sins of economic injustice were thriving unopposed.

I knew from experience that much of what he said was true. I'd heard rich and poor people alike in my own Okie world talk about heaven the way he depicts it—a balm that quelled the pain of dealing with the sins right in front of them. But my own experience of God's grace in the midst of Freddy's death wasn't like that at all. It didn't cultivate a view of heaven where Freddy was enjoying the pleasures life had denied him. That never occurred to me. The whole experience was of a different sort altogether. I felt that in the mysterious love of God, the living and the dead existed together in the eternal here and now. Freddy never stopped being Freddy, a young man whose beautiful existence was destroyed by injustice. And I never stopped being Serene, a child of relative privilege who was never charged with grand larceny or had to steal to eat. Held in grace, our connection didn't let me off the hook; quite the opposite. His continued presence kept my anger at his plight constantly fueled and my desire to fight against it growing ever stronger. It eventually sent me to seminary, to learn more about the power of theology to challenge social systems. His life and his death were the compelling force that drove me into a spiritually fired life of social activism.

As for Freddy, this vision of his eternal presence ran counter to a world that didn't care if he existed at all, in life or in death. Against the claims of an unjust world, grace insisted on his ultimate value, not in some distant heavenly place but in the fleshly life he lived, in the dirt of our earthly life, held in grace forever. This vision of divine love didn't drain the living world of value; it illumined its sins and glories all the more vividly. Including those sins of the past that the living want to lop off and forget, preferring instead the lie of false glories.

And that brilliant light illumined a powerful truth about our young love.

When our masks—mine and Freddy's—came off our faces, they fell apart in our hands; their construction was flimsy, their material paper thin. To think that the walls that divide us—class, race, gender, sexuality; our different abilities, religions, nations—might be as flimsy as those masks, well, it's hard to imagine, isn't it? If we believe those walls belong there, then there they will stand. But if we dare to see them as the flimsy lies they are, regardless of how sturdy or well defended they might be, they will fall.

As for the presence of Freddy in my life, five years later—because of him, really—I was on a plane to, of all places, India. I was headed into poverty the depth of which I could not imagine but craved experiencing after having been so moved by Gutiérrez's writing. Somehow Gutiérrez and Freddy together tapped into the social justice side of my Disciples faith. My social justice activism in college had expanded and grown more global. Loving Freddy theologically gave me the inspiration to go there—however misguided and naive that may seem now. Truth be told, even now, more than forty years later, he's still alive in my hopes and dreams, frozen in time, never more handsome, never more ornery, never more theologically provoking and connected to me. His love, our love, pushing me forward.

STATION III

Hatred and Forgiveness

CHAPTER 7

I Once Was Found but Now Am Lost

Apathy flourishes in the consciousness of the satiated.

Dorothee Soelle

After Freddy's death, the prairie faith that held together my childhood confidence in God's grace was blown about like tumbleweed. My grief was lodged in my chest, tight and snug against my heart, and I realized that you have to feel faith as much as think it. But when it came to feelings, my insides churned more with anger than love. I didn't blame God for Freddy's death and believed Freddy was with God. I still felt God loved me and loved the world. These parts of my faith feelings held strong. But a loud, screaming "So what?" echoed in my head and pounded in my chest. All that divine love didn't make one bit of difference when it came to how the world actually worked. Divine diffidence appalled me.

Life now seemed to me a cruel invention, untrustworthy, oppressive, and fractured. God may love it, yes, but why should I care? That love hadn't saved Freddy. Or the hundreds, thousands, millions of people—in my mind I saw masses of Freddies everywhere, generation after generation of them—whose lives were crushed and wiped out by the same evil that wiped him out on a dark highway. Born into systems of sin, never given a chance to thrive, Freddy and his doomed tribe of the deplored had died under the weight of that sin. That God loved them all the while they were being ground under by sin was true, yes. But this truth now seemed cosmically pointless. Amid the grinding powers of injustice, grace was weaker than sin, overwhelmed by it.

After hearing "Amazing Grace" sung at Freddy's funeral, it played in my head all the time, replacing the "Be Thou My Vision" of my youth. I focused on that short phrase "a wretch like me" because I felt wretched. A wretched soul in a wretched world. That winter, I went to the OU library to find out more about the song, hoping it might illuminate my fractured faith.

But my research only made matters worse.

I'd grown up hearing Mahalia Jackson and Judy Collins sing the hymn. Like Woody Guthrie's "This Land Is Your Land," "Amazing Grace" was a staple of our youth group's protest campfire songs.

As my youth group leader had once explained, "John Newton, who wrote the song, was the captain of a slave ship, and when he got stuck in a storm at sea and survived, he had such a powerful conversion experience that he became a Christian and turned his ship around to go back to Africa to set the slaves free." For my all-white church group, it was the perfect story of how Christianity embraces social justice and marches onward to freedom.

My library research revealed another story—another falsehood.

"It's not true! It's just another lopped-off American-style story!" I practically shouted from my plastic library chair amid the stacks of books. The OU library had become for me a sort of mother lode of knowledge, a place to find out the real truth about my home, my family, my myths, and now my first love. That Saturday afternoon, I remember hearing the rise and fall of cheering fans in the football stadium around the corner. That year, OU won the national football championship. The camaraderie and excitement the team generated felt alien to me. I was alone with my grief, rage, and doubt.

Newton's so-called conversion happened during a storm off the coast of Ireland, when he was a sailor on a slave ship. He felt grateful to God that he had lived when others had died in the storm, yes. But his gratitude to the Divine did nothing to immediately change his views on slavery or lead him to turn the ship around. When he recovered from the wreck, his gratitude simply changed him from a personally wretched slave ship crew member to a personally pious Christian one. He continued to trade and ship enslaved Africans for years, his growing success all the while fueled by his deepening gratitude. It was only much later in his life, when he began to study theology, that he penned "Amazing Grace," and became the abolitionist he is now heralded for being. Before that, he reminded me more of Okemah's lynchers and Dick Jones than Idabel or my dad.

That Freddy had died and I had lived didn't make me feel particularly grateful for God's grace. In fact, it made the grace game feel rigged. I was angry about the whole notion of grace I'd been spoon-fed, and the lie behind the man who had written "Amazing Grace" further weakened the power of the idea.

I remained involved in the church during college, though restlessly so, and eventually made the decision to go to seminary at Yale Divinity School. I didn't want to be a pastor—the thought of leading a congregation made me feel sanctimonious. I simply wanted to wrestle with the big ideas of faith and religion and, perhaps more so, theology's vision of social justice and activism. Freddy's death had not weakened but had strengthened this part of me. While my faith was in flux, my commitment to joining the struggle against oppression was firmer than ever. Social justice was sure as hell one of Jesus's main ideas, I told myself; I'll worry about the salvation and grace stuff later.

In 1983, now twenty-two years old, I left Yale Divinity School for a year and traveled to South India—ostensibly to study liberation theology at the small Protestant seminary, Tamil Nadu Theological Seminary, in the town of Madurai. The seminary had been founded in 1969 by a group of radical Marxist professors and Indian pastors who were involved in the then-growing worldwide "people's movement for freedom." If my hunger for grace was diminishing, I had thought, then joining a grassroots revolution informed by the ideas of my theological youth seemed a virtuous alternative. I subconsciously still craved the divine, but the earthly would have to jar me back to it.

FROM THE PLAINS OF OKLAHOMA TO THE DUST OF INDIA

The day I arrived in India, I took a sixteen-hour bus ride from Chennai that let me off at the gate of a large compound filled with scattered, open-aired concrete buildings. The garbage collector for the campus, John, found me there and took me to the women's dorm. The dorm mother, Ms. Thomas, looked me up and down like an odd museum specimen and called the president's office to figure out what to do with me. I guess he told her I was expected because her suspicious glare turned to a welcoming smile as she showed me to a small room I was to share with Retnam, an eighteen-year-old Dalit village girl who had a scholarship to study Indian sacred music.

"Here's your bed," Retnam said in halting English, hugging me and pointing to a slender slab of wood on four small legs with a small bright orange cotton sheet at its foot. "And your own desk!" she added with such enthusiasm that it was clear having one's own desk was a special luxury. That first night I dreamed I was sleeping next to my grandmother in her sod house, safe and warm. I awoke at dawn with bruised hips and the sound of a rooster crowing outside the dorm window. The sounds and smells of India were already dizzying, the early morning heat already heavier than any "devil's day" my grandma had lived through.

In those days many of my peers were going to India to find spiritual gurus, imitating their favorite rock stars, or for the drugs that flowed freely in the white hippie enclaves scattered across the country. In large part I went because I was reading more and more liberation theology and had realized it held the most promise of all the global social movements fighting against social injustice. I selfishly hoped, too, that being in India might help me knit back together the hope in grace I had lost when Freddy died on that Arkansas highway.

In 1983, liberation theology was still a relatively new term in North American theological circles. My beloved teacher at Yale Divinity School, Letty Russell, had introduced me to it in a class on faith and activism. We read Gustavo Gutiérrez, James Cone, Rosemary Radford Ruether, and M. M. Thomas, the luminaries of this groundbreaking theological movement. The term "liberation theology" had first emerged in the late sixties inside the South American Catholic Church where Catholic priests, theologians, and lay leaders were arguing for theology done from "the underside"—from the perspective of the poor, the marginal, the outcast. When Christian faith was seen through the eyes of the underclass, Jesus's message of liberation for the poor became starkly clearer. For those who listened to the perspective of the poor, the message of the Gospel was a clarion call: Go become political activists and join the struggle for the liberation of the oppressed. For these theologians, liberation wasn't an otherworldly hope or a personal stance; it was a political and religious idea of a world in which all people could flourish.

In the United States, Cone argued that God was black and that theology done from an African American perspective was inescapably about black liberation. Similarly, Rosemary Radford Ruether wrote that women needed to break free from the male-dominated theology that had held them under for centuries and do feminist theology. Womanist (African American woman-centered) theologians like Delores Williams, Emilie Townes, Kelly Brown Douglas, Jacquelyn Grant, and Katie Cannon, and Latina Mujerista theologians like Ada Maria Isasi-Díaz brought their own powerful voices to the liberation conversation as well, showing how white and privileged feminist theology was and urging that more diverse theological insights be brought into the public realm.

At first, all of it sounded to me a lot like the social justice theology I'd grown up with—nothing seemed radically new about it. But as I read more books by people whose lives differed so dramatically from my own, the limits of my Disciples theology became clearer to me. Where you stood when you studied theology profoundly changed how you viewed God and how you lived theology. In a small way, that's what I had been slapped in the face with when Freddy died. I had supposed we were more or less the same, but we weren't. Because of our extreme class differences, our view of life—and our chance at succeeding at it—were dramatically different.

Among the Indian liberation voices, M. M. Thomas and Arvind P. Nirmal were the most prolific and outspoken. Thomas advocated for Indian independence and the promise of socialism. Nirmal wrote about the struggles of poor Dalit (untouchable) Indians for water rights, education, fair wages, and basic health care. At the heart of his theology was a searing critique of caste in India, a social system that categorized as "outcastes" large segments of the population. These officially "untouchable people" renamed themselves Dalits, the word for "waiter" and "servant." The name reveals the fact that the whole society depended on their labor, their service, but higher-caste people hid this fact by treating Dalits as if they were dirty and worthless. Dalit theology wisely used this word for servant to not only expose the injustices of caste but, more important, deployed it as the basis for envisioning a casteless nation. In such a nation, everyone would be a serving Dalit, caring for the needs of others because everyone's purpose would be to contribute, as equals, to the collective good of the whole. It was a powerful Indian version of socialism at its best.

At Yale, I happened to hear a lecture by a liberation Indian scholar who oversaw the small Tamil Nadu Theological Seminary. Knowing nothing much about India except what I'd read in books, I went up to him afterward.

"Would you take an international student like me for a year?" I asked him.

"If you can find the funds, you would be welcome," he responded. "But please know we have never hosted a student from America. You might find it challenging. There is no place more different from the United States than South India." The quickness of his invitation—as well as his warning—thrilled me. Within twenty minutes I was on the phone to the Disciples of Christ's Division of Overseas Ministries, the branch of my church that worked outside of the United States. Within a week, I received a commitment from them to sponsor me. Funny, but the very church whose theology I was wrestling with was the church that quite eagerly gave me the support to go to India and continue that wrestling.

On the TTS campus, I quickly became an object of great fascination for my fellow students. From the first day they called me "Yank," and when I laughingly accepted my new title, they opened their lives and their arms to me. The majority of the students were young men who had grown up in small churches in low-caste and Dalit villages and aspired to return to them as their ordained pastors. They came from all over South India as well as nearby Sri Lanka. Among them were a handful of Christian-raised women from churches that did not believe in women's ordination. They dared to come to the seminary anyway, carving a path for themselves that they hoped would one day lead them to pastorates. By the end of the first week, Sudundura, a young woman from Sri Lanka, quickly became my closest friend and had taken me on as her new project.

We first shopped for lighter clothes at a chaotic local market, buying a bright turquoise sari and two long red tunics with flowing pants beneath them.

"No one ever owns more than three pieces of clothing," Sudundura whispered to me when I asked if we could shop for even more. In converted U.S. dollars, the Indian rupees I'd spent amounted to barely five bucks. "Even three is the mark of a rich person," she said, cautioning me against buying another sari as she watched my eyes behold their bright and captivating colors.

She showed me how to wrap the long sheetlike sari around my body, carefully pleating the fabric that formed the skirt and then looping it over my shoulder and down my back. I felt so honored, like the mother of God was dressing me. My legs were fully covered, even my ankles, but my white-skinned midsection was awkwardly bared to the world. The girls in the dorm painted elaborate brown henna patterns on my hands and rubbed thick oil into my hair. They then gave me a string of jasmine flowers to wrap around the slick black braid that now ran down my back.

I'd spent my young adult life wearing jeans and oversize black T-shirts, trying to hide my stomach (which my mother had one day offhandedly told me was flabby), keeping my hands clean, and washing the natural oil out of my hair every morning. Now I looked and lived just the opposite, a greasy-haired, bare-bellied, henna-handed white girl lost in yards and yards of color. The delight my new friends took in my transformation was uplifting, but sometimes I felt acutely awkward, my mother's critical voice pointing out the flaws in my body and the absurdity of my attire.

For several weeks, I sat in theology classes taught in Tamil. I was taking lessons in Tamil, but my learning was slow, its swirly letters strange to me; speaking required sounds my mouth and throat refused to make. In my theology classes, I tried to understand the lesson by reading the professor's body language and picking up a word here or there. Much of the time, I drew endless spirals in my schoolgirl notebook. Along with all the other students, I ate rice and dhal three times a day at a long wooden table in the open-air dining hall. Carefully following my fellow students' example, I used my right hand to roll the food into little balls I shoved into my mouth as I sat hunched over my metal plate.

My left hand, Sudundura had confided to me the first morning we met, was for the toilet only. "Your new Indian toilet paper," she had quietly joked, just out of the hearing range of the many male students in the seminary. There was a bucket of water beside the porcelain hole I squatted over. I was to use that water for washing the hand that I was told to never use for other purposes, especially touching other people or eating.

By the end of the first month, I was still carrying my body around, but I didn't recognize it, its gradual diminishing and reconfiguring astonished me. I didn't understand the words my ears heard or the smells and tastes my nose and mouth took in. The only time I found rest in the familiar was when I dreamed at night, believing I was at home, usually eating some kind of store-bought casserole around the family dining table. So foreign was my body to me that I didn't recognize at first that I was losing weight.

One day I saw the full, protruding arch of my hip bone while bathing. By the beginning of the third month, my ribs were showing and I had stopped having a period or wearing a bra—nothing was left of my breasts.

"I think you should see a doctor," Sudundura told me in her gently lilting Sri Lankan English. We had just finished our Caste in India course, and I had fallen dead asleep during the lecture.

That afternoon, we walked two miles to a concrete building that housed the clinic students used. In the crowded waiting room—a large cinderblock square with bare walls and no chairs—a woman lay on the floor, huge wounds covering her legs. Another man, without legs, sat propped against the wall, balancing on a flat wooden cart that he used to move around. A young woman sat cross-legged cradling a small girl, maybe three years old. The girl never made a sound, not even a whimper.

The quiet in the room was more eerie and disturbing than any noisy, scream-filled emergency room I'd ever visited in the United States. Sudundura steered me toward a clear space in the far corner, where we squatted, Indian style. She had told me not to touch the floor, much less sit on it. After several hours, a young cheerful nurse in a white sari brought us back to a spare examination room with one chair. She nudged me down into it. An older man in a white doctor's jacket soon came in and took my vital signs and checked a few boxes on the chart he held, not bothering to introduce himself or say hello.

"You're dehydrated and you probably have amoebic dysentery," he finally announced like he was handing out homework assignments, still looking at his chart, not me.

The words scared me. Before leaving home, countless people who had been to India had warned me about this debilitating diarrheal disease that afflicted most Western travelers for a day or two. But the idea that there were actually amoebalike bugs that had been swimming around my insides for months was horrifying.

"What should I do?" I asked, assuming some medication would fix it.

"I could give you medication, but as long as you stay in Madurai, you'll just get sick again. You should consider going home." He then looked over his shoulder, already preparing for the next patient.

"I can't leave! I just got here." The words tumbled out faster than my mind could manage them.

Looking up at me, he said, "Then you'll just experience what it feels like to be Indian, not a tourist. Many people here live their whole lives feeling like you do." With that, he flipped the chart closed and left.

Some stubborn Okie desire not to be deterred by a seemingly common illness stiffened my back, and I stood—feeling the bones in my feet pressing painfully into my flip-flops.

"I'm not going," I whispered.

Sudundura looked at me, puzzled. "Are you sure?" Her expression was asking, without words, why anyone would choose to live like this if they didn't have to.

I thought of Freddy. I realized my life in that moment was a frivolous, random privilege, even more so now that I was surrounded by the overwhelming poverty of South India. I didn't want to die—that was very clear to me. But my decision to stay was made more out of lethargy and obstinacy than any grand humanity. Freddy's death had made me, for the first time, feel the despair of faithlessness, and its devilish ways were undermining my judgment.

Walking home from the clinic, Sudundura's arm linked in mine, I saw the world so differently. Did the Dalit street cleaner, wearing a tattered rag around his waist, feel this bad? All the time? The rickshaw driver? The cooks in the dining hall? The small thin woman who swept our dorm floors every morning? The quieter students who fell asleep in class even more often than me? The young Bible professor who walked with a cane and sat down to teach? How did they get up each morning and go to work, living with this god-awful dysentery not just for three months, but for thirty or forty years? That walk home was perhaps the most profound lesson in liberation theology I would ever experience. I was learning it in my body, with my body, with my gut.

For the next month, the evil, oppressive bugs kept eating away at my insides. Physically, I was wasted, spaced out, and exhausted most of the time. Even walking in a straight line became a challenge. The air itself felt increasingly hostile; hot and thick, it smelled of soured curry, rotting dogs, diesel fuel, floating street sewage, and the pungent sandalwood of temple incense. The small room I shared with Retnam became my only sanctuary. I began to miss more classes, preferring my wooden bed to lectures on indigenous Indian Christianity and the injustices of India's all-pervasive caste system (even in the church). Every student and professor on the campus was low-caste or Dalit—I had yet to even meet a Brahmin.

The only consolation to me during those sick months was the companionship of the dorm, the women taking care of me with a tenderness and simple generosity I had never experienced. My primary experience of so-called girl culture until that point had been catastrophic—fighting with my sister Kindy, schoolyard nastiness, inane chatter at the lunch table about our constantly changing array of new clothes and new boyfriends. There was gossip in the TTS women's dorm, much of which I surely missed because my Tamil was so shaky. But most talk was about family events and arranged marriages and about the men—students, faculty, workers, family members—who should be avoided at all costs. This included the sordid tales of the girls who hadn't avoided them. I never knew how to ask what the Tamil word for rape was—or if there was one. But my friends' constant anxiety about sexual assault was palpable.

Not all the young women were Christian, for some Hindu and a few Muslim students studying at other schools in Madurai roomed there. But I rarely noticed the difference except through glimpses of the objects perched on their window ledges: a prayer mat, a cross, a statue of the goddess Shakti dancing. What drew everyone together was their fear of being made impure by any number of interactions they might have with men. Together, the women wove a cultural veil of protection around themselves to keep out these looming threats to their purity—and safety. Among them I felt a snug sense of safety and care—what kept me going. I had never in my life experienced such unearned love from a group of people. I didn't realize it then, but it was all grace. At night when dehydration chills would wake me, Retnam, who was Hindu, would crawl under my cotton blanket and hold me, her arm making a pillow for my head, singing soft songs to lull me to sleep.

NEAR DEATH

One afternoon, when classes had emptied the dorm of its residents, I decided to leave my cocoon, alone, and catch a bus outside the school's front gate. I wanted to find a phone to call my parents to tell them how sick I was. Maybe I hoped they'd convince me to come home, given that I'd thrown away the will to convince myself. A fellow student had given me the address of a government building downtown near Meenakshi Temple—India's largest Hindu temple—where there was a public phone booth that made international calls.

But my brain wasn't working right. So not surprisingly, I got on the wrong bus. Leaving town, I looked outside the dust-smeared window and knew, within minutes, that I was going the wrong way and would soon be lost. I did not panic; I did not foresee danger. I accepted it like the heat and my illness.

I was squeezed onto a bench next to an old village woman. She stared at my face with bold, toothless fascination, her mouth bloodred from the betel nuts she chewed with her few remaining teeth. A teenage boy stood over me, holding on to the bus's overhead bar, his stare openly lecherous, the brown checks of his sweaty, tight polyester shirt inches from my cheek. Jostled as we rolled over potholes and washouts, our bodies kept touching, moving apart, and then bumping together again. At each stop, more people crammed in; the smells got stronger, the stares harder. And still I couldn't figure out what I was supposed to do about being on the wrong bus.

Unlike the sense of security I felt in the dorm, I so clearly remember the feeling of being completely different from this old woman and this teenage boy, as if we hailed from distant planets, aliens locked in different worlds of meaning. My hand rested on the back of the green vinyl seat in front of me, next to hers. Her skin held a darkness that centuries of equatorial sun had emblazoned into it; her hands were calloused by the million grains of rice she had probably harvested into the basket of her sari skirt, the pots she had carried on her head, the bales of straw she had strapped together with indigo-blackened hemp. My hands, soft, temporarily darkened by the sun, bug-bitten, shaking, still so young, embarrassed me. They were hands my mother had washed, hands that had tightly gripped ink pens and filled pages with words crafted carefully for professors' eyes.

I knew, in some corner of my grasping brain, that I was in big trouble. But I couldn't get that thought to actually matter—it simply wouldn't land on any competent brain cells.

Instead, a mantra began to slowly pulse its way into my fuzzy mind. The words of the Psalmist:

All flesh is grass.
All flesh is grass.
All flesh is grass.

Grass. Grass. Grass. All of us so intimately and unceasingly the same and yet distinct. Grasslands. The rice patties of South India. The wheat fields of Oklahoma. Each vast and full, rippling like waves in the breeze of a cloudless afternoon.

For another half hour we rolled along, the rhythmic beat of those words ticking off time, holding me to the earth, to my seat, to the woman and the boy and the smell and the heat and the fumes. I didn't even ponder the unknown destination toward which we were slowly moving.

The bus finally pulled into a large station in a town whose name was written in a script I couldn't read. A huge village, it seemed, the platform busy with the scuffle of sandaled feet, chicken claws, goat hooves, the yellow split hooves of scrawny cows, the wheels of a tea vendor's rusting metal cart, piles of sheet-wrapped clothes, bundles of possessions being hauled off to somewhere.

But still I couldn't move. I couldn't grab ahold of my situation, decide what to do. It seemed not just impossible but unimaginable. The bus slowly emptied out. The old woman crawled over me to leave, the boy winking as he walked away. But I sat there pretending not to see the bus driver's suspicious stare. He finally came back and kicked the base of my seat, scolding me with a string of words I couldn't understand.

It was in that moment that my befuddled musings on sameness and difference, my lullaby about grass and flesh stopped. As quick as a heartbeat, my confusion turned into fear, raw and animal enough to propel me out the bus door, stumbling onto the bus platform floor and, as quickly as I could, finding a support beam to lean against.

Churning in the core of that fear was one thought alone, one singular truth that possessed me with overwhelming force: If I disappeared right then and there, drifting away into nothingness or succumbing to some unnamed violence, no one would know where I had gone, forever. If I were to die, my clothes would never make it back to my mother; my sisters wouldn't touch my hair in a coffin; no one would kiss my lips goodbye; no one would watch my earthly leaving with sadness or even recognition. Dying or disappearing, it didn't matter which, I, Oklahoma

Serene, the girl who had grown up among the Disciples of Christ and my father's theology and my family's stories and sins, would just be gone.

A blade of grass: the thought lost all consolation.

Filled with sudden purpose, my focus sharpened, and with all the adrenaline I could muster, I tried to make a plan. I slid down the support beam and sat on the platform and remembered Karl Barth and Jesus and Kierkegaard; my mother and that father of mine who never lost his way; my cat from second grade; the geometrical formula for calculating the corner tilts of triangles; and the conversion standard for moving from ounces to kilograms and the cost of cigarettes in the United States versus India. I piled up memories and tables of numbers and ideas that I hoped would focus me. I didn't realize it, but I was losing my mind.

But then this desperate grasping for numbers and memories and writers began to slow down as India stormed back in. My effort to overcome my state of being had failed. Later, having witnessed loved ones die, I would compare it with the last keen moment many people experience before dying.

A black fly landed on my knuckle, and a flat-bedded wagon filled with stacks of flattened cow dung rolled up to the platform next to me. The driver was shirtless and turbaned. The radicalness of his difference broke me once and for all. I could not do what I knew I had to do; I could not harness or direct my conscious thoughts and energy.

I was overcome with hatred. I hated him, I hated them, all of them—their stench, their poverty, their ragged nasal language, their fantasies of caste and rules of dress, their running noses and hunger-rounded bellies, and the leper and the child with no hands or legs and the mother with her cleft palate, her bloodied gums exposed, the man wearing the pocks of gonorrhea, the teenager with his worn-out polyester bell-bottoms, the dung seller. All of them, I felt, all freaks and monsters not even worthy of the food they would never have. And slopping around in the muck of that hatred, my rage grew larger, wider, shadowed, thicker, and the more it grew, the more it took me over and pulled me down, down so deep that I despised myself worst of all and my stupid searching for whatever I had come to search for. I had been found already, back in Oklahoma. I didn't need to find myself again. It was a stupid indulgence, a searching for something I didn't need.

But soon that churning, gratuitous hatred was too much for my drifting mind to manage, and my disgust dissolved into the loose abandon of a dozing sleep I could no longer fight off. My brain shut down and my head fell forward to rest on my raised knees.

I am not certain how much time passed or what I dreamed, but something—perhaps India's late-afternoon sun—awakened me, and I looked up from my cement seat on the platform's floor. With startling clarity, I saw a middle-aged, well-dressed man pouring burning-hot tea from one tin cup to another, widening the space between the cups each time, the arc of brown fluid growing larger each time. The flow between cups was mesmerizing, the arc of liquid smooth and perfect. Finally, he opened his mouth and, tilting his head back, poured the hot liquid into himself, the steam seeming to rise out of his mouth.

It couldn't be, I thought. Had I fallen into complete madness? Was his throat not blistered, his esophagus not scorched, his stomach not on fire?

Staring at him with feral determination, I forced myself not to blink. I wanted him to look at me, to glance in my direction, to prove my vision was real.

But he never looked my way.

And gradually, unintentionally, I just gave up. I curled my head down, past my knees, toward my gut, closed my eyes, and came undone. My warm, watery insides seeped out underneath me in a relentless stream. Through one half-opened eye, I watched the stream run out from between my sari-wrapped legs, forming two small rivers, each one twisting and turning down the slightly tilted platform. I let go of my life.

Following the course of the rivulets, I flowed away down the filthy street, my body now liquefied and being stepped on and driven over.

I felt death as a fluidity and not an annihilation. I was no longer a physically bounded person, a center of ego—I dissolved into the vast waste of humanity, thousands of years of humanity, an endless flood of flesh, decaying and dying and seeping back into the muddied earth, everything one.

The man lit a cigarette, drank slowly from the cup of steaming tea, and finally turned his head slowly to look directly at me, his gaze serious, his eyes piercing, intelligent, glowing like hot coals.

Was this God?

An angel?

A divine messenger?

It surely wasn't the cool divine jug of my grandma's prairie faith. The man showed no sign of repulsion at my disembodiment. Nor did he show empathy. Or even particular interest in whether I was alive or dead. To him, what was just was. Still looking, he folded a newspaper under his arm, took another drag off his cigarette, and with a slight nod, walked off toward the ticket office. Then turning the corner, he was gone.

His disinterest in my undoing somehow brought me a perverse peace. I had become nothing, to no one, neither to humanity nor God. I was dissolving, and my unimportance, my liquidity, flooded me again with overwhelming consolation at the blending of the world into one infinite flow. The words of the Psalmist passed through my head again, this time as a gentle, rhythmic chant. This time they came and went not with the thrill of discovery but with the steadiness of descending, all-encompassing, indisputable truth.

All flesh is grass.

All flesh is grass.

I awoke hours later. Night had fallen; the stars were bright and the noise of the platform had calmed. A motherly looking woman in a faded red sari was crouched down close to me, softly petting the top of my head. It was Maggie, a cook in the TTS kitchen. She had been coming home from work and saw me there.

"TTS?" she asked me as I reached up for her hand.

I vaguely remember two men helping her get me on a bus and my head bumping softly in her lap, her hand resting on my forehead, as we headed back to Madurai. It was past midnight when the dorm mother turned on the outside light and yelled up to Retnam and Sudundura to come help her carry me up to bed. Retnam slept wrapped around me, Sudundura on the concrete floor next to us, a bucket of cool water beside her for the damp pieces of cloth she laid on my forehead, off and on, all night.

THE MYSTICAL

In the Disciples world I grew up in, no one ever talked about mystical experiences or visions of God. My people got nervous when anyone claimed to have direct contact with anything godlike. In their minds, making such claims tended to make the people who had visions feel they were better than others or that they had special knowledge that set them apart from your average mortal Okie. Given this flattened-out view of the mystical, I had no theological template to help me understand what I went through that day. Was it a hallucination caused by my sickness? A bad dream? A poetic metaphor that got stuck in my craw and started to feel real? Or had something broken through the veil of the ordinary and left me with an insight of a special nature? How was I to tell the difference between what was divine and what was delirium?

Despite my family's mistrust of anything unorthodox, I had always enjoyed reading about medieval women Christian mystics, especially

Saint Teresa of Ávila, a sixteenth-century Carmelite nun whose contemplative practices and bold visions are legendary. In her *Autobiography*, she describes four stages of prayer that are like stairs one ascends if one seeks ever-deeper union with God. I tried to make her steps fit my experience that day.

In the first step, you practice "meditation" and work hard to discipline your mind to focus on divine things. I suppose my version of that first step was my refusal to go home when I got sick and instead stick it out to see what I might learn. The second step, Teresa tells us, is easier: "quiet prayer," in which you learn what it means to be still and to let God come to you, to fill you with insight and presence. For me, the sicker I got, the more I craved the quiet; the emptier I became, I lost not just bodily weight but the weight of so much of my homespun version of life. Was God filling that emptiness with wisdom?

For Teresa, the third stage is even easier. Your senses still work as you allow the water of God's love to flow into you and you "behold the divine" and fully feel the presence of God's spirit. I believe I was in a state like this when I watched my divine tea drinker light his cigarette and slowly look my way, though I'd be hard-pressed to call it rapture. But the notion that everything is interconnected and of my being nothing was as accurate as the bugs attacking my intestines.

The fourth and highest stage of prayer is beyond feeling and knowledge. In Teresa's "rapturous unknowing," you become one with the Divine—no memory or sight or sound or feeling is there for you to grasp at. It is just a profound, soul-deep presence. According to Teresa's pattern, I believe I went into such a state when I just decided it was okay to die and I let go of life.

It was in the writings of Teresa of Ávila's close friend and coworker, Saint John of the Cross, a sixteenth-century Spanish mystic and priest, that I found a mystical description of the "Dark Night of the Soul," which rang even truer. With unflinching directness, John of the Cross describes the terrible theological experience of losing oneself. When one descends into the dark night of the soul, the self—which is made up of all the stories we tell ourselves about our identities and place in the world—is slowly stripped of all its attachments, not just to worldly objects but to our most precious ideas about who we are, our memories, thoughts, even our concepts about God and love.

The language he uses for this stripping away is harsh, but it resonated with my experience. "Utter desolation," "violent purgation," "complete aloneness and lostness"—and all this even before he describes coming undone. Referring to his own experience of that final undoing, he quotes from Psalm 18:5: "The breakers of death surged round about me, the destroying floods overwhelmed me." He describes a profound sense that you have been rejected and cast out, not only by your friends, but most horribly by the God you believed you knew and who loved you. It is "enduring a kind of living hell" in which God rejects you, tossing you aside as an object of his own anger. Or as Saint John writes, "One feels utterly alone, cast out of the shelter of God's favor like an unwanted stranger."

According to Saint John, this process of mortification (a fancy theological word for "dying") forces upon you two profound realizations. First, you realize that the God you have created in your own mind or have learned at church may not be God at all. Realizing this, you are opened to an even more radically loving reality of divine life, one that comes to you, not one that you reach out and grab. Second, as all your pretenses dissolve—most important, your own ego—you have the disorienting but consuming experience of pure consciousness. You become simply part of all that is, in God. There is no time or space or boundaries to your existence. You simply are. As all that is, is.

All flesh is grass.

All flesh is grass.

It took me weeks to feel well enough to start processing my vision at the bus terminal. I had come to India to study liberation theology, and I was doing the best I could to take in all the wisdom the movement had to offer. But what stood in the way of my true immersion in India—and just about everything else—was my own encumbered ego, my own aggressive and needy self. Tied around me like thick ropes of twisted hemp were obvious things: my American, white privilege; my sense of my own ultimate importance; my saturation with a Western culture of acquisitions and accomplishments; my education, my family, and my love of "great knowledge" and books; my self-centered, naive yearning to be among the poor of India so that I, myself, might learn more.

There were also other, deeper-cutting ropes that held me tight: guilt about my family's racism; shame and trauma around my grandfather's and my mother's relationships with me; and the raw rage at and confusion about all the flaws and gaps and wounds that pocked the landscape and life in Oklahoma. But the strongest, most lacerating rope of all was the preciously held notion of grace that I had begun to question when Freddy was killed. To untangle these ropes, I had to first touch them, feel them, know they were there. I had to find what bound me so that I could finally see how truly lost—and tied—I was.

I'm certain that God did not send my illness upon me in order to test me or bring me to new heights of awareness. The poverty of India did that all by itself, and I would never recommend it to anyone. What the illness did, though, was force me—physically, mentally, and spiritually—to break through the unacknowledged walls of my ego, the core self that held me together.

The day after my bus trip, rumors of my adventure spread across the dorm. The president of the seminary even broke the "no men" rule and came to visit me to make sure I was intact. Late that evening, Alice slipped through the door of my room. She was older than most of the girls, in her early thirties, and had been hired by the seminary to help students with their English. Everything I learned about Hinduism that year, I learned from Alice, a devout Hindu and an ardent reader of South India's Tamil ancient sangas.

She sat on the side of my bed and handed me an eight-inch dark blue statue of a big-breasted, many-armed goddess holding knives and daggers in her hands, her neck and waist girded with the armor of war, her helmet and necklace made of human skulls.

"This is Kali. Here, she's yours. You need her, Serene." Alice perched the little figure on the side of the bed facing me. "Her name means 'the black one'—that's why she is painted indigo blue. The word 'kali' is also associated with 'time,' meaning she is the one who 'makes time by bringing forth from nature both life and death.' People also call her 'the divine protector' and 'the bringer of liberation.' She is a consort of Shiva's. It is said she sprang from the forehead of Parbati, Shiva's wife, to protect her from a charging enemy. Her fierce warrior energy is powerful."

Alice slipped out as quietly as she had entered, leaving Kali by my head as I drifted back to sleep, dreaming not only of broken ropes but also of battles yet to be fought, liberations yet to come, life still yet to be lived, gods still yet to be revealed.

(NO) SELF?

I stayed at TTS another eight months, during which time I got well enough to think straight and stay off the wrong bus. But my physical battle with those stomach bugs never stopped. No medicine was strong enough to fight off the effects of India's poverty on my body. But through rest and a steady diet of soured milk and rice, I gained some of my strength back.

What I didn't realize then was that it would take me years to get better, even after I was back in the sanitized halls of Yale Divinity

School and under the care of some of the best infectious-disease doctors in the world. Even now, my immune system doesn't behave right.
My body gets tricked into thinking it's sick when it's not, setting off
fevers and fatigue for no real reason. And when my body is fighting off
some bug or another, it is slower to respond than it should be, forcing
me to rest more than I want to. One doctor explained to me that my
immune system is like a wall of defense against whatever antigens come
my way. Because I was sick for so long in India, that protective wall got
battered down and its signals got confused, not knowing what to let in
and what to keep out.

Looking back, I realize common sense should have sent me home
from India earlier than it did. It's also a reminder to me that harms
from the past are not just mental states, they are physical, too. And in
physical form, they often exceed our mental capacity to manage them
or banish them altogether, as I wish I could do with dysentery's afteref-
fects. It's a constant reminder, as well, that millions of people around
the world suffer what I did, but with no help in sight. When they are
young, in fact, it kills them. In 2016, a million and a half people died
from diarrheal diseases that are completely preventable. All it takes is
access to clean water. If there's a medical version of sin, it's hard to
imagine a more wicked one.

I realize it's dangerous to turn an experience with a deadly disease
into a spiritual metaphor, so I do it with great humility. But for me, my
illness symbolizes more than the immune system barrier it destroyed.
When those bugs shut off my capacity to manage the walls around my
body, it also broke down the walls around my mind and my sense of
self, walls that I didn't even know I had. In Western culture, particularly in its Christian form, we carry on as if there is a core "self" that
distinctly defines us, gives us our borders and identities. So present is
that "self" that we view it as natural. Ask me who I am and I'll haul out
a list of words that describe my "self"—Okie, female, white, Christian,

mother, daughter, middle class, educated, and on and on it goes. We all do it. In America, the land of individuals, it's a hallmark of our glory. And for Christians, well, that self is the person we imagine God loves, the person who loves God.

But what if, like those masks Baldwin tells us we need to take off, this self and all its attendant descriptors is really just a flimsy fabrication, a fiction spun out of our self-centered imaginations? A centuries-old lie? That's the question the mystics ask us to consider. That possibility enveloped me on that train platform, in my delirium—I am nothing but a temporary invention of my own mind, and my spiritual imagination is merely a figment of that falsehood, another "self-deception." If this is true, then who is the "self" that carries the weight of being sinful and graced, asleep or awake, just or unjust? What kind of existence, then, does God relate to? Are we merely blades of grass, a multitude of wheat chaffs in the infinite fields of eternal time?

It may well be true. Since India, I haven't been able to say with absolute certainty, one way or the other. I'd like to believe we have souls, those inextinguishable markers of our individual existences, the source of our fundamental rights and responsibilities. But it could be otherwise.

What I do know with certainty: Until one is able to consider the possibility that the life markers we hold most dear, even our souls, are mere grass, then whatever faith you may think you have is just one more game you've conceded to play without questioning. India, even more than Freddy's death, made me realize faith was no game. It needs to be tested, shaped, reconfigured, adapted, and nourished in the face of pain, defeat, and loss. The two are inseparable, really, faith and the dark night of the soul. I would return to America and confirm this new truth to be universal.

CHAPTER 8

Hatred

It hit her like a sledgehammer, and it was then that she knew what to feel. A liquid trail of hate flooded her chest.

Knowing that she would hate him long and well filled her with pleasant anticipation, like when you know you are going to fall in love with someone and you wait for the happy signs. Hating BoyBoy, she could get on with it, and have the safety, the thrill, the consistency of that hatred as long as she wanted or needed it to define and strengthen her or protect her from routine vulnerabilities.

Toni Morrison, *Sula*

The most enduring and satisfying lesson of my quirky, complicated Christian childhood was the connection between the personal, the social, and the divine—between individual deeds, the collective good, and God. I had a strong sense of my individuality, but given the frontier-fed cohesiveness of the Disciples community, I always saw myself as part of this group, this culture, or this people banding together amid a larger group of people, all of us blessed by the grace of God. Be it singing fireside songs at church camp or delivering food to migrant labor camps, I believed that every good social act was a faith act, and vice versa. The heavens were little on my mind; earth, if we did the right thing, was heaven enough. God was above us and around us but also within us—and we realized that Divine presence through works of love.

Even during my time in India, the closeness of my dorm companions reminded me of the religious "club" upbringing of my Oklahoma youth. We young women—my Indian roommates and I—doted on one another, warned one another, advised one another in our effort to move forward in our spiritual, educational calling. Today I still go back in my mind to that dorm made of concrete blocks and feel and smell and hear the divine. Sorority is such a scarce thing in the lives of American women, and it often requires my imagination to remember it can exist. Sometimes I feel Retnam holding me; at other times I see Kali perched at my bedside.

This inherent, reflexive inseparability of myself and my community—of the individual and society—remains, even today, a fundamental premise of my theology. God created me among us, me inseparable from us, me for us and them for me. The necessity of collaboration and collegiality on the American frontier, ingrained in me, did not waver as I went out into the world, read South American, Asian, and African theologians, and sculpted a new theology that married diverse influences and wildly different worldviews. Instead of creating problems, my sense of community was expanded by these encounters, and in my midtwenties, I began to feel myself part of a worldwide movement for positive social change. In the eighties and nineties, in fact, I regularly talked about being part of "the movement," which referred to the loosely woven web of political and social justice movements around the world. Not a week would go by when I wasn't in touch with community organizers somewhere on the globe who were trying to coordinate their work with the work of "the movement" people in the United States. The sense of global connection was intense and strong.

After finishing my master of divinity at Yale Divinity School in 1985, I began my doctoral studies in theology in the Department of Religious Studies in the Graduate School of Arts and Sciences at Yale University, still aspiring to be a teacher of theology, not a congregational minister. During my graduate student days, my faith-grounded involvement in social justice took on even more zeal, driving me, as just one example, to take a key leadership role in a recently successful organizing effort aimed at creating a graduate student union to advocate for our interests as teachers and employees. During these years, I spent the daylight hours working on my dissertation on Calvin's role in the political world of his day, and in the evening light I led strategy sessions on how graduate student labor might best be organized. It was a heady and wonderful time, full of an unstoppable hope that, globally and locally, "the movement" could dramatically change the world. During this time, I married a man I met in seminary who shared these same passions and commitments. We even put in our self-composed wedding vows, made in a church perched on the wide plains of Enid, Oklahoma, a statement about our common desire to struggle against oppressive systems wherever they might be. My marriage, my political involvements, my studies, and my faith were all part of one seamless whole.

To my amazement, in 1991, during the last year of my doctoral studies, I was hired for a tenure-track position teaching theology at Yale Divinity School. That decision to stay east, more than any other decision up to that point in my life, told me I was ready to break free from the place that had formed me so deeply. From the minute I started teaching, I loved it. Channeling my hope for global justice and change into accessible theological language, I discovered, was my calling. Of course, like most callings, you don't realize you're in the right place until you've arrived there.

But the tension between my inherited, inchoate Christian visions of life and my evolving, more global theology would regularly trouble my spirit and challenge my imagination. For years after India, I would still occasionally struggle to banish from my brain an old-fashioned image of God as a massive judgmental orchestrator of a constant cosmic battle between good and evil. Liberation theology, at times, fueled this image through its call to political struggle. My burgeoning feminist sensibilities, along with my reading of womanist theology, had at least on the surface stripped my language and images free of white male versions of God. But no matter how committed I was to his banishment, he'd reappear.

In 1992, the year I completed my doctoral studies, I was asked to read from the book of Psalms at the graduation ceremony. I blew it. Even though the program organizers had put into the "order of service" a beautiful nonmale (no male pronouns) version of the Psalms, when I stood up to speak it from memory, in front of hundreds of students and family members, my brain turned every gender-inclusive pronoun back into "him." I recited it proudly and with passion, saying "him," "he," "Father," "Son," over and over again. I was not even aware of what I had done until I sat down and the reality of my inadvertent retranslation washed over me. There I was, an emerging feminist theologian, showing to the world that God the Father was alive and exerting his power inside my head. I was mortified. Thankfully, it was more so than the occasion warranted. Even though I'd spent years self-righteously correcting everyone's male language, my friends laughed and used it as another chance to remind me, Little Ms. Perfect Feminist Social Justice Activist, that I was just as human as the rest of the world.

Childhood images live in you—they cling to your brain cells. I was taught early on in life to believe that God—most assuredly male—was a sovereign moralistic figure doling out his delight or displeasure about your daily behaviors, good and just or bad and unjust. I had no concept of hell, for that dark, fiery place never really made it into my Disciples imagination. But I did have a vivid sense of a vast, cold realm into which you tumbled if God deemed your actions wrong. When I was young, it was a traumatic image; as I grew older, it became a merely irritating one.

Then on April 19, 1995, I was blown backward, back into the depths of my immature, image-rich religious mythology. It wasn't the shock of sudden grief that rocked me, like it had when Freddy died. It wasn't the threat of annihilation, like in India. It was literally an explosion the magnitude of which our country hadn't felt on its soil since Pearl Harbor. And standing atop that rubble was a stranger, Timothy McVeigh. For the first time in my life, I wanted a God who threw people into the dungeon of eternal damnation and slammed shut the door. Screw grace. I wanted blood.

AN ATTACK ON HOME

My Tuesday morning lecture had finished early—the curious question I was exploring with the students had to do, oddly for such a class at such a place, with the notion of hell. We were reading Jonathan Edwards's famous "Sinners in the Hands of an Angry God," and as always, my students viscerally hated his image of a harsh, judging God who so viciously meted out punishment on people who failed to follow the path of virtue. I had to admit I didn't much like it, either, but I pushed them to imagine what it would be like if they were part of a marginalized, traumatized group of people who were being actively persecuted and killed by people more powerful.

"If you know you have absolutely no chance of seeing God's justice enacted in this earthly life—in fact, if you are about to die at the hands of the unjust—wouldn't you find solace in the belief that ultimately God sets accounts straight and punishes the evildoers, even though they seem to be getting away, literally, with murder?" I asked them. I hoped they'd come to see why "hell" seemed to matter so much over time, to so many people.

I could see the question had given them pause. No one was looking at me. Most of their eyes were staring at their notes, their pens still. The silence was thick, so I decided to end class and let them sit with the question until next time.

Mokhtar, a theology major from Egypt, trailed after me as I went to my office.

"I just think your idea about Edwards's views on divine punishment could be pushed a little further," Mokhtar said.

"Run with it, Mokhtar," I said. He was a dedicated student, but occasionally overzealous.

"You won't mind?"

"As Edwards would say, 'The Glory be all yours.'"

As I spoke with Mokhtar, I spotted Sue, my closest faculty colleague at the seminary, standing just outside my office. She took my arm and essentially steered me inside, closing the door behind us.

"Is everyone in your family all right?" she asked, pain on her face.

"What are you talking about?" I asked. I backed into my desk and sat down.

"Serene, an hour ago, a bomb went off in downtown Oklahoma City."

"A bomb?"

"It blew up some government building."

"The Murrah building?"

"That's the one. The whole thing has collapsed. They're saying terrorists."

"Terrorists?"

"You don't know anybody who works there, do you? I mean, your family and all?"

My sister Kindy, now thirty-four, was the director of the Oklahoma Disability Law Center, having left behind a lucrative job in a law firm and before that a job in the Oklahoma City public defender's office where she did soul-breaking work on death penalty cases. Her new office was near the city's center.

Immediately I thought of her and how close both her and her husband Rand's offices were to the Murrah building. And Dick Jones's office was mere blocks away. I knew that downtown skyline by heart and could hardly get my mind around the fact that a bomb had blown its centerpiece building sky-high. I tried calling Kindy, and then Rand, and then my grandpa, and no one answered. I moved on to my parents, who I knew were nowhere near the building.

I reached my father on the first ring. My parents had moved to Indianapolis several years earlier, where my father was now teaching theology at Christian Theological Seminary, one of our Disciples Church's best schools.

"No. Nothing. I don't know," he said. He started out in his professor voice, but it didn't hold for long. "Your grandpa's okay. He had already left for the day." Dick Jones usually got to his office by 6:00 a.m. and, now retired, was ready for lunch at home by 9:00 a.m. The bomb had blown at 9:02, just as most people were arriving at work.

"Why is Kindy not answering her phone, Dad? She isn't answering," I screamed at him. I heard him coughing, which meant he was trying to cover his own panicked tears.

I then called my sister Verity's church office in Colchester, Connecticut. She was now twenty-eight, a recent seminary graduate serving her first call as an associate pastor.

"Have you heard? Have you heard anything from Kindy?"

She dropped her usual ministerial calm the minute she heard my voice. "Nothing. Oh my God, Serene. What are we going to do? Where is our Kindy?" She began sobbing along with me.

"We have to keep trying. She'll call us. I know she will." My big-sister side kicked in for a quick second. "Who the hell would do this? What maniac would blow up a building filled with people? Our people."

"They are already saying it was probably Muslims. But why Okla-homa City? We're nothing." Verity pointlessly tried to figure it out. We hung up so that Kindy could call, if she could.

I walked up five flights of stairs to the top of a nearby dorm build-ing to watch the news on the television in the student lounge. The mass of young bodies glued to the news parted as I stepped into the room and moved toward the TV to see the images. No one at Yale missed the fact that I was an Okie through and through. I looked at the screen for less than thirty seconds before I turned away, the images too un-bearable. I walked to a side window of the lounge that looked out over the hills of New Haven to the harbor and the Long Island Sound in the distance.

For years, when I'd get homesick for the prairies where Kindy, Verity, and I had played as children, I would climb to the top of this building and look at the open expanse of sky that stretched across the city to the ocean sound beyond. The view somehow reminded me of home—a wide, flat space. The bigness of the sky always comforted me. I imagined the sky as arms or a blanket, holding, surrounding, sustain-ing the earth and my small life here and my sisters' small lives on the prairie, all held in a secure but endlessly expansive embrace, the love of God. Grace.

Now, as I looked out the window, I saw only menace in the sky. I remembered standing at the window in Kindy's disability center law office the summer before, looking out at what she called her "pent-house" view of downtown Oklahoma City: concrete buildings rising up out of flat, treeless plains of red dirt, their lines cutting sharply against that cloudless sky. Today, I could envision only black smoke.

Our sky of grace was churning with wrath. And Kindy and Rand and so many others were lost within it. . . .

I headed home a few minutes later, canceling my classes to sit by the phone, pace, cry, and watch my own TV, out of view of students and colleagues. Around 11:00 the phone rang. As soon as I picked it up, the panic in Kindy's voice was so clear that I started to cry even harder.

"I can't find him," she said. "Rand's not answering his pager. Nothing. After he dropped off the boys, he was going to renew our membership at the YMCA. God, Serene. It's right across from the Murrah building."

"Kindy. Kindy, honey," I said, trying to put on a strong front. "Where are you? Are you hurt?"

"I'm in my office. I'm okay. At first I thought it was a sonic boom. It shook my building hard. Then there was smoke everywhere. It looks like the whole downtown's on fire. I begged a friend to drive us closer to see if Rand was okay, but we couldn't get down there, the streets are blocked. What am I going to do?" She was sobbing now.

"I'm sure he's okay," I said. "Calm down. Breathe." I was curled over, my forehead on the kitchen table, my legs shaking, seeing an image of her husband, Rand, laughing with my nephews piling on top of him on the family couch.

"You're right. You're absolutely right. He'll call soon, won't he? Tell us he's fine?"

"Yes."

"Serene, I think he's dead."

"Don't think that. Stop!" I begged her, suddenly becoming the more irrational one. "Please put that thought out of your head."

She hung up to call my father.

I called Verity again, needing to hear another person that I loved breathing.

Years earlier, Kindy had decided to study constitutional law and contracts at Boston College Law School, while Verity had chosen Yale Divinity School, where I was teaching. My much younger sister was now closer to me than Kindy. Caught in the swirl of similar theological passions, we often talked about the finer points of feminist biblical criticism and third world liberation theology. Now, Verity donned black robes and pastored a congregation of Connecticut church folks who'd taken the leap of hiring her fresh out of seminary.

"I'm going," she said. "Driving. I'll be there by midnight."

"I can't stop shaking," I said. "Had to get off campus so the students wouldn't see what a wreck I am. Where were you when you heard?"

"I was in the middle of a Rotary meeting when someone announced what had happened," she said. "I'd been invited to give the opening prayer. When I heard, I got up to leave, but when the Rotary chapter president, a member of my church, remembered that I had family in Oklahoma City, he tried to reassure me from the lectern that whoever did this would pay. Would pay 'big time,' he said. He started talking about Arab terrorists and the car bomb at the World Trade Center in 1993."

I thought again of the Oklahoma City skyline and grace and decided that for me, prayer was too hard right now. Out the window of my kitchen, I had noticed a rabbit eating the buds off my crocuses. I had run out of Tums. Shepard, my husband, hadn't yet called me.

"I ran into one of my Arab students, a nice fellow named Mokhtar, as I was leaving campus," I told Verity. "He looked terrified. I hugged him. Needed to somehow tell him it'd be all right."

Mokhtar had been surprised when I approached him in the parking lot as I had fled the student lounge earlier that morning. The previous year, he'd stopped by to ask if I would be his adviser when he started divinity school. He'd told me he wanted to change his studies from engineering to religion but knew his father would protest. Back in Cairo, they needed people who could build roads, not someone studying Kierkegaard. He'd pulled two articles out of his backpack I'd never seen on Muslims in early America. An interesting dissertation topic, I'd thought, surprised. It wasn't a far stretch to imagine him in graduate school somewhere, chain-smoking as he argued over the finer points of Aramaic influence on early modern Christian doctrine. My cautious encouragement had brought tears to his eyes. His family, I had guessed, would have other reasons to cry. Today, I assumed those reasons had grown even more complicated.

"I was terrified for him, Verity, for what craziness might fall on him if it was Muslims who did the bombing. Here Rand is God knows where and I'm worrying about this Muslim student's safety."

I spent the next hour trying to get a flight into Oklahoma City. I booked a flight to Atlanta and then booked a car. I knew I was going to drive like a bat out of hell across an America that would forever be changed.

Around noon, Rand had finally called Kindy. By late afternoon, my family had assembled the story of what had happened—the story that would eventually earn Rand Eddy a name among the wounded inscribed on the memorial wall at the site of the former Murrah building.

He had indeed been renewing their membership at the YMCA when the explosion hit. The next thing he knew, he was lying on the other side of the lobby, glass all around him. Dazed, he stood up. His suit was shredded, pants ripped and matted with blood against his legs. A gas line must have burst, he thought at first. Stumbling from the building as it quickly filled with smoke, he found the outside air even darker.

He stood staring, seeing no one. The world seemed empty; car alarms sounded a deafening chorus until a second round of explosions began. Every ten seconds or so another would split the air. He could feel the ground shake. He thought the city was being bombed from the air. We later discovered it was the sound of car gas tanks exploding from the heat of the blast. The cuts in his legs forced him to lean against some nearby wall. He didn't remember how long he stood there. Then he was wandering down streets, people staggering around him, appearing and disappearing like ghosts. He wanted to get out of the thick fog, but he didn't know which way to turn. At some point, a man grabbed him by both shoulders, asked if he was able to keep walking, and when he nodded, the man physically turned him around and pointed. He told Rand to walk straight ahead and keep going until he could see the sky again.

He didn't remember how long he walked or what he saw. He ended up in a red vinyl booth at a Pizza Hut whose windows were shattered. A waitress asked if he wanted to use the restaurant's phone. It was only then that he noticed his pager was missing. His wallet, keys—all ripped from him by the blast. The woman handed the phone to Rand, but he couldn't think whom to call. Another woman asked if she could take him to the hospital. Rand asked her to take him home, finally remembering his address. He called Kindy and then fainted in the car as they drove away.

That night when I called their home, Kindy had just finished tweezing more of the small glass shards that covered Rand's face. The TV blared in the background.

Kindy wearily tried to tell me more but stopped when her tears began to spill out. She didn't want her sons to see her cry.

It wasn't until two days after the bomb went off that speculation about Arab terrorists was replaced on the news by that now iconic picture of a clean-shaven, white-skinned young man with severe eyes and a military haircut.

"I tell you," Kindy said to me, "he sure looks like about half a dozen guys I knew in high school. Well, actually, he looks more like the guys *you* knew in high school." Her friends had worn Izod shirts; mine, like Freddy, were the ones in combat jackets.

She was right—McVeigh looked hauntingly like a shorn and malnourished version of Freddy, the boyfriend I'd forever lost.

Kindy told me their family minivan had been parked two cars down from the truck McVeigh had probably used. Its remnants had been impounded. No one inside Rand's office had been injured badly, but the building was unstable, most of its windows gone. They wouldn't be able to get inside for several months. The boys' elementary school was already being flooded with crisis counselors. A psychologist who'd been in Bosnia had talked with their youngest; she'd told Kindy that their son seemed fine. All the children were having a hard time believing it wasn't just another Arnold Schwarzenegger movie; they'd figure it out with time, she had assured my sister. Kindy also told me about two people we knew from college who had been in the federal building. They were no doubt dead, their bodies still buried in the rubble.

There were other things we couldn't talk about. From the distance of New Haven, I watched rescue workers scramble to dig bodies from the ruins as the number of dead crept higher and higher. The hardest pictures were those of the children. There had been a day-care center on the second floor above the lobby of the Murrah building. From it, firefighters had carried out one lifeless child after another. Children's toys were scattered across the sidewalk where Kindy had stood so many times. A small shoe. A rattle. Kindy told me she clicked off the television when these pictures came on. Everyone knew not to mention it, even though one of the kids whose bodies they carried out had been at their church only weeks before.

No one in Connecticut, however, understood the need I had for silence. In the days immediately after the bombing, I'd been afraid to go on campus, afraid of the sympathetic faces of students and colleagues who were also eager for details about what I knew and how my family was. The college chaplain asked if I wanted to speak with students after church on Sunday to share my theological perspective on this kind of violence. "The only thing students would learn from me right now is what a theologian looks like when her mascara runs from crying and she can't stop spitting out an endless stream of curse words," I told her.

A Connecticut news station had heard I was close to people who had been near the bombing; they wanted an interview, an emotional testimonial to the event by a local leader whose life had been directly touched by what was now being labeled as the largest national attack since Pearl Harbor. I foresaw a middle-aged, Oprah-style version of my nephews' action adventure.

I said no. Except for phone conversations with my sisters, I found it difficult to talk about it. Not a drop of blood had fallen on my hands, not even a grain of concrete dust had touched my lungs. I was embarrassed by my distance from the events, but at the same time I was quaking inside. I fled to my couch and the comfort of the telephone lines and TV cables that connected me to Kindy and Verity, to my parents, and to my city.

ONE OF US

It still surprises me how, after all these years, when I hear McVeigh's name or see that immature, angular face, in a flash of recognition, something deep inside me catches—a pull, a little cringe at the base of my skull, a tightening of my shoulders. For the very briefest of seconds, the world tilts slightly out of kilter, my mind goes blank, and I feel an anger, a trembling rage that I know is pure, burning lust for revenge. And I don't resist it. It's called hatred, the least divine impulse there is.

Then, with remarkable speed, I flip some mysterious switch in my head and it all turns back on: I am able to think again. But my vision of my beloved Oklahoma, or, better said, my beloved vision of my

Oklahoma, never quite looks the same each time I imagine the building exploding in my head.

After a few days, I got on my flight to get me to Oklahoma City.

"Damn, Verity, I swear he looks just like that flyboy Denise dated in high school. What was his name?" Kindy said the moment I walked into the house with Verity, who'd been on the same flight as me. Denise was a friend of Verity's who eventually became our foster daughter. I realized the absurdity of how we kept comparing McVeigh to boyfriends. I guess we just wanted some small familiar touchstone to connect us with an event so horrible that it exceeded our capacity to grasp it in any other familiar shape.

Kindy was looking at the television. She didn't even greet me.

"Steve. Denise's boyfriend's name was Steve. And no, they don't look anything alike," Verity quipped back, "except for that military look." Having expected an emotional reunion that would help me make sense of the devastation and evil, I instead felt peeved that we sisters were already bickering. And God was still the furthest thing from my mind.

Kindy reached for her walker as she struggled to get out of her favorite La-Z-Boy. During the trauma of the bombing, I had stopped paying attention to the horrible incident that had happened to her only six weeks earlier. She had been taking her usual Sunday afternoon nap and had been awakened by a terrible pain in her lower back. Trying to roll over, she realized her legs wouldn't move. Then it hit her that her arms, too, were useless. She was paralyzed from the neck down. Yelling down to Rand, she knew immediately that she had to get to the hospital. After two days of tests, they told her she had had a rare "stroke in her spine." They had to admit to her that the paralysis might last who knows how long. Forever, maybe. But my indomitable sister had started rehab within the week, and even though she still had little feeling below her neck, she slowly learned how to walk and use her arms. She had been back at work only a day when the bomb blew.

How could anyone carry so much weight all at once? I thought as I watched her struggle to rise, a determined smile on her face.

That night, Rand, Kindy, Verity, and I sat around the kitchen table after the boys had gone to bed, and did shots of tequila. A strange communion, but it felt somehow sacred. Kindy had insisted there was no better medicine for her spinal injury than this particular firewater ritual—licking salt and sucking on lemon slices as accompaniments. The four of us lit one cigarette after another, the room filling with smoke, so different from the fog of violence that had descended on Rand only a week before.

"I hate him," I blurted out after our third round of shots. "I want to kill him. I've never wanted to kill someone so badly in my life. I want him to slowly suffer and then just die." I could have gone on, but Verity put her hand on my shoulder to gently stop me. Her cherubic baby face had calmed me as a child, and still did, even though her face was now thinner and exhausted, with dark circles under her eyes.

Kindy jumped in. "Yeah, so much for our Sunday school belief in the inherent goodness of people. All that children of light and darkness crap. There is no light in that man. I don't care what Dad taught us, I am not like him. Not one tiny bit." She lit another cigarette. "I channel my anger into workouts to make my legs and arms stronger. I imagine myself punching and kicking him. Over and over and over again."

Rand just listened quietly, which is what he had done since that day downtown. It was as if the shock of the explosion had lodged in his voice box and clogged it up with fear and rage so dense that no sound could break through. He did another shot on his own.

Verity's and my visit lasted a week. As we were leaving, my mom and dad arrived to take up the slack. My mother went straight into her therapist mode—she'd been certified as a marriage and family counselor a few years before, a professional move that left me dumbfounded. She immediately focused on Rand, his trauma, his struggle, his lethargy. My dad went into professor mode, as if we were students waiting to be quizzed on our weekly reading assignment. He asked detailed medical questions about how Kindy was recovering from her stroke and how the city was managing a crisis of this magnitude. Of course, he also wanted a full accounting of what local churches were doing, asking specifically about congregations where his former students were pastors. My parents' urge for order was overwhelming to the three of us, who for the full week of our visit had been in the kitchen mostly crying and drinking and raging against our white terrorist nemesis.

The inevitable family blowup happened when my dad finally asked Kindy if she'd taken the boys to church. He knew their pastor well and wondered how he'd preached about it. Was it good theology?

"No, Dad, I haven't been to church. I haven't even been to the goddamn grocery store. I haven't left the house," she retorted. She failed to mention our frequent liquor-store jaunts.

I was standing by the front door, my roller suitcase in hand, waiting for the cab to the airport.

Reeling from Kindy's outburst, Dad turned his attention to me.

"You visited your grandpa this week, didn't you? He's all alone in that house." My grandma had died the summer before, and Dick Jones had crawled into his dimly lit Forest Park home to drink and whimper, mostly about days past and his lonely life.

"I called him and he didn't want to talk. But the answer is no, I didn't visit him," I said, perturbed but dutiful.

By this point in my life, I had no desire to ever see him again if I could help it. His creepiness, now unconstrained by my grandma's presence, meant no woman was safe near him. It infuriated me that my dad would even consider my visiting him. What I didn't tell him was that in my short call to my grandpa, he had spit out a string of anti-Muslim curses. It wasn't worth talking him down from his tirade; he enjoyed it too much to stop, even though he knew, like everyone else, that a white man-child had been the real terrorist.

I left with a soul as arid as the Oklahoma plain. It had been one of the more sisterly times of my life, for sure, drinking together late into the night, caring for Kindy's children, raging at every bad person we'd ever met. It had also been one of the least spiritual periods of my life— I hadn't set foot in church, had no craving for prayer, no longing for divine consolation or even consideration. Theology had abandoned me, or I had abandoned theology, or both. And it would take me years to understand that this was just fine, that abandonment, loss, and doubt are as much a part of being a believer as constancy and faith. And even though my sisters and I were too wrecked to drag our hungover bodies to church, we knew it was there, waiting, ready for us whenever we might decide to return. Verity, the pastor, had no choice but to walk back through the doors of her own church and figure out what to say in her sermon next Sunday. Kindy and I felt for her, knowing she was as lost as we were when it came to finding God in the midst of a catastrophe.

NOTHINGNESS AND THE HOLY

Six weeks later I was back in New Haven, at Yale's Battell Chapel, standing in front of a crowd who had turned out to hear me sound theologically profound. Everyone surely wanted to hear some resolution, some homegrown comprehension of homegrown terror. I once again felt neither erudite nor pious, just nervous and, yes, still quite profoundly out of sorts.

Why had I let Kindy and Verity talk me into giving this stupid public lecture, anyway? The question had pounded through my head all day, even though I knew the answer.

For the past month, we had spoken several times a day as the number of deaths rose. As far as soapboxes go—as a public advocate lawyer, Kindy loved nothing more than a big soapbox—Kindy hadn't yet found one to stand on. She was too busy trying—and still failing—to keep her legs working, her husband from falling apart, and her sons focused on anything other than the event.

So when I told her on the phone one day that Yale University's chaplain's office had called to see if I would give an evening talk about the Oklahoma City bombing, she begged me to do it.

"Come on, Serene," she cajoled. "For a theologian, isn't this the perfect moment to help the rest of us understand this mess? I mean, when else will you get a chance to talk to people about God and faith right in the middle of such a life-shattering event?"

Later that same afternoon, Verity had joined in the push. She argued that people needed to see how someone of my theological training dealt with tragedy when it was up close and personal like this and not just some far-off historical event. She had preached about it and survived, she said. Why couldn't I? It was my Christian duty, wasn't it? A divine calling? A heralding from on high? She knew, of course, that this last plea would probably do the trick. Why? Because like her, I was a guilt-ridden, mission-driven Jones girl with a long line of grace-filled Okie sinners standing behind me, constantly uncertain about whether to cheer or growl.

My sisters had a way of getting me to do things—tricking me, nudging me, barnstorming me. I called the next morning and told the chaplain, yes, I'd do it, noting to myself that for the first time since the bombing, names like Calvin and Edwards passed through my brain in a sincere, methodical way. I had agreed to speak without even thinking, until now, what it was my duty to speak about. As a theologian, I would have to use theology as the lens for understanding, or at least discussing, the bombing and my people's suffering. All I'd been thinking about for weeks were bombs and death and blood and rage-filled skies and shredded families. Now I'd have to find God in there somewhere, somehow.

The day of the speech was the first day I felt relief from the massive shock of the event. It didn't feel like I had climbed out of a hole but rather had been lifted out and set feetfirst on the ground. I immediately realized that my sudden sense of liberty from so much worry and fear was a direct consequence of the theological mandate of the speech. I had been forced, by professional necessity, to return to being who I was, to return to my true nature. Politics and family anxieties, interactions with colleagues and engagement with the media—all of this was pushing me away from a calling to ponder theology with my whole mind and soul. The world had intervened—some would call it evil, some would even call it the Devil. But now a clearheadedness—and a clear soul—brought levity back into my existence. By levity I don't mean laughter or good humor. I mean the very sense of lightness, of weighing less, of carrying less of a burden, that a theological vision of life brings.

Out of the scores of talks and lectures I've given, it is still the only speech I can recite in full to this day:

Let me begin by thanking you all for coming tonight. I know it's exam period and there are many grand and noble thoughts you are being asked to master in these next few days. But I also know that something happened last month in our land that was not grand or noble but which demands of us a form of personal mastery that no one expected to need. We have, all of us, experienced an act of terrorism on soil so close to home we could feel the tremors in our hearts here when it happened. We have seen children that could be our own, our little brothers, our baby sisters pulled from rubble that looks like the concrete used in the Phelps lab up the street. We have watched firefighters that could be our neighbors trying desperately to save lives, and we have watched mourners, who could be us, weeping as the remains of their loved ones are finally uncovered. Perhaps most shockingly of all, we have seen the face of a young man who looks like many people sitting in this room tonight, and we have discovered in his eyes an American-bred hatred that could, without remorse, without so much as even a tear, decide to annihilate us all, right now, right here.

With these last words, a silence settled over the room that surprised even me. There were no planned theatrics here. I gripped the podium and tried to quell my trembling arms. Please don't let me cry, I prayed. If tears came, I knew they wouldn't be the misty kind that appeared when I was moved in class by "the miracle of grace" or something along those lines.

Breathe, I thought. Take a deep breath. Now let it out . . .

And get your holy shit together.

Cursing at myself seemed to work. That and the fact that I'd just found Mokhtar—whom I hadn't seen since that day in the parking lot—sitting in the front row, a place he never assumed in class. And he was, believe it or not, taking notes. I had to smile. He touched me, graced me in the way grace usually appears—out of nowhere. I continued, sturdier, not so much inspired as becalmed.

It's hard to act with integrity when you're utterly terrified and all your rational thought processes have been knocked out of kilter by a violence you didn't expect and can't possibly understand . . .

. . . and it's almost impossible to feel loving and faithful when intolerable pain has left you so shocked and numb you can't move . . .

. . . or so damn enraged your whole being strains against the bridle and passionately yearns to kill someone in return, to see your offender tortured, maimed, harmed . . .

. . . I don't like to admit it, but that's what I, a so-called peace-loving and very politically correct feminist theologian, have felt these past six weeks . . .

. . . mind-blanking grief and behind it, volcanic rage.

I paused again and stared out at my audience. No smile. No calming warmth. No barely repressed tears. All of their eyes revealed that they were trying to grasp the dissonant shock of seeing a well-heeled professor/theologian and a bloodthirsty bitch-warrior inhabiting the space of a single person.

It's not exactly a picture of pious perseverance, is it? . . .

As the silence settled even deeper, I looked over and found Mokhtar completely engrossed in his note taking, seemingly oblivious to the fact that every other eye in the room was fixed on the angry woman standing at the front of the hall. I couldn't help myself; one corner of my mouth curled up into the ever-so-slightest of grins.

. . . Or is it?

As I walked back to my seat, I felt holy, but in a chilling way. I had touched the divine, saw it with such shocking clarity that my feet carried me to my pew while all the while my eyes saw a vision of something so indescribable that I have never, until now, tried to put it into words. I saw sheer space and sheer light.

This God is big, so vast that the far reaches of the universe or of our minds fail to mark her edges. In her, there is no edge, no moral judgment, no outreaches or inner sanctum, no measure of goodness or sorrow or ultimate meaning. She is, in one word, contradiction. All creative, perhaps all destructive, too. Just light, blinding light, and more sound than the ear can tolerate. In the light float wisps of that reality we call history, my life and yours and every other one that was, is, and will ever be, all swirling in a tumble of light and sound.

And in that swirl, everything is simply what it is. Brutal, cruel, and sickening, or gorgeous, graceful, and loving, all exploding together with the force of a building in Oklahoma City.

My feet took me to my pew and my body sat me down. I've almost become an atheist, I thought for a moment. And I wasn't afraid. And in the years to come, I would realize the fine line between the two, atheism and divine vision, nothingness and the holy. I would realize, because of Timothy McVeigh, that the divine is more complex than anything the human mind can grasp.

But at that moment the woman next to me put her hand gently on my knee, which was shaking. And her hand felt so cool and so warm at the same time that she transported me back to the place of my theology, back to my original theological site with the cool jug and the hot sun and my grandma Idabel there putting her hand on my knee as we sat together in the shade, the wind of a storm in the distance starting to sweep down on us. And I felt graced.

CHAPTER 9

Forgiveness

Anyone who is devoid of the power to forgive is devoid of
the power to love . . . There is some good in the worst of us
and some evil in the best of us. When we discover this, we
are less prone to hate our enemies.

MARTIN LUTHER KING, JR.

"Covenant" is a beautiful word. I probably heard it for the first time
when I was five years old, as it tended to pepper Disciples services
and Sunday school classes; I probably intuited what it meant for the
first time when I was seven and heard about the covenant rainbow God
promised Noah; and I surely understood the notion by the time I was
ten and my Sunday school teacher made us sign a covenant with the
church stating that we would tithe our allowance for a year.

Covenant means "contract," even in its biblical connotation. In
the Hebrew Bible, God executed contracts with a whole host of people:
Adam, Eve, Noah, Abraham, Sarah, Hagar, Moses, and the idea of a
God who negotiated, who made deals with God's people—and that
we had to honor our own end—resonated in my religious upbringing.
Oklahoma was, in many ways, a God-covenant kind of place. My
grandma's family believed God had given them their homestead; in

turn, they were obligated to live faithfully. For my grandpa's family, they no doubt felt God's divine hand at work in their lawless escape from Tennessee. In turn, they owed God, at the very least, a visit to church now and then. These weren't contracts in a strict sense, but nevertheless, people struck deals with God all the time.

In our Disciples theology, a softer version of a covenant was captured through the word "bond." "Covenant" comes from two Latin words, "con" and "venire," pairing the words "coming" and "together." We believed God bonded Godself to the world by promising to love humanity. That God-bond is another word for *grace*.

With respect to the human side of that bond, it's complicated. We are bound to God no matter what. Our names are on the contract of grace, even though our hands never actually sign off on it. Our covenant with God is not a two-way street. If we know grace, then we can consciously participate in God's love, although never as an equal partner. If we don't know it, God's love holds steady, anyway. That's how strong divine love is. Given how unsteady and conflicted we are, God's covenant also includes the promise to forgive us our sins. Grace and forgiveness, in God, are two sides of the same divine love coin.

Of course, when it comes to covenants made between people, we are most familiar with the term "covenant" as it applies to marriages. When you marry, you bind yourself to the other person as an equal partner, promising to stay together come hell or high water. Over time, Disciples have thankfully recognized that such promises aren't limited to a woman and a man. Our covenants to partner with others can be made in many different ways, with varieties of people and for multiple reasons, especially including marriage covenants shared by same-sex couples. But no matter who does it, when you make a covenant it is serious business—because it is symbolically a smaller human version of the bigger, everlasting divine covenant. The same holds true for forgiveness between people. Our smaller human version of God's forgiveness, in relation to other people, especially those partners we make conscious covenants with, is really hard. Maybe the hardest thing we ever do. Forgiveness and humanity are not friendly bedfellows, to put it mildly. Hatred is our favored reaction when hell or high water pulls us under.

MARRIAGE

When I shared matrimonial vows with Shepard Andrew Parsons at age twenty-four on June 22, 1985, in Enid, Oklahoma, we both took it very seriously. Especially the forever and always part. If God's love was forever, so, too, would be our love. Of course, we updated our vows, putting in stuff about laboring together in the struggle for justice and adding words affirming same-sex marriages, which back then wasn't even mentioned in Enid churches. Both my family and his shared a sense of its seriousness. Shocking as it may sound, no one in either of our families had ever gotten divorced. The Joneses and the Parsonses were damn good at keeping their promises.

"Dad, what's that noise?" I whispered to him when Shepard and I had processed into the church and were standing in front of him, ready to say our vows. He was performing the ceremony but could hardly hear me because what sounded like a blaring tornado alarm was shaking the sanctuary. Wedding guests were holding their ears and looking around, panicked. Not your normal start to a blissful wedding.

"A key seems to be stuck on the organ. I'll fix it." Dad put his hand on Shepard's shoulder and then walked behind the chancel and pulled the plug on the big instrument. We listened as it slowly faded.

Shepard chuckled as he took my hand, quietly kidding me. "Do you think it means something that our wedding is starting with what sounds like a storm alert?"

"Means we can weather anything," I squeezed his hand, ready to make it all nice, to get on with the service and our lives.

During our early years together we weathered a lot, but happily so. He was called to pastor his first church and I finished my doctoral studies at Yale. About eight years in, that changed. We started trying to have a baby, but it didn't work. I had three second-term miscarriages, and we were just about to stop trying when I got pregnant with our daughter, Charis, who was born on March 19, 1996. The losses hit us hard, setting off what would eventually turn into tornado-strength winds. In 1995, Shepard was pastoring the founding church of New Haven, a hard, huge job . . . I was writing books like a crazed woman, frantically trying to climb the tenure ladder at Yale, and when I wasn't burrowed in my office, I was traveling for work, giving talks around the world. The market for God talk, I had come to realize, was big, despite the seemingly massive decline in official believers in the West. And more and more the marketplace wanted a woman to channel and help understand the more accessible, accepting God of the late twentieth century.

When we celebrated our fifteenth wedding anniversary in Taos, New Mexico—our four-year-old daughter, Charis, in tow—I was outraged that he'd spent seven hundred dollars on a turquoise necklace for me. I made him return it. He was furious that I cared so much about the money we didn't have—and that I had forgotten to buy him anything. By that point, the easy chatter between us had dwindled to practically nothing; shared laughter was nonexistent. He moved out in 2001. A year later, we were divorced.

If there's such a thing as a spiritually grounded divorce, we tried to have one. The morning before the judge officially uncovenanted us, we shared "no longer married" covenant vows in church, pledging to still hold as dear the other's life and to never seek the other's harm. Basically, we promised to be nice to each other—something it took us only a day or two to blow.

"I promise to raise our daughter in harmony with you, putting her well-being always before us," he told me standing in the front of the sanctuary with a handful of friends around us. She was six at the time and in school for the day.

"I promise you the same, to share in the care of Charis, with joy and patience," I pledge back to him, holding hands, both of us tearing up, most of our friends weeping.

Later that afternoon, when the judge's gavel fell, we officially ended it, eighteen years after that June day when we promised to stay together forever.

I realize ours is not an unusual story. Nationally, marriages last, on average, only about eight years. We beat those odds. Almost half of all marriages end up like ours, in divorce court, probably not in church. The reasons for divorces are as diverse as the intricacies of our varied lives. When there's violence in the marriage, divorce can literally be a lifesaver. In our case, there wasn't violence, just failing hearts and loss of will. But for both of us, that failure had a painful spiritual side. Because marriage mirrors God's bond, the severing of our bond felt spiritually devastating. If India had left me wondering about God, my divorce left me feeling like an outcast from the land of covenants. If I couldn't keep my promises, I wondered, could God keep hers? Or was it all a silly, deluded game to start with?

RAGE

Charis stood face-to-face with me that Monday morning in June 2001, still months away from my official divorce. We were in the front hall-way and she was glaring at me, hands on her hips. She was six. I had lived for several months as a single mom (we were separated), shuttling her back and forth, from my house to her father's apartment on Friday and then back to mine on Sunday, for the school week. Her bare feet were planted firmly on the floor. "No, Mom," she said. "I am not going to school without my new blue Nikes. I won't go."

Her head was the shape of her father's—the high forehead, the thick curls of hair, the square jaw. She had her father's legs, too. Long strong calves, muscled thighs, compared to my stubby, dense ones. She was an athlete through and through, heir to her father's love of sports.

Too tired to argue with her . . . or with him, I wanted to sit on the floor and throw my own fit. The last time I'd talked to Shepard, the evening before, he'd said that it was my fourth call of the day.

"You're counting? Now you count?"

"I'm just saying the phone rings and it's normally you."

"You'd rather it be your new girlfriend?" I snapped.

He already had one. I was not jealous of his girlfriend, who would soon become his wife. But in those early days, I was jealous of how quickly he seemed to have moved on, how little he seemed to have suffered from the pending destruction of our covenant, how solid he seemed while I still felt so shattered.

"Serene, I wish you could hear how you sound."

As the memory of that comment jarred my brain, I felt the awful urge to plant my daughter on the floor and force her old worn-out white Nikes on her feet.

"Please, honey. These shoes are fine. You wore them last week."

"So?"

"I'll call your dad as soon as you get to school and find out what he did with your blue ones."

The buzzer sounded suddenly, announcing that her friends had shown up to walk to school. I was not going to let them leave for school without her; Charis had had enough abandonment to last her a lifetime.

"Charis, you know what? I'm the boss. Put your shoes on. You're leaving for school. Now."

The phone was ringing in the kitchen. God, let it be him calling me for a change, I thought. Let his calm voice do its work on his daughter. Let him try to get her out the door. She still hadn't left.

I heard my youngest sister instead. Verity's far-off voice sounded tired. She spoke slowly, deliberately, her Oklahoma accent less eroded than mine. "I've been up all night. It's over. I'm pretty sure they're going to kill him today."

Back in the hall, Charis tugged the white Nikes onto her feet. She stomped a few times, pretending they were too small.

"Do you want your sandals instead?" I cradled the phone in my hands as I shouted to her.

"No!" The door slammed behind her; her friends were now halfway down the street, their parent escort fast-walking behind them.

Still cradling the phone in silence, I watched her run to meet them—she ran like her father, too, heels kicking higher than most. But she had my focus, my will, a Jones gumption that had left behind a battlefield of shoes. Reaching down to pick them up, I remembered that Verity was on the line. Would Timothy McVeigh wear sneakers today, I wondered, his toes curling under and then easing inside them in that final moment?

"Verity, I'm sorry. It must be hard for your whole church group. Have you talked to Kindy?"

"No, I couldn't reach her this morning," she said. "If you do, tell her that I'll be at the prison for most of the day. We've set up a larger camp down the road from the prison, with our signs, begging to stop it. I'll call one of you when I get a chance."

Verity and I had grown closer over the years; our days together in seminary had been full of zeal about social justice. Back then she had had two pairs of baggy jeans, ten T-shirts, and enough protest buttons to line a path on the Mall to the U.S. Capitol. Now, fifteen years later, I was still at Yale, teaching kids in tight jeans and T-shirts that said NO FEAR; she was now wearing pastoral-looking suits and black robes on

Sunday. Since the bombing, she had moved to be the senior pastor at a church in Terre Haute, Indiana, a midwestern community that felt more like Oklahoma to her than her New England congregation in Colchester.

But when we three sisters heard the startling news that McVeigh was being transferred to the Terre Haute penitentiary for his execution, we were stunned. It didn't seem possible. Would he follow us forever? My two sisters' lives, one in Oklahoma City and the other in Terre Haute, seemed destined to bookend a history of violence that started with one hundred and sixty-eight deaths and was now ending with his singular death in an executioner's chair. The symmetry of their places in this arc was uncanny. That my marriage had just blown up added to the drama of our interconnected lives. Granted, my personal drama was trivial compared to the violence of his, but its place in the mix of our mingling traumas was nevertheless unavoidable.

When Verity stepped into a leadership role in the anti-death-penalty protests that surrounded the execution, no one was surprised. She had always been the quietest, most composed and thoughtful of the three of us, and her faith-anchored activism was as sturdy as the prison walls she had been protesting outside of. She was the strongest, wisest pastor I knew—and because I had taught hundreds of future pastors, not because she was my sister, I knew how rare she was. She never reveled in the power of her pulpit; she saw it as her humble calling to lead with compassion, not ego. She had the soul of a pastor, which meant she put others' needs and worries before her own, always committed to discerning what words of grace they needed to hear, not whatever theological brilliance she needed to share. Unlike Kindy and me, who couldn't help but blurt out every feeling and thought we had, Verity's quiet circumspection made her harder to read. But I knew she seethed at this man who had done so much harm. It had to be hard for her, knowing as we did that she shared Kindy's and my rage at him.

But she had better managed to move herself forward, into a place of forgiveness and compassion, while I remained stuck in my fury.

A testament to Verity's pastoral leadership was the fact that when she went to the jail to protest, as she had done every day for the last month, she had large groups from her own church with her. They brought plates of deviled eggs and bologna sandwiches, cookies, and coffee to share during each vigil. Her congregation wasn't known for being particularly radical when it came to controversial social issues. It was a mix of Republicans and Democrats with a smattering of both far-left- and far-right-wingers. When it came to the death penalty, though, they were of one mind.

It wasn't a sudden thing that changed them. A longstanding member of the church had just lost a son shortly before Verity arrived. It was a drug deal gone bad; his twentysomething son was stabbed multiple times and died alone in the back room of a run-down trailer. Verity sat for days with the church member through the trial of the man who had murdered his son. Even as he was grief-stricken by the murder, he came to feel the deadly weight of a death sentence against the assailant. And he was stricken again. He wasn't an activist or a particularly political man, but the thought of paying for one life with another struck him as profoundly perverse. He talked regularly with Verity about it and eventually the whole congregation was drawn into his struggle. The church eventually did a Bible study on the themes of punishment and revenge. After a year of heated debate and gut-wrenching testimonies, not just by this man but by others who had experienced violence and sought revenge, the church together decided that the death penalty was contrary to the teachings of Jesus. They had watched *Dead Man Walking* together and had heard lectures on the racist and classist nature of the criminal justice system. Some of them had even begun to visit the nearby prison, meeting incarcerated men, listening to their stories, reaching out to their families.

"Jesus refused to respond to violence with violence," one of their elders said when he summed up the Bible study's conclusions. "And he asked his followers to forgive their enemies, not to kill them."

Another elderly deacon added, "And Jesus himself was executed by the state. We can't turn our back on the horrible truth of the cross."

All of this happened before McVeigh had been brought to their town. They had already started letter-writing campaigns to overturn the death penalty in Indiana and faced pushback from other congregations that called then unchristian for their stance. Verity had patiently and wisely led them through it all. So, when McVeigh arrived and his execution date was announced, they knew the time had come for them to personally bear witness to the truth. And so began their vigils. Their number was small at first but soon hundreds of people, many of them from other Indiana congregations, joined them near the prison.

"When we kill people for killing, it means violence has spawned violence. It's a vicious cycle we have to stop," said the man who had started it all to Verity in one of their first meetings. She had listened and, as Kindy and I watched from a distance, her own blood-lusting fury at McVeigh had dwindled away, replaced by compassion, not vengeance.

As we followed her transformation, we had become more awkwardly self-conscious of our own unrelieved fury. Verity didn't talk much about what shifted inside her; she just explained to us the events that were changing her community and talked about her steady desire to be a good pastor to her flock.

And today was the day their protests at the prison would end.

Everyone knew by now that he would be killed, no matter what they did.

"Verity, honey, I wish I could hug you. You amaze me. I'm so proud of what you're doing," I said. I stopped short of saying that I wished I could be there with her, because I didn't. My own rage at McVeigh was still burning. All I could think to add was a simple statement of truth. "You're my hero, little sister. I love you. There's a reason your name means 'truth.'"

"Thanks, Serene," she said, her gratitude clear. "How are things with Charis and Shepard?" Always the pastor, she turned the conversation to my troubles.

"Just the same. Awful. Just awful." My urge to start ranting about my failing marriage stuck in my throat, so instead I lied. "But we'll be okay."

"You will be. I know it," she gently answered back, her voice quivering with exhaustion. "I love you, too, and I'll keep you posted on what's happening."

Hanging up, I turned on the TV to see what, if any, coverage their protest might be getting. On every news channel the execution had top billing, but on screen the church's witness was nowhere to be found.

I washed out my coffee cup and called Shepard again—why did I keep doing that?—and he picked up on the fifth ring. I heard him clear his throat twice before offering a studied, laconic "Hello." For almost two decades of marriage, I had listened, every morning, to that same raspy cough and rough hello; they were cues. He wanted me to know that he was still asleep, but that, as always, he was cheerfully willing to get up . . . for me. He also knew that I had most likely been up since five, that the house was clean, the breakfast dishes washed, and that I had a list of items I needed to discuss about the day. His pleasant hello never failed to make my list sound like a long series of complaints. A burden he would cheerfully bear.

"You forgot to send Charis's blue shoes home with her. She's been hysterical all morning, in case you want to know."

"What time is it?"

"If it's not too much trouble, could you bring them to her when you pick her up for dinner? You are still taking her to dinner, aren't you?"

"It's too early for this."

"This is your daughter's life."

"I'll look for the shoes and let you know if I find them. And yes, I am doing dinner. Thanks for calling. Have a great day."

He clicked off. The covenant wasn't just breaking; it had been shredded. Between our separation and McVeigh's imminent execution, I was angry all the time.

I wasn't hungry but forced myself to make a ham and cheese sandwich. As I was finishing the last bite, the phone rang. I knew it was Shepard. McVeigh's haughty face stared out at me from the television, his execution still the day's top news.

"Are you sure you don't have them?" I asked incredulously.

He said he had spent the last hour looking. "This is really weird. I'll look a little harder. But they are not here," he said, getting ready to hang up again.

"You just don't get it," I said. "These little things are really important to Charis. She thinks she's lost you from this house and now you go and lose her shoes, too."

I imagined her blue shoes carelessly stuffed in his closet or under a pile of his dirty clothes.

"She doesn't seem all that angry when I'm with her, Serene," he said, hurt in his voice. "I think you're the one that's mad and projecting it onto her."

His reliable dagger—astute psychological analysis couched as an offhand remark. I thought of Charis's stomping feet, the door slamming behind her. She had enough fury in her to fuel a jet; she didn't need the added hit of my rage as well. I hated it when Shepard was right, even if only a little bit. I changed the subject.

"Don't you even know what today is?"

"It's June eleventh," he said.

"They are going to finally kill McVeigh," I said. "They'll probably do it late tonight or in the early morning. Verity called this morning to say that she would be holding vigil at the prison until it's finished."

My words delivered the desired shock. "Oh my God, I completely forgot. I read about it yesterday and was going to call. How are you?"

Of all the people I knew in New Haven, Shepard alone understood what the day meant to me, the awful five years that had led up to it. For a brief moment, I recalled the feel of his arms, the comfort of his body. He was the only one to whom I confessed that McVeigh had made me question, if not lose, all the grace beliefs my theological life and career had been built upon. He was the only one to whom I had confessed that, some days in the classroom, I felt like I was teaching lies to my students—especially when it came to forgiveness, something I couldn't muster myself.

"Honestly? Not so good," I said, ever vulnerable to a glimpse of comfort from the man I had once needed. "I'm trying to grade papers and I can't seem to concentrate. Thought I'd worked through the whole thing. Guess I haven't."

"How are Kindy and Rand?"

"I don't know. You could call them yourself." I had tried to reach Kindy several times in the last hour and failed. The sound of her answering machine brought my mind and body back to the day of the bombing. I tensed, felt the same pain in my lower back and shoulders.

"When you talk to them, give them my love." He paused. "I really have to go, Serene. Hang in there. I'll call later if I find the shoes."

He hung up and left me once again alone, holding the kitchen phone in my hand.

I promised myself that after two more papers, I'd try Kindy again. I'd finished grading only one before I gave up, found some ice cream in the freezer, and called her law office again.

"Verity called from the parking lot of the prison yesterday," Kindy said as soon as she answered. "This execution thing is going to make her have a stroke."

She fully grasped the irony. All I could imagine were the two of them, my two be-stroked sisters, dragging their feet along the road side by side.

"I know. All I have been able to do . . ." I couldn't finish the sentence, feeling guilty at being so far away from . . . what? From another death? From my sisters? From my home? From myself? From God and faith? From forgiveness?

"I'm trying not to think about it," Kindy said. "Just a coping strategy I've developed after years of handling death penalty cases. Don't think. Don't feel. Just move on." She forced a chuckle. "Spent a couple of hours slogging away on the exercise bike. My legs aren't doing so well."

During the five years since the bombing and her spinal stroke, Kindy had struggled fiercely to regain use of her legs. After several surgeries and hours of ongoing physical therapy, she had become pretty good at walking. Her steps were still labored; her left foot dragged and her right hip torqued awkwardly forward when she moved. But much to our family's amazement, she was eventually able to drive and even to walk her dogs, with only a cane in hand.

Her relentless determination had sustained me. During this long period of recovery, I talked with her often on the phone. She kept me apace of her daily progress, and together we followed closely the unfolding of McVeigh's trial, conviction, and eventual sentencing. She watched news reports about his case carefully, oftentimes while sitting on her therapeutic bicycle, forcing her legs to stretch and push. She kept me abreast of the legal intricacies of it all. The saga of "the executioner," as she described it.

Before the bombing, Kindy had been at the center of a big capital case in Oklahoma. Sean Sellers had been sixteen when he killed, execution style, a convenience-store clerk a couple of miles from his house. It was never clear why he did it; he would later say that Satan told him to. It was even less clear why, when he was seventeen, he shot both his parents in the head while they slept.

Only a year out of law school, Kindy had eagerly agreed to be the second chair on his case in the public defender's office. While no one ever doubted that he did it, Kindy had absolutely no doubt that the state shouldn't kill children. Pregnant with her second son, she had waddled in and out of his court trial for seven months, going back and forth between arguments against trying him as an adult and trips to the bathroom with morning sickness. Her arguments had failed, on all counts. He was tried as an adult, convicted on three counts of first-degree murder, and sentenced to death. The day McVeigh bombed the Murrah building, she had been on the phone with Sellers's lawyers planning one more appeal. In 1999, the state had filled his youthful veins with enough burning poison to down a herd of steer. Oklahoma-style revenge, she'd called it.

She told me that she was relieved when McVeigh's trial was moved to Colorado—not only did she think it ensured a fairer trial, she welcomed its distance from her family. Sean's own legal saga was far too close to her. She had developed empathy for the teenager during his trial. Since his conviction, she had visited him every few months in prison. She was devastated the day he was killed, shaken to the core by the state-sanctioned ritual that ended his life. Unlike Sean's execution, however, McVeigh's fate never drew feelings of compassion from her, only a sense of coldness . . . and a greater determination to walk.

It was only in the last stages of McVeigh's sentencing that she got involved. Even before his conviction, families of survivors as well as those who had lost loved ones in the bombing began to lobby for the death penalty. Local and national news had joined in the conversation. She had watched as people she knew testified to the grief and rage they still felt over their losses and the violence he had perpetrated against so many. The tearful testimonies were wrenching. They wanted the murderer to pay. Truth had to triumph and accounts had to be righted—and I admit that I found myself nodding in agreement, stunned at how quickly my anti-death-penalty sentiments had dissolved.

As these stories reached out across the nation, Kindy told me she knew from her experience with Sean's trial that killing McVeigh would do little to lessen the living agony of those he had so viciously harmed. She knew that her own legs would gain little strength from his execution. But half of me, or more, rebelled. I couldn't summon her power—and I really saw it as divine power—to fight for this murderer's life. We had always been an anti-death-penalty family and our theology backed it up. And here I was, at the moment when the rubber really hit the road, breaking ranks. I wanted him dead.

The chorus shouting along with me for his death eventually grew so loud that Kindy felt compelled to join a small group of victims' families who were speaking out against the state's use of lethal violence. Their voices had been ignored by the media, for the most part. In the silence, though, her resolve to stop his execution grew stronger as did the voices of those who berated her for her vocal opposition to killing him.

"Did you hear the last McVeigh interview?" she asked.

"Yeah, caught part of it," I said, lying.

"Pathetic," she said. "I kept thinking about what you were thinking, you know, as a theologian. About this blood thirst we have for revenge."

"Yes, yes," I remember saying weakly. Five years of doubting my own theological vision of life. And I couldn't bear to admit my faithlessness to her. And my own blood thirst.

"The only relief I'm feeling, frankly, is that all those fucking reporters and their cameras will finally take their Hollywood sympathy and get the hell out of Oklahoma," she said.

"He still doesn't show any signs of remorse," I said, trying, I realized, to get a reaction from her, to see some slight weakness with which I could identify.

"I know," she said. But she was much less angry than me. "Never said he was sorry. Never even admitted it was wrong. But he wants us to kill him, anyway. I've seen it before. Guys like him get turned on by the thought of people watching them die in the spotlight, being famous and all. Not that they get it, you know, that they are going to *actually* die. Be gone. No more."

"It's creepy how cold he is about the whole thing," I said. "Cold as winter in Enid." I didn't know if I liked my simile or not, but it was what I felt—Oklahoma winter cold from the universe. "He looks a lot older, though."

"Looking at him made me think about Sean. That's the part that really hurts." Her voice cracked for the first time. Her pragmatic opposition to the death penalty suddenly turned to an emotional, personal one.

"The dirty blond hair, the pointy nose, that smirk—I keep seeing Sean's face, wondering what he'd look like if he'd lived to be twenty-six," Kindy said. "You know, it's weird, but I feel completely detached from McVeigh. No rage. No pity. Nothing. That little kid's another matter. I grew to like him in a strange, motherly sort of way. He depended on me and I failed him when I gave up the case in the final appeal."

"You did all you could, Kindy," I said.

But my mind was elsewhere. I couldn't give her the consolation she needed right now. My big-sister compassion was buried by my rage. I encountered anger everywhere—not just when I saw McVeigh on TV but about my marriage, my failed covenant, my disconcerted daughter, and the distance I felt from my two sisters, both of whom were walking down a path toward a forgiveness that completely eluded me. I was the oldest sister and was supposed to take care of them, leading them, guiding them. And yet now, in the midst of their pain, I felt steeled inside.

Not only could I not lead them, I couldn't even stumble along behind them.

So many times in my life as a teacher and a theologian, I have failed to summon the strength to be pastoral, to encourage theological thinking, to give comfort. I used to be ashamed of this, but the McVeigh event would soon make me more patient with myself as a theologian.

I sat in my kitchen sipping tea for the next couple of hours, haphazardly reading student papers. Five years later, and my hatred and rage had not yet subsided. They had lodged in my soul, rearing up whenever I was frustrated, tired, or weak. At times I thought the light had reasserted itself to battle all my darkness inside. But McVeigh had become an enduring test to my theology.

Even now, I find it hard to reconstruct the events exactly. Sometimes, out of nowhere, I will recall with sharp clarity an insignificant detail—pressing the phone keys to call Kindy when I first heard about the bombing, the sky without the federal building in it, the call from the television station, the color of McVeigh's car and his military-style jacket. Other details, once important, have faded. I no longer remember the exact nature of Rand's injuries or how my nephews got home from school that afternoon. The series of events that led to McVeigh's arrest elude me. I feel perturbed with myself, frustrated that the darkness has blotted out the light—the light I grew up with, the light I studied and wrote about, the light I taught, the light I professed to live by.

THE EXECUTION

Later that afternoon, my colleague John, the only other Oklahoman I knew in New Haven, called to see if I wanted to meet him for happy hour at a bar just a few blocks from my house. He hadn't mentioned the upcoming execution when he called, but just hearing his Oklahoma accent, so close, felt comforting to me. Charis wasn't coming home with her father until after dinner, so I decided to walk over and meet him. Before leaving, I tried to call Verity again, but she wasn't picking up.

At the bar, John and I ordered beers, and he asked how things were going, how Charis was doing, how I was. The television on the wall behind us was tuned in to CNN, the sound off. McVeigh's face kept appearing every ten minutes or so. We knew why we were together.

I no longer froze up when people asked about Shepard. After months of shamed silence, I was finally able to talk about it without feeling embarrassed or awkward. John's sarcastic stories about his three exes had often provided me with welcome relief from the silent grief and anger that gripped me.

"Well," I said, eyeing McVeigh on a screen above the bar, "the crisis of the day is that Shep seems to have lost Charis's favorite shoes. It's exhausting, shuttling a daughter between two households." I took a long drink of beer. "He bought her those shoes to try to cheer her up when he announced to her that he had a girlfriend, and now he can't find them. She told me the other night that she hated her daddy for moving out. Sometimes I want to tell her I can't blame her."

With these last words, I felt a brief wave of satisfaction pass through me. It would hurt Shepard to know that she had said this; I wanted him to hurt. I had long ago realized my hatred for McVeigh had found its milder companion in my distaste for my soon-to-be ex.

"Sorry about that," John said. "I'm glad I didn't have children to deal with through my many breakups. It's tough." His ex-wives all lived somewhere else. They never saw each other. I told him that I envied that distance.

"Think they'll finally do it?" I asked at last, looking over John's shoulder at McVeigh's face on another television, the penitentiary in the background.

"I hope so, just to get the damn thing off the news. It's a circus." He told me a story—his sarcastic wit in rare form—about his Oklahoma relatives who had wanted to actually see the execution on closed-circuit television. "They had planned to have friends over for a barbecue to celebrate."

I told John my sister Verity was most likely protesting at the penitentiary as we spoke.

We sat in silence for a moment.

John glanced again at the television and then looked back at me, smiling. "I hope you find Charis's shoes. I feel for her."

"Yeah, me, too." I grinned slightly, then paused to drink more beer. "Hey, John, you don't happen to know whether or not people wear shoes, or socks, or house shoes, or bare feet, or whatever when they are executed, do you?"

"Well, sister, you got me there. Let's think about it." He was a Native American religious history professor at Yale; I could see him putting on his history hat. "Barefoot seems too crude, too bodily; people won't want to be reminded that he's a regular person with ugly feet. Shoes strike me as too formal; they would lend him an air of dignity. Not good. House shoes, maybe, but they seem a little too homey for people's comfort, too domestic for a public killing. I bet he'll wear socks. White socks. Thick white athletic socks. Yes, that would be my guess."

"I bet you're right," I said, just to say something.

We left the bar around seven and I walked home alone. The lowering sun was just beginning to cast a light orange glow over New Haven and the evening air felt damp; the sky was darkening on its western edge and the wind had picked up. A summer storm—it would be raining by morning. And I felt colder than I'd ever felt on the coldest, windiest Oklahoma winter day.

I passed by the hill I loved to climb to see the harbor's open air and to think of Oklahoma. The beer had left me too lazy to go up, but visions of the sky above the southwestern plains loomed large in my mind nonetheless. I looked up and saw the storm clouds coming closer.

When we were kids, my sisters and I would sometimes huddle together on an old workbench that sat on the back porch of our house and watch storm clouds gather at a distance; we could see almost ten miles out across the open wheat fields. In early summer, the storms could be fierce. We would watch the dark front move toward us, waiting excitedly to spot tornado funnels that would dip down and up again, as the churning heavens moved closer. I remember well the thrill of seeing the future before it arrived, anticipating its power and then quaking under the force of its torrential waters when they finally paused above us. We would then watch the storm, now past, travel on across the fields, our own air cleansed in its wake, the land flooded, the wheat soaked. In the sky above us, the three of us thought we could see time as it traveled, forgiveness coming only as it moved past onto other fields, other skylines.

In a trash can by the door, Kindy would collect rainwater to wash her hair. She liked the shine. Verity loved to play in the mud puddles left behind, browning her body with wet, fresh earth. I, the oldest, would stand on the porch looking out at them, brow furrowed, hands on hips, worried about the tornado that hadn't hit but might, later, and the floods, the future and the past, and the cruel force of a sky I couldn't control.

Forgiveness. I had taught it, preached it, even practiced it. And yet, for five years, I could not summon it. I had tried my darnedest, especially by reading a pile of books a colleague had given me by Howard Thurman. He's considered a mystical theologian whose writings about slavery, racism, nonviolence, forgiveness, and the spiritual work of activism had led Martin Luther King Jr. to study with him at Boston University, where he was the chaplain and a teacher for many years. He was born in Florida in 1899, and his grandmother had been enslaved. His most famous book, *Jesus and the Disinherited*, gave spiritual guidance to generations of civil rights activists.

He wrote about the deep but often ignored connection between our inner spiritual landscape and our outer public lives. If hatred fills the former, the latter mirrors it. And that hatred, he believed, was something the "human spirit cannot tolerate." It destroys us from the inside out by allowing the harms of others to define who we are. He spoke a universal message but never spared his readers the luxury of forgetting he was writing as a black man living in Jim Crow America, a world riddled with hatred and violence. His wasn't a polite or sweetly naive faith. His life made his message all the more uncomfortable to hear, especially because he dared to speak about the soul-corrupting force of violence and, hardest of all, the spiritual work of forgiveness.

When I got home, I pulled one of his books off the shelf in my study and opened it to a passage I taught in class. He described with pointed clarity my anger at McVeigh, my grandpa, my mother, my disappearing husband:

> [H]atred tends to dry up the springs of creative thought in the life of the hater, so that [one's] resourcefulness becomes completely focused on the negative aspects of [one's] environment. The urgent needs of the personality for creative expression are starved to death. A [person's] horizon may become so completely dominated by the intense character of [this] hatred that there remains no creative residue in [one's] mind and spirit to give to great ideas, to great concepts.

His words hurt me because they were so accurate. I then turned to one of his prayers.

> I purpose in my heart that I shall not use my memory to store up those things which fester, poison and destroy my living, my

life, or the living and the life of others. I shall make it my study to preserve my soul in balance and liberty. I will use my memory to store up the excellent things of my experience.

As I read further, he forced me to see my own ransacked bloodlust for McVeigh's murder as part of a larger human will to violence and the delusion that it will cure the pains we suffer:

> A cursory glance at human history reveals that [people] have sought for countless generations to bring peace into the world by the instrumentality of violence. The fact is significant because it is tried repeatedly and to no basic advantage. . . . Violence is very deceptive as a technique because of the way in which it comes to the rescue of those who are in a hurry. Violence at first is very efficient, very effective. It stampedes, overruns, pushes aside and carries the day. It becomes the major vehicle of power, or the radical threat of power. . . . Violence is the ritual and the etiquette of those who stand in a position of overt control in the world. As long as this is true, it will be impossible to make power [economic,] social or political—responsive to anything that is morally or socially motivating. . . . This is true, whether in the relationship between parents and children in the home or in great affairs of the state involving the affirmation of masses of the people. . . . To believe in some other way, that will not inspire retaliation and will curb evil and bring about social change, requires a spiritual maturity that has appeared only sporadically in the life of [humanity] on this planet. The statement may provide the machinery, but the functioning of it is dependent upon the climate created by the daily habits of the people.

Most challenging of all, however, were his discomforting words about the necessity of forgiveness. He never suggested that black people en masse should simply forgive and forget, with a shrug of their shoulders, the ravages of harms perpetrated against them. That was nonsense. What he pointed to, instead, was the danger of holding on to internalized rage that makes you captive to the very thing you seek to resist. For freedom to find us, as human beings, we must step out of our own internal prisons and imagine a different future. That's what forgiveness looks like. Freedom. Freedom inside you that, when you join with others, demands freedom outside you, from the social sins that bind us.

The more I read Thurman, the guiltier I felt. I knew that my puny rage had turned into my own gargantuan prison. He made me question: How can I be an activist for social change if I can't even imagine a world beyond the pain of my own divorce? Or beyond an executioner's chair in Terre Haute?

HOW COULD HE?

When I finally laid Thurman aside it was almost 8:00 p.m. I sat on the front porch and waited for Charis and her dad to return from dinner. Neighbors passed by offering friendly hellos. A lawn mower hummed a block away. The calm of early summer had begun to settle on the street. The evening felt like it wanted to be peaceful.

They pulled up in his minivan around 8:15 p.m. I could see his new girlfriend sitting in the front seat. Charis bounded toward me gushing about the dessert she had just eaten. "Piles of chocolate," she told me.

I stayed seated on the steps, arms opening for her. Her father stopped, relaxed and friendly, in the middle of the yard. He looked quickly around at the homes of friends he had once called neighbors. His girlfriend came over to say hi with a gentleness that made me ashamed of my ire.

"I still haven't found her shoes. But we sure had fun tonight. I think she's warming up to the whole new arrangement." He nodded toward Charis, who was hugging his girlfriend goodbye. "The three of us have big plans for the weekend." Charis climbed into my lap and was now pulling a colored drawing from her backpack. She had kicked off her white sneakers; her bare heels knocked against my shins.

"That's great," I said as I feigned a smile and wrapped my arms around her little body. She felt warm and happy. "Did you look in the van for the blue shoes?" I asked with cheerful blame.

"Yep. They aren't there, either. Sorry." He looked back at the van again. "Listen, I gotta run. Bye, Charis. I love you, sweetie. I'll see you on Friday." He squatted down to her level, waiting.

She looked up briefly. "Bye, Dad. Love you, too." She then wiggled out of my arms and continued, still perched in my lap, the task of unpacking artistic treasures from her bag.

As they drove off, she chattered away about the day's events. Gym was fun. She had a new library book about dogs. "Let's go in, Mom. I want to take a big bath." I picked up the shoes she had tossed on the grass, and we went inside to begin our bedtime ritual.

About midway through our routine, things began to fall apart—somewhere between the bathtub and homework. I had come to expect rough evenings, but it was clear that this one was going to be particularly hard. First, she didn't want to get out of the bathtub. It was late, so I encouraged her with the promise of a short reading from her favorite book of poems—if she finished a little bit of homework first. When we finally settled down to do the homework, it was only a few minutes before she threw her pencil across the room in frustration. She couldn't do what we both knew was an easy math problem.

We laid the paper out carefully on the desk. I read her the instructions. She was to count the coins depicted in five boxes; dimes, nickels, pennies, and quarters all arrayed in different configurations. It took only an instant for the full force of her six-year-old panic to set in. I knew she did not yet understand money. What I had not anticipated was how much her not knowing would scare her. She looked at the mysterious figures before her and burst into tears, then sobs, then wrenching cries of despair, "I can't do it, Mommy. I'm stupid. I'm stupid. Mommy, no. Please!" She kicked the top of the desk, pushed her chair away, and ran blindly toward the bed, collapsing on top of her stuffed animals, her body a heap of heaving anguish.

I sat down next to her. "Charis, it's okay. It's only homework. Coins are hard to understand, but you'll learn. It's okay, honey." I asked if I could hold her and I could see her half-buried head nod slightly. I picked her up and, sitting cross-legged on the bed, I cradled her sideways in my arms, the weight of her body in my lap. We rocked and rocked, her fists clenched against her chest, me drawing her closer and closer gently, ever tighter. I whispered into her hair, a mumbled chant, repeated again and again. "I know, sweet girl. I know."

Her crying continued. "I want my shoes, Mommy. Please, where are my shoes? My new shoes. I want them. I want them now. How could Daddy lose them? How could he? I hate him." With the word "hate," her sobs grew suddenly loud again.

I kept rocking her.

How could he? Was it a real question to me? Should I answer? Or should I tell her why shoes are only shoes, why some things matter so much more? In a flash, years of rage churned up inside me. McVeigh had taken up so much space in my home, my life, my relationship with my daughter, my impending divorce. He had poisoned the underlying emotion in almost all of my intimate interactions.

"I don't know!" I said, way too loud. Red-faced; my whole body clenched and heaved like hers. "I don't know how he could do such a goddamn awful, awful thing." I was shouting by then.

"Mommy, are you okay?"

She didn't understand my vulgarities, my sudden loudness and intensity. Then her mind wandered back to its preoccupation.

"Mommy, how could he lose them?"

Her tender voice, now a softening whimper, brought me back to the room, the bed, and the child I was holding. I looked down at her small toes and matted blond tangle of hair. With a flash of emotion compelled by a power beyond even my rage, I knew that I loved this child more fiercely than I had ever loved anyone before and that I had a choice before me. How would I respond to her question?

With a simple turn of phrase, I could show her how to hate a man, a woman, any other human being. I could turn her confusion into growing anger with gentle coaxing. Without even trying very hard, I could take her from him. It would be easy. It seemed so natural. No one would know. Not even Charis. I held in my hands the power to kill and the raging desire to do so. I saw the future tornado coming toward me, cloudy, turbulent, the downpour soaking every inch of my life's parched ground.

How could he?

FORGIVING

I couldn't lie to her and make it all right. I couldn't forgive him—either of them—the pain still cut too deep. But I could decide not to harm her with my rage, not to let my fury distort her vision of life and love. Then and there an image from Thurman flashed through my mind:

> There is in every one of us an inward sea. In that sea there is
> an island; and on that island there is a temple. In that temple
> there is an altar; and on that altar burns a flame. Each one of us,
> whether we bow our knee at an altar external to ourselves or not,
> is committed to the journey that will lead us to the exploration

of our inward sea, to locate our inward island, to find the temple, and to meet, at the altar in that temple, the God of life.

Suddenly, all my reading and writing, all my devotion to the minds that had grappled with God and faith, all the books and photos of theologians and discussions with my dad cohered into one logical, powerful vision. On my own inward altar, in the temple of my rage, the God of life was still vibrantly present, awaiting my return.

I stepped toward that grace when I made my choice.

"Charis, remember how your daddy taught you to tie your shoes? He did it when you were only three years old. At the time, you were the only kid your age on the whole block who could do such a wonderful thing. Oh, you were so excited, so proud of yourself. You spent three days running around, showing anyone who would watch how you could make bows with your laces." Her body stopped shaking.

"You know what else I remember, sweetheart? After you finished tying your beautiful bows, there was a special knot that Dad would tie on top of it. A double knot. It was so secure that it would keep your shoes from coming untied all day." She lifted her head and gently pushed herself away from my chest. Her eyes were red, her face streaked with tears.

"Tonight, when you came home, I noticed you had that double knot in your shoes again. Did your dad tie that for you after school?" I grinned at her quizzically.

Her eyes lightened. "Yeah, he did. First thing when he saw me. Mom, was I really the first to tie my shoes? Even before Sophia or Noah?" The thought of doing something ahead of her two best friends delighted her.

"Yes, you were. And you know what? Anyone who can tie shoes as well as you can surely learn to count coins." Her fists had come unclenched. She smiled when she figured out that I had pointed her back toward her father and, yes, toward homework. "Let's try to figure out just one box tonight. We'll do the others later."

"Okay, Mom."

Thirty minutes later, she was sound asleep. I debated turning on the television but instead lay down in bed. In the darkened room, I thought of my sisters: Verity, holding vigil, Kindy straining on her bike, trying to blot out the pain of Sean's execution. I thought of Timothy McVeigh and his white socks. I thought of my profession, my books, and my title: theologian. I stared at that island in my inner sea. It had become cluttered with all the wrongs I had piled up there—other wrongs against me, my own wrongs against others, the wrongs of the world against itself. Looking at the island, I saw that the past debris was piled so high I couldn't find that altar I knew was buried somewhere under it.

The urge to uncover the altar was strong. I imagined tossing each piece of clutter aside, but every time I looked at the particular wrong I held in my hand ready to fling it away, I couldn't bring myself to let it go. It felt comfortable, familiar; it told me who I was. All these wrongs had become extensions of myself; that vast pile had become my arms, my legs, my gut, my heart. I saw it so clearly: anger and hate took up all my inner space and made me feel secure. Somehow less vulnerable. I didn't want to be that person anymore. But the risk of letting it all go was terrifying. Who would I be without these adopted parts?

The dizzy freedom of forgiveness felt scary. But the growing weight of not forgiving, I knew, would eventually destroy me and poison my daughter. It was then I realized why forgiveness is so hard. It wasn't because forgiveness lets people off the hook—which is what I had so often tricked myself into thinking. We can forgive and still hold people accountable. What makes forgiveness hard is its demand that we give up the snuggly warm blankets of hate we believe will protect us from future harm. We fear that if we let go of that protection, the evils of the world will ravage us further. But this animallike fear hides the fact that we are already being ravaged, not protected, by the hatred enveloping us. The hatred that we believe shields us is the hatred that kills us. And—caught in this very human, very fearful state of being—it is almost impossible to see that choosing life, not death, requires letting those warm blankets of hate fall off our shoulders. That's what forgiveness is. To forgive is to let go of what weighs us down so that we are freed to do the work of love in the world. Freed also to let ourselves be loved.

Only then are we able to actually address the real source of the wrongs that burden us and all of humanity. The most powerful, visionary movements for social change in society and in our hearts have always been fueled by compassion and love, not just by rage and bitterness. I thought of my grandma's cool jug. I imagined reaching for it, unscrewing its rusted top, lifting the dented and weathered metal container over my head, and letting its fresh water pour down, running in streams across my face, washing away the heat of the day. The waters of grace, I imagined, had the power to cleanse me, wash away the debris that hid me, flush the dust of hatred from my clouded eyes, return me to myself.

And on that island in the middle of my inner sea, I could suddenly see the shining, ancient altar where the God of life awaited my return.

When I beheld that altar, I didn't see a kingly figure in robes of gold. I saw myself holding Charis in my arms, her little arms wrapped around my neck. That was a bond worth living for, a beautiful bond of love. It was, in truth, all the security I needed. That, and my slowly returning knowledge that I was now, and always had been, wrapped in the never-ending love of God.

That night as I dreamed of flowing waters, Verity met a small group of parishioners in the state park perched on the edge of the Wabash River, several miles from the prison. They left their cars there, and after being searched for weapons, they were loaded onto a local school bus and driven past tall prison fences and the wide fields that separated the penitentiary from the city. It was raining hard by the time they pulled up to the gate in front of the main building, and through the downpour, they could see, off to the right, a large crowd of people who had gathered to cheer.

They found a field off to the left and quietly joined hands, forming a line. In silence, their line moved in a spiral motion that, as it turned, drew their bodies closer and closer until finally they were wrapped together in a tight circle. They sat down, on plastic trash bags, umbrellas overhead. Around 3:00 a.m, they began to pray. They prayed in stilled silence for one hundred and sixty-eight minutes, each minute honoring the life of one of McVeigh's victims. Verity told me many of them wept for almost three hours. Children, parents, a janitor, a businesswoman, an FBI agent, a car attendant. All sorts of human beings praying.

As the first signs of dawn began appearing, their prayers ended. They added an extra minute, only one minute, to the end: a prayer for Timothy McVeigh. At 5:45 a.m. he was injected with Sodium Pentothal; he died fifteen minutes later. The prison guards let them know when it was finished. The cheers from the other side had been unexpectedly soft.

That morning, I got out of bed at 6:00 and looked once again at the television and saw the face of Timothy McVeigh. He never showed any pretense of regret and now he was dead, gone, murdered.

At that moment, I felt no overwhelming sadness. But I wondered, briefly, what it felt like to die with a cheering crowd around you. To feel thick socks on your feet. To flinch at the needle's prick.

As Kindy—and Thurman—predicted, I didn't feel any satisfaction, either. No release had taken place. No bloodlust had been satisfied. And there was a whispering sense somewhere within me that a profound wrong had been done in his dying.

"We need the state not to kill," Verity had once said to me, "not because we are so just and good, but because we are so broken. In the swirl of misery and loss people in our land suffer, we need to believe in a country that seeks life. We can't be a place that ritually kills people if we also want to be a place that praises freedom and goodness. If we can kill him righteously, then there's nothing to stop us from building more prisons than schools and throwing anybody we don't like in them. Because if we can kill this way, we make ourselves God. And under God's mantle, we can do anything we damn well please. That old Bible saying is dead-on: Violence begets violence."

I knew she was right; the horrific spectacle of mass incarceration, particularly of black and brown bodies and of many poor white bodies, is still growing more powerful each passing day. Our culture hoards its hatreds and praises punishment, feeds on its own people like vultures circling over the decay of death, craving the taste of its prey. And my own life's traumas had thrown me into that righteous circling mass, my own insides decaying.

It was pouring rain in Connecticut by the time Charis awakened. I decided to drive her and her friends to school. As I opened the back door and urged her to climb in, I noticed her blue Nikes lying on the floor behind the driver's seat. My driver's seat.

"Charis, look. Your shoes! They've been here the whole time."

Together, we looked, at first in stunned silence. And then, remarkably, we laughed.

The accusation had fallen back upon the accuser. And in the lightness of knowing that, we glimpsed, she in her child's way and I in my sullied adult's, the release from the anger we held.

It would take me a long time to actually forgive both Shepard and myself for our failure and even longer to let go of McVeigh's place in my mind and my grandpa's violent legacy. But the first step was to imagine its possibility. I could finally feel the bondage of the harms I was hoarding, and the joy of my release from it was slowly dawning on me.

Driving home from Charis's school, I thought about covenants again. The one I blew. The covenant to protect and shelter its masses that our nation has blown. The covenants with God that my Okie ancestors had foolishly and greedily made to justify their own gain. And then there was God's covenant with us, to love us regardless, to forgive us without ceasing.

The ending to Thurman's reflection stunned me again with its beauty, with its own forgiving acceptance of anyone who tries to covenant and fails.

> Before that altar [of God] impurities of life are burned away; before that altar, all the deepest intent of your spirit stands naked and revealed; before that altar, you hear the voice of God, giving lift to your spirit, forgiveness for your sins, renewal for your commitment. As you leave that altar within your temple, on your island, in your inward sea, all the world becomes different and you know that, whatever awaits you, nothing that life can do will destroy you.

I reread the passage when I got home. As I did, I realized that nothing I could do to myself could destroy me. No foible or cheap thought or sinful grudge or self-destructive wrath could undo me. There was nothing to fear. I would always be forgiven; I already had been. And in God's love, so had everyone else, all the McVeighs of the world included.

With my raging fears now quelled, if only for a moment, I walked out of the house into my backyard and turned my face upward to feel the pounding force of the pouring rain, and now, alone with just myself, the waters flowed over me, running down my arms, drenching my T-shirt, my sweat pants, making puddles around my bare, muddied feet. That sweet, sweet rain soaked me from head to toe, washing me almost clean.

STATION IV

Redeeming Life and Death

CHAPTER 10

Breath

The human being is made of matter but also of breath.
Breath is, indeed, what can be shared by all.
It demands just one thing: the respect of the natural and
spiritual life of the self and of the other.

LUCE IRIGARAY

A life spent trying to accept divine grace rarely leads to resolution. I achieved a certain settling of my theological half certainties and modest convictions after the McVeigh tumult and my divorce. I am by no means devout or holy, but life's experiences—its joys and tragedies, hatreds and forgivings—have finally led me to a basic assuredness about my theology.

I didn't arrive at this assuredness, mind you, because I am a theologian. My training in theology provided me with the language to talk about what I've discovered, but finding this solid place is something anyone can do. All it takes is a willingness to look at your life honestly—what you've done, or not; how you've loved, or not; what tragedies you've lived through, or not; what joys you have discovered, or not—and then ask yourself what truths about life have surfaced for you over time.

What lessons have you learned? What truths that once captivated you do you now see as lies? What glimpses of the divine have you occasionally caught?

If you have the courage to do this, then theologians can help give you the language for what you've discovered and assist you in pulling those truths into a meaningful story about reality. That's the gift that the theologians in this book have brought to my life. But the hardest work of all is that first step: your own honest assessment of the true things you know. Until you take that step, any theology or philosophy book you read or sermon you hear or self-help book you cling to will simply clang around in your head and eventually mean nothing,

FINDING THE PILLARS THAT HOLD US UP

I think of the truths that surface, when you dare to look for them, as pillars. When you discover them—the most fundamental things you know to be true—you suddenly realize that even though you haven't always been aware of them, they are the basic weight-bearing structures that hold your insides together and give sturdy meaning to your life. Quite often, when these pillars appear, they replace older pillars that you've been depending on but that no longer have the capacity to bear the weight of your life. That replacing can be disturbing, especially when those old tumbling pillars were put in place by religious institutions or wise people whom you once thought you could trust but no longer can. The previous three stations of this book are accounts of one pillar after another of mine being knocked over, often violently so, by new truths life has shown me, new truths about my faith, about America, about humanity itself. Crashing pillars still startle me when they fall, but over time I have learned to trust that there will be people to help me recover and new pillars always waiting to arise.

When I sift through my wiser, hard-won imagining of God, four pillars now stand out: breath, justice, mercy, and love.

As I wrote in the preface, these four pillars of my theology may feel abstract, clichéd, and overused. But theologically these words exist in another, always fresh dimension. Contemporary culture and media have left them haggard; but theological writers like Luce Irigaray and Howard Thurman redeem them every time I turn to their pages. I literally feel these sacred truths alive in my bones as much as I intellectually recognize their spark in my brain; they shape my unconscious actions, like how my body responds to an encounter with a stranger or a friend. They dictate my conscious plans, as I carefully try to solve a challenge I face. They course through me like the pulsing of blood and spirit, flowing through everything I do and think. I strive to fulfill their challenge and so often fail to heed their urging.

They usually direct my deepest desires, guiding what I think I want, what attracts me, what I yearn for, what I believe will ultimately satisfy me. These sacred truths are not just inside me, though. They also course, pulse, and flow through the world, imbuing everything with their power, suffusing all life with their light and energy. They illumine life's sacredness. Even though I might not always see them or feel them, these concepts are the divine.

PILLARS OF IMAGINATION

The only way I know to describe the support these pillars give me is to talk about the imagination. We all have an imagination—it simply refers to that vast web of images, thoughts, memories, words, feelings, experiences, fantasies, meanings, desires, dreams, hopes, and relationships that make up how we perceive and engage the world and ourselves. It's impossible not to have one, and even more, it's not something you turn off in order to see things as they really are. Our imagination is the lens through which we experience everything. We can't help it. There is no way to get around it. Imagination is not always logical and it's not always obvious to us, but it's always there.

When one awakens to God's love, this is where it happens—in the vast land of the imagination. Without imagination, there is no theology, no lived-faith, no meaning to life. Theology and imagination are inseparable.

That said, the imagination is also the place where our lives and our thinking about whatever gods we worship can get tricked and contorted by forces that aren't worthy of our humanity. Call it sin. Traumatic events can dramatically impact our capacity to imagine, throwing us off-kilter and thwarting our ability to grow. So, too, the daily grind of a culture filled with trivial matters, manufactured fears, and empty promises can create ruts in our imagination that prevent us from seeing new and more satisfying paths forward. Our minds trod over these paths again and again, hemming in our thoughts and feelings to a small terrain of possibilities. Good, honest theology, I believe, has the power to get us out of these ruts and heal traumatic wounds so that we can imagine the world as God beholds it.

For me, breath, justice, mercy, and love are the most vivid manifestations and visions of my hungry, urgent theological imagination. When I see God, my imagination beholds the transformative power of these four sacred truths flowing through me and through the world around me.

Like this:

The world, as I imagine it, is filled with breath, divine spirit, air that moves in and among us, wedding us to one another, making all that lives one fluid, breathing organism, expanding and contracting in love. And it is beautiful. Not as in pretty or movie-star gorgeous but beautiful in its power to attract and wondrously fulfill our ultimate desire for one another and for the flourishing of all. Think "beatific"!

For all of this to flourish, there must be justice. I don't think of justice as some big Roman measuring instrument where everyone gets equal parts; it's bigger and more beautiful than that. To seek justice is to work to create environments where life and love flourish and the God-created value of each life is cherished. Justice keeps us restless and questing and struggling for the good, for justice's fulfillment usually stands as a distant hope. It's what we strive for—realizing the divinity in each of us and treating each person and the planet as cherished and divine.

Mercy? It is a more complicated word than justice, often confused with bland forgiveness. Mercy is greater than that. It reminds us that as we seek justice, there is no grand God-calculator in the sky making sure good is rewarded and evil punished. Mercy is the promise that divine love ultimately wins and life is fulfilled in God's love despite its brokenness or unfairness. It is something we have a hard time recognizing in our score-keeping lives because it exists in another, incomprehensible dimension. It is beyond us, yet it defines our lives.

And then there's love. For me, the other word for God's love is grace. Grace sums up all of these sacred truths in one word. The light that shines on all existence is the light of love from beginning to end; it is the truest reality there is, our most natural impulse, our core, and our creative expression. You do not have to earn it and you can't lose it. It just is: God.

BREATH OF LIFE

In the foggy days of early motherhood, the only thing more shocking to me than the fact that I'd given birth to a living being was the chilling fear of her imminent death.

It happened on a rainy Sunday afternoon in late fall 1996. Charis and I had stretched out on the family room floor on her favorite blanket for a long lazy nap. I didn't really nap; I dozed to the rhythms of her breathing. And in dozing beside her I relaxed more richly than in my deepest sleep. As she emerged from sleep I could tell right away she was hungry—her tummy was rumbling the way it always did when she wanted to munch with me. It delighted my ears, the sounds heralding the anticipation of sharing a snack with her. She would always put both hands on her tummy before opening her eyes. She did that, too.

"Peanut butter," I whispered.

I carried her to the kitchen and dug out a big jar of creamy peanut butter. After putting a big spoonful in my mouth, I stuck my finger in the jar and let her lick a little off. She was just learning to taste and swallow food; its sticky thickness amused and confused her. With her still perched on my hip, I looked away to put the jar back in the cabinet. When I looked back, I saw red splotches on her upper throat and looking at her face I could see her eyes reddening and starting to swell. I hurried upstairs to show Shepard, who, as the son of a doctor, said to give her a little Benadryl. By the time I slurped some into her mouth, hives covered her face and her eyes were starting to puff closed. I had no idea what was happening but knew it was bad.

I scrambled for the phone to call the university's urgent care line.

"I just gave my eight-month-old some peanut butter and her face is—"

"Ma'am," the nurse cut me off, "if you gave her peanut butter, then she is most likely having an anaphylactic allergic reaction. You don't have time to call an ambulance. Just get in your car and drive as fast as you can to the nearest hospital. Now! Go. Don't even grab your purse."

"I'm going to Yale New Haven Hospital Urgent Care. It's ten minutes away," I shouted, then slammed down the phone, adrenaline sharpening my every sense.

I called to Shepard as I raced out the door. I threw him the keys as he ran behind me.

"Drive to the hospital's emergency room now."

As we screeched out of the driveway, I held Charis in the backseat and told Shepard what was happening. Gripped tightly against my chest, she slowly stopped crying and started wheezing; soon she made no sound at all. Her face began to turn purple, her eyelids turning inside out. Could she hear me? I rocked and sang to her as we ran red lights and rushed down one-way streets. Two blocks from the hospital, I felt her breath start to slow. Then I felt it quicken. Then I felt it stop. The feeling of breath stopping, of your child's breath stopping, is indescribable. I felt like I could see her last breath floating in the air. I remember wanting to grab it, collect it, and stuff it back into her.

"Shepard, she's not breathing," I remember saying.

"No. No. You can't die," I whispered to her. "Sweetie. Come back. Breathe, honey. Please God, breathe."

I tried to push my breath into her tiny mouth, but her tongue had swollen so much that it blocked her throat.

When her breathing stopped, time slowed and slipped away for an eternal instant.

I felt the rage of utterly helpless mothers who, throughout the ages, have watched their children die; it consumed me. In the howl that erupted from my gut when she stopped breathing, that cosmic maternal bond with stricken children everywhere was visceral and vast and unspeakably terrifying.

When we reached the far corner of the hospital entrance, two nurses were waiting for us on the curb; in one single motion, they opened the door, pulled Charis out, and pushed a syringe into her limp thigh. I saw her foot jerk once as they ran with her across the parking lot and through the hospital doors.

Five minutes later, she was fully awake in my arms, shaking and coughing, and alive.

Big gulping breaths ran through her lungs; once in a while she managed a frantic infant cry.

We went home from the emergency room two hours later, having been thoroughly educated on the seriousness of peanut allergies and the fact that, for the rest of her life, she would need to carry an EpiPen to inject herself if she ever suffered such an attack again.

Well into the evening, after she had stopped crying and was drifting into a groggy sleep, every part of her little being continued to quake and shiver, sometimes jerking, her nerves and brain fighting to come back from depths of death toward the surface of life.

Around eleven, I relaxed my vigil, lay down on the couch, and stretched out her tiny sleeping, shivering body on top of my own, her belly against mine, her small bald head turned sideways between my breasts. Her convulsions were growing smaller, but I still felt them, jerky and irregular next to the smooth rhythm of my gently inhaling and exhaling lungs.

We lay like that for hours and then again each night for days, breathing together, the edge between the two of us dissolving.

All the while, in the darkness of the night, I imagined the spirits of countless frantic mothers flowing around our living room, wailing for their lost children, and I was flooded with both guilt and relief. My access to good health care had saved my child. Most of the world's children would have died from the reaction she'd had. But strangely, prayers of thanksgiving never came, even as she lay alive on my belly. I didn't dare, for fear I might sound, even to myself, like I believed God had somehow harmed her and had then worked a wonder with her. And if I were to believe that, then how could I accept that the same God had decided not to work such wonders with other children, those who never made it to a hospital, who never had a fighting chance to live. I felt more grateful than ever before in my life, but it wasn't aimed at God. Maybe it's not normal for a mother to feel no gratitude toward some divine being when her child is saved from death. But that pious impulse completely evaded me. If I had raised a thank-you to some divine being for saving her life, it would have been to a God I hated for all that God had left unsaved.

What I did feel was the strength of our human tug back against death, a tough, grizzled persistence. A universal gasping for breath and the calming balm of air.

I had her. And she was filled with sweet, sweet breath.

Breath was all the God we needed.

THE DIAGNOSIS

Eight years later, it was my turn to deal with death. I was diagnosed with cancer.

I don't want to die. I hope I don't die. What will my daughter do if I die? How will my family survive my death?

They assault you, the questions, and the internal interrogations about your final moment when it suddenly seems about to come sooner than you think. They're usually the same handful of stinging doubts and fears. I've found in talking with friends who've also been given a cancer diagnosis that the thought of God goes away for them, too. That luxury cedes to the here and now, to raw life and the ones who depend upon us.

Cancer is a very special condition. I call it that and not a "disease" because it distills and clarifies for me precisely what the human condition is: uncertainty, doubt, vulnerability, and utter contingency. Cancer also distills all that defines life—and does it every day, every hour, every minute on some days. It gives definition to our desire to live. Love comes to the forefront. Cancer perversely exposes the force of love. It shows us why it is we want to live.

I was diagnosed with advanced endometrial cancer by accident, in 2005, at the age of forty-five, three years after my divorce. It was a severe case of a severe condition, and I began to contemplate my death the minute the doctor told me I had cancer. I could see it in his eyes, I could hear it in his voice: This woman is quite possibly dying soon.

That abrupt realization was utterly different from the sensory, almost psychedelic contemplation of my death's arrival when I thought I was decomposing in that bus station in India. Then, at twenty-two, my head was filled with poetry and divine imagery. It was also different from my daughter's near death. Then, everything was focused on her. I was outside myself in a way. By 2005, however, death had become a much more practical, prosaic concept.

Death, more than birth or falling in love or the sight of overwhelming natural beauty, is the defining theological moment in almost everyone's life. I almost dare to say it is that moment in everyone's life, for I have seen the most self-reliant individualists, the most self-certain intellectuals, and the most self-deceiving and all-conquering money-makers grasp for theology, for the consolation of the sacred, in their waning days.

The birth of a child is still often turned into a self-aggrandizing moment by the self-obsessed; so, too, is falling into romantic love or getting married. But death is the one universal reality that makes almost all of us at least think about God, or cosmic reality, or the great mystery that we inhabit. It can't help but force the questions: What is the purpose of my life? Why am I here? Particularly trenchant questions when you are faced with losing it. Of *not* being here anymore.

What comes with the shock of possibly not being is the stunning truth that the possibility of "not being here" had been, throughout your whole life, always there, every step along the way. Every minute. Even when we are not consciously aware of it, the fact that we could and will die defines the fact that we are alive.

Of course, I had thought about God and death a lot before my cancer diagnosis—I even did that thinking for a living as a pastor and theologian. Theologians love to ponder death. But cancer, even more than Freddy's death, or the realization at age twenty-two that I was nothing more than a blade of grass, or the rage I felt when I almost lost my daughter, did not push me away from God but drew me closer to the divine—in a radical way I never expected and to this day marvel at.

Why? Not because of panic or fear. Cancer made me, with much effort, sit still. Cancer, like any life-threatening illness—its treatments, its debilitations, its waiting-room visits, its recovery requirements (if you're lucky)—creates time outside of time. It reinvents time and in so doing forces a glimpse of the divine in a more precise and exacting way than any other human experience than death itself, with which cancer is obviously an intimate partner. For the first time, I found the stillness I needed to find a new connection to God.

My staging, as the professionals call it, was well advanced. My cancer had been stealthy, devouring my reproductive organs silently and, for me, relatively painlessly. Within a week of the diagnosis, I was in surgery.

Kierkegaard has a wonderful book called *Stages on Life's Way* about the theological life. My brain went to that book title as soon as I heard "advanced," and then I twisted the title around: stages on death's way. I was on a fast track to the final stage. For Kierkegaard, however, the stages were really overlapping spheres—aesthetic, ethical, and religious, both a progression and a cumulative journey. But I knew I wouldn't be in this sphere long—that "immediate surgery" in medicine meant seven days until I would have all my reproductive organs removed and until the doctors would be able to determine "if" (they never said "how much") it had advanced through my uterine wall and moved into other organs. All the overlapping spheres of my life—my daughter, my family in Oklahoma and their lives, my childhood and youth there, my life now as a professor—were immediately and densely compacting into this perhaps final one.

It had all begun as a knee injury the day after the 2004 presidential election. Hailing from Oklahoma, I had had some proximity to the politics of the Bush family all my life. My family in the Texas oil business knew them well and most of the Joneses supported Bush father and son. My immediate family, not surprisingly, held down the alternate fort, vehemently opposing the Bush worldview, especially its economic and international policies. As I walked into my class at Yale on Christology (a class about Jesus) that afternoon, I knew I would face a distressed and angry class. University divinity students tend to vote Democrat and I decided, in order to try to help them (and me) make sense of the results, to turn that political moment into an eye-opening religious one.

My right knee hurt a bit as I walked up the steps of the Sterling Divinity Quadrangle to the classroom. I remember writing it off to having stood instead of sitting at an election party turned funereal assembly the previous night.

I walked into the classroom and avoided making eye contact with any of the chagrined students seated in the chairs in front of me.

"I want all of you to take five minutes to do an exercise with me," I said, finally looking at them as I folded my left leg under me, sitting on it to make myself a little taller. "I want you to describe what the face of Jesus might have looked like in the minds—or better, the Christian theological imagination—of someone who pulled the lever for President Bush yesterday."

They looked at me, puzzled.

"Pick one, or ten, or a hundred voters, I don't care," I said. "Draw or describe the Jesus they imagined. Male, female, old, young, white, brown, blue. What kind of Jesus entered the voting booth with them?"

I paused and then added, not wanting to dump all the ire on Bush supporters, "If you'd rather, you can describe the Jesus that followed you in."

I picked up a pen and paper and began the exercise myself. Gradually, my students followed suit as I wrote my own description of a Bush-supporting Jesus. A white male, blue-eyed, steel-jawed, gun-slinging Jesus with a Texas twang emerged, looking much like my high school friends. I felt my own tension and anger rise and fall and rise again. I felt the same thing happen in the room. Our theological imaginations were coming to life with concentrated urgent force.

I picked a student at random. "Okay, Amy, let's hear your depiction."

We then spent the remaining ninety minutes of the class sharing our quickly scribbled word-portraits. With each presentation, we would talk about why that picture. Not everyone imagined the same Jesus I did, although quite a few did. Like me, they imagined Bush voters seeing that standard picture of a serene-faced, white-skinned, long-haired, blue-eyed Jesus—an angelic mirror of all that comprises white ideals of beauty. Others chose to describe the Jesus they saw: a dark-skinned Arab face, closer to the probable face of Jesus. One described the poor Lakota mother version of Jesus who had followed her into the booth. Another, going back to the imagination of the winner, drew a white-hooded Klan member. Still another, shifting to his own experience, scribbled out a description of a young Latino police officer named Jesus. The whole display of Jesus portraits was moving. Our deepest fears and our hidden hopes were physically poured out on the page for us to look at together, honestly and with spiritual scrutiny. Did I really think my Bush-supporting, high school friend saw Jesus the way I described? Probably not. As we laughed and mourned and pondered our inner thoughts, our common origin, fate, and humanity all cohered into a messy but God-grounded picture of life in its wild diversity.

At the end of the class, I stood up and felt my knee bark. I had never been a huge football fan, but I had heard enough football conversations from my days studying at the University of Oklahoma to know that the sound and sensation of my knee did not bode well. I also knew a few football clichés, so I told myself, "I guess I left it all on the field today." To this day I remember it as one of the best classes I ever taught; I felt like a conductor who had directed the class from one emotional state to another with rhythm, nuance, and charisma. But in that moment I could not take any pleasure in it; I sat back down and asked a student to call security to get me help. I could not walk. My knee popping, I did not realize then (as is so often the case), was really my world popping.

I would learn in a few hours in the emergency room that I had torn my meniscus and I blamed it on the stress of American politics. I had arthroscopic surgery a few weeks after the swelling subsided, and the doctor sent me home with a prescription for a megadosage of ibuprofen.

By the end of the second week on the meds, I was feeling faint; by the fourth week I felt so woozy that I fell; on a Sunday afternoon at the end of the fifth week, I collapsed on the kitchen floor, unconscious for a quick minute. But it was long enough to send my eight-year-old daughter into a howling panic as she shook me, asking me to stop pretending. When I came to, I told her to go across the street to get Noah's mother, Beth, who immediately came and called an ambulance.

In the ambulance, the paramedics asked me the name of the medication I was taking, and as soon as I told them the dosage of ibuprofen they suspected a bleeding ulcer. That wouldn't be the only culprit. The blood work taken in the ER revealed that I was extremely anemic; I received a transfusion of three quarts of blood and commenced a three-day stay in the hospital. My ulcer soon went away, but my anemia didn't. Puzzled, the doctors began a five-month process of trying to figure out why my blood count wouldn't rise, filling me with iron supplements and telling me to eat lots of red meat and beets and to drink red wine. Not such a bad regimen, I'd thought.

But nothing worked. Finally, in late August, after an awful summer of anemic exhaustion, they decided to see if my previously benign uterine fibroids might be the problem. They did a procedure to look inside my uterus that included a randomly located biopsy.

I absurdly ran the New Haven Labor Day half marathon for my fourth time a week later, this time dragging myself to the finish line with the last group of stragglers. Stumbling into bed that night, I thought back to India and realized, once again, that I had failed to measure my body's incapacity to match my mind's will. Tuesday morning, the first day of classes for the fall semester, my doctor called around seven thirty and asked me to come in as soon as my first class ended. My mind refused to think much about it, so when he told me the biopsy had revealed cancer, my mind flew into a state of panicked confusion.

"This kind of cancer is hard to diagnose because you have to directly biopsy the exact spot or it doesn't show up on tests," he told me calmly. "That this random biopsy landed right on the site of your rapidly advancing cancer is a one in ten thousand chance. That's the actual statistic. You are very lucky. You could have carried this around with you for another couple of months and been out of options by the time we found it. I'm setting you up for surgery—a hysterectomy and oophorectomy—for next Tuesday. I'm sorry to tell you this, Ms. Jones."

My father was teaching theology at Yale that semester; we were going to teach a class together of our shared father-daughter reflections/debates on God talk. I drove from the clinic to his apartment, and in a state of manic shock, I told him I had cancer and would be operated on the following week. Joe Jones, ever a philosopher and a realist, changed from his professor mode into my comforting dad before my eyes; he told me I would be fine, even as he fought back tears. As he tried to encourage me, he never said the silly things religious people say at times like this, that it's God's will or some version of that.

I didn't believe that when Charis nearly died and I didn't now. Neither did he. Too many innocent people die senseless deaths for us to blame it on God. That God, I would despise. Instead, what echoed through my memory were my father's words that day by the hardware store when the men spat on him. "We are all children of light and children of darkness," he said. "You and me and those men, we are children of the same God." He was then a young man educating his young daughter on the loving ways of God, even in the awfulness of shame and hate. I was now tumbling from sunlight into shadows and he could do nothing. I went home to have the hardest conversation of all—with my own young daughter.

I set down my book bag and joined her and the babysitter on the living room floor as they played Dogopoly, her favorite game and a constant reminder to me that she wanted a dog.

"Charis, I found out today that I have a little sickness in the part of my body that makes babies," I said as I put my hand on my lower stomach, "and the doctors are going to take it out of me in the hospital next week. I'm going to be fine, but I won't be going to school this semester, so I'll get to play this game with you a lot."

"Wait. What?" She looked up, trying to fit what I had just said into her child's picture-book understanding of how babies were made. "You're going to stay home for a long time? No work? Just play with me?"

"Yes, that's right," I said.

She thought further. "If they take out your baby-making parts that means you'll never have another baby?" You could practically hear her mind clicking.

"Yep, that's how it works," I answered.

"I'll always be your only baby? Just me?"

"You've got it. Only you."

"Mom, this is great!" She jumped up and hugged me, pushing me over, her legs kicking with joy.

I laughed with her, relishing the happiness of this child who had come so close to losing her own life. Whose unfiltered, vital self-interest made leaping-good news out of bad.

It was then that the possibility of my possible death overcame me, causing the sort of fear I had never experienced as a young woman in India. The tears of our laughter covered what for me were tears of fear and anxiety. I could be days away from never holding her again. Even worse, she could be days away from never feeling my arms around her again.

The night before the surgery, I lay in the hospital bed thinking, naturally, about my eight-year-old daughter at home with my ex-husband. And when I was not thinking about her, I was thinking about what it would be like to not have a uterus, for I knew that a total hysterectomy would be the least devastating outcome in the morning. I felt, oddly, selfish about the impending loss of my creative, reproduction power, even though, honestly, I had no plans for more children. Still, giving birth had been a wildly life-changing experience, and I longed to keep alive the possibility of that creativity. It ran so counter to the death I had come so close to with her. I also, I realize now, longed simply for the female power I never really thought about until the moment before I lost it. I had menstruated every month since I was fourteen. The ability to do this seemed, in some profound but inarticulate way, to be an essential part of my being, a sexual, fertile, life-giving female being. What would I be when I woke up?

The images swirled. The surgery was going to be laparoscopic, which meant that after detaching my uterus, the surgeon would pull it out through my cervix. In the morning I would give birth, in a sense, to my own womb. If things went well, because of this birth, I might not yet die. I was hopefully giving birth to myself, not just in some feminist folk-song way, but in a quite literal and physical way.

But then another, more troubling emotion nagged at me. Female reproduction in Western society is tied to a general obsession with productivity in the capitalist sense. Our obsession with fertility, I believe, is directly tied to our fixation on productivity, newness, excess, endless abundance. The unproductive female body is dubious in its utility. And

I felt suddenly useless, worthless. My feminist hackles rose as I fought against false despair.

By turns, a terrified mother, a lamenting woman, a cultural failure, a despairing feminist.

I woke up in the recovery room at Yale New Haven Hospital on September 19, 2005, to the voice of a doctor telling me my uterine wall was strong and hadn't been breached, and he had gotten all the cancer. I would most likely live a long time, he said and smiled. The surgery was one hundred percent successful, he assured me.

In my head, I wondered: How does he know I will live a long time?

Still in the haze of the anesthesia, I began to laugh at the absurdity of the whole thing. President Bush's reelection had saved my life by stressing me out so much that I tore my knee, which led to extreme anemia, which then led to the discovery of the cancer that didn't kill me. None of it made cosmic sense or even some special kind of theological sense. All I knew in that moment was that from here on out, the rest of my life was—and I know this is a silly image for something so profound—icing on the cake. I thought of carrot cake with rich cream cheese frosting. I had extra time, unexpected, undeserved, especially sweet, and thick and rich time to keep on living.

Little did I know what was still to come.

DOING YOGA WITH JESUS

Like having been hit by another wrecking ball, I woke up the morning after the surgery to life without ovaries and in the throes of full-fledged surgical menopause.

At first, I found myself forgetting simple words. Then I realized I could not read. My eyes ran across a page but couldn't translate what they saw to my brain to make sense of it. My breasts lost their fullness.

My skin immediately felt drier, my hair limp. And this had all happened overnight. Even though I knew I should be savoring the licks of my icing on the carrot cake, negative thoughts consumed me. Sometimes strange ones, theological ones.

Over the next several weeks, I became obsessed with the image of my uterus as an upside-down three-point triangle: two ovaries at each side on the top and a cervix at the bottom, holding between them the space where life begins. Three points that together create existence. Father, Son, and Holy Spirit. Creator, Sustainer, Redeemer. Source, Spirit, Destiny. Could the Trinity be imagined as a womb?

Once my mind had shifted to the Trinity and uterine triangles— and I was thinking constantly in threes—I asked myself over and over again why Western thought had so wrongly decided to divide the world into twos that were binary opposites. Men/Women. White/Black. Bad/Good. I/Thou. Nature/Civilization. Emotion/Reason. Animal/Human. The list was endless. It defined all parts of our thinking. But . . . but . . . if life was held in the mutual grasp of three, be it the angles of the uterus or the Trinitarian Godhead, don't these binaries disappear into the play of infinite, interdependent, triadic realities? Moving fluidly between the three, combining in endless configurations of meaning and forms of life? My theological imagination was on fire. We needed a new kind of cosmic mechanics to grasp how the world worked, not one marked by dualistic boundaries and differences only but by borders that were permeable, where fluid and air moved through all difference with ease. Granted, these thoughts had the funny side effect of making my Dogopoly tournaments with Charis a trying exercise in regular old binary competition.

I also became acutely conscious of a great absence between my hips, an open space, an emptiness without edge or form. I felt guilty for thinking about this loss, given that I should have been happy just to be alive. But it haunted me. What was there now? How could I hold "nothing" inside myself? Being alive was filled with so many things that were "something." How could it also hold "nothing"?

One day, about three weeks after the surgery, my friend Laura showed up unexpectedly at my house and announced that she was taking me to a yoga class. Holding me by the arm, she lovingly insisted that I had no choice; she had already paid for it. Relieved to leave my metaphysical musings about triangles and absences behind, I went with her to what turned out to be my first serious yoga class (I'd played around with yoga for years) and a major turning point in my life. She had set up a special session for just the two of us with a wise, older yoga instructor, who was outside smoking when we pulled into the yoga studio's parking lot. I trusted her immediately. Laura had already told her about my cancer, and she kindly informed us that for the next year, twice a week, we would practice "restorative yoga" together. I'd never heard of such a thing, but she explained that it involved putting our bodies into relaxing positions and resting for an hour or two. Being still and breathing. That was all we had to do.

For the first few months, within minutes of becoming still, my feet propped up on a chair and blankets surrounding me, I would fall into a deep, dreamless sleep. But as the months passed, I became more awake to the sensation of the stillness and of my own breath and found myself in a space where there were no boundaries or loss or obsessive thoughts of triangles. I could feel my breath filling the empty space in my body with air, with each fresh inhalation and expiration. I remembered again the borderless feeling of Charis on my belly as together we found breath again after hers had been taken so suddenly.

One day, I thought of Christ on the cross, say, half an hour before his final breath. I imagined him vividly, how the noise of the spectators had to diminish in his ears as death approached; how the people around him must have blurred into one moving mass of color and emotion; how the shortening sound of air, moving in and out of his lungs, must have consumed his mind. Sharing breath with the world, flowing in and out through his own broken body.

And suddenly, as I lay there on my yoga mat, I heard what he heard, the last thing he surely heard in the minutes before he "gave up his last breath": just breathing. That was surely the last sound he heard. But I didn't hear it next to me or as if I were watching a film. I heard it through my own ears coming out of my own mouth and nostrils. I was sharing his breath, his air, suddenly. The breathing, in and out, of the world itself.

As my recovery progressed—as I grew more and more at ease lying still—I kept hearing the uncanny sound of my own breath in my inner ear. Even though I had done yoga before, off and on at the gym, like almost every woman my age, and had hummed the "Ohm" and focused on my breathing, I had never truly heard it; it was pronouncing itself, pronouncing its existence. The air itself, which was giving me life, was also distinguishing itself as another entity, almost another being, but not quite. There was no form or substance to it, no personal identity or concrete reality. God for me had for so long been about sight and sensation—what I saw or what I felt. It had rarely been about sound despite my love of music. It had almost never been about the utterly invisible. But here I was, marveling at the air—at the noise it made, at the life it gave me, at its composition, at its promiscuity, at its generosity.

It's moving how the accidents of life can change how one views God and the meaning and purpose of one's life. For me, the most profound changes I've undergone were not the product of intellectual study or particularly good sermons or even conscious thought itself. My most profound shifts began from some physical experience that then caused an insight to rumble up from my unconscious mind. This time it emerged out of the disorienting fog of loss and trauma surrounding my daughter's near death and my own almost dying and then living. In each instance, the rules of thinking that governed how my mind worked were unable to hold the experience I was having. Both experiences exceeded my capacity to make sense of them and sent me whirling into spaces of imagination where what mattered most looked and felt very different from what I'd been taught to feel, not just about God, but about humanity and the cosmos.

IMAGINATION AND GOD

The thinker who was most helpful to me in grasping the depth of this shift in imagination was the French philosopher Luce Irigaray. She began her intellectual life immersed in the classics of Western thinking, reading philosophers like Plato and Aristotle, much like I read Kierkegaard, Calvin, and Niebuhr. I don't know what exactly provoked the shift for her, but early in her career, she began to ask deep questions about the patterns of thought that undergirded Western thinking, like the tendency to see everything as either/or. It is our knee-jerk desire to divide everything into dualism, with one being good and the other bad. She asked simple questions: What if we tried not to think dualistically? What if we rejected hierarchies? What if we opened ourselves to new patterns of being? To use her words, she asked us to let go of our usual ways of knowing and let ourselves enter new "imaginaries"—which for me meant a new theological imagination.

I have found it helpful to explain Irigaray's thinking to my students in the hope that they might reconfigure their imaginations, too. Her strong focus on the imaginary empire of the male-female binary was cutting and convincing. As she put it, "woman" had been defined throughout history according to the role she played in defining "man." She is his mother, his lover, his other. Who she is depends entirely upon what his identity needs. That meant, of course, that she was never allowed to define herself, her desires, her own endlessly unique existence. It made complete sense to me as I thought about my mother and my own mother-lover-other self-understanding. Did I even know what I, apart from the world of male definitions, wanted? Did the word "woman" even define me anymore? Were there multiple ways of being that this core binary had rendered invisible? My whole world of human definition exploded, gloriously so, before my eyes.

Irigaray also helped me come to some fundamental realizations about my life and the divine, bringing my theology to a higher level of awareness, creativity, and imagination. First, when you have a child, whether you bear one or four or adopt one child or commit yourself to a whole community of children, from nieces to neighbors, whatever form it takes, it displaces your sense of being the center of the world. From the minute Charis entered the world, I felt that my life would forever be inextricably connected to hers. Not a moment would go by in which my place in the world wasn't measured according to her place, wherever she might be, even when I wasn't thinking about it explicitly. Even when I had no idea where she actually was. I also knew, way down inside myself, that her life mattered more than my own. In this way, I quite happily let go of myself to give myself over to another. The self that my favored theologians had talked about all the time was no longer the self-centered self they described. It was love that changed things, a love so expansive and unromantic but forceful that it broke through my sense of being a purely separate self.

Nearly losing it made it viscerally clear to me how much more her life mattered to me than my own. The experience of breathing her back to life—with her on my belly, night after night, tuning her biorhythms to my own—let me see that the boundaries we create between ourselves and others are fictions in our minds. Charis showed me, as her quaking body learned to follow my body rhythms, that we—not just her and me, but all of us—are profoundly interconnected. We are part of one another, not distinct dyads of you and me. It's both of us, we. That interconnection is not something we earn or create; it simply is the way things are. The world is more of us than we are of ourselves.

As I let go of myself, I realized that when faced with my own imminent dying, my fierce desire to live—so I could love and be loved—was as undeniably present as the inevitability of my death. When desires—call them wants—become that strong, they cast skeptical, judging light upon the other less important yearnings that occupy your life: wanting to be successful, to accumulate worldly comforts, to endlessly build up your mind and your strength with the aim of achieving . . . what? The perfect family? A great reputation? True love? A strong military? More money? Invincible walls? A totally fulfilled, lie-filled life? I was only able to see all of these unrealizable and ultimately unfulfilling desires when forced to sit still and hear the breathing of the world.

Irigaray, in a book entitled *The Way of Love*, explores the theological freedom that comes with using breath to understand our relationships with one another and with God. She asserts that in Western thought and theology, thinkers have been "in love with wisdom"— trying to rationally analyze the nature of our humanity and the character of our social lives. She insists that this approach misses the truer "wisdom of love," which requires us to pay attention to our bodies, our emotions, and our interconnections with one another; she asks that we turn our attention to what love bids us to see about life together.

Instead of imagining our world as a collection of isolated, bounded selves that bump into one another, we are better served by recognizing all the physical and emotional ways in which we are connected, in our dazzling, wonderful, fraught differences. Until we are able to shift to this view of human and planetary interconnectedness, our political and social lives will flounder and the path forward will remain cluttered with conflicts and violent competitions. The alternative way—the way of love—allows for deep democracy to be imagined, as we recognize, spiritually, the sustaining bonds of air, body, water, and life that bind us together. This way of love, she tells us, opens us to wonder and mystery rather than to reductive conclusions and unquestionable certainties. It also allows us to see God not as another object, distinct from us, but as the air, the flow, the spirit, the life force that moves between us and through us.

At the center of all these insights is breath. Through breathing, and paying attention to it, I learned to be still and experience that divine reality. For me, it reconfirmed, in a new way, that old notion of grace I was taught by my grandmother. We are constantly being given life by other life that is beyond us and yet within us. Irigaray called this the grace of God. I now think of it as the grace of raw existence, the ebb and flow of everything, together. With each breath, life comes to you. Love comes to you, not from above but from between and through, the between and through of the time and space in which we breathe.

Learning to be still and listen to your breath—our breath—is the most radical path we can take, in our day and age, as we search for new ways to direct our misaimed desires and create a new imaginary for the divine. We need a path that gets us out of measuring everything according to productivity, utility, and dominating power, and reminds us of the precious reality that we are alive, by grace. And one day we will not be, and yet the breath of grace will go on.

All this talk of breath can sound a little airy—especially when it is tested in the practical fires of day-to-day life, both personally and politically. What does breathing have to do with gerrymandering voting districts? Stopping mass incarceration? Racial profiling? Dismantling the cruel culture of whiteness? Attending a funeral for yet another opioid-addled life?

In my mind, they have absolutely everything to do with one another. To explain that, however, I need to tell the story of a place where,
for me, the practical force of these spiritual pillars exerts itself every day.
It's the place where I unexpectedly landed on the other side of cancer
and divorce, Union Theological Seminary in the City of New York.

CHAPTER 11

Justice

> What I try to encourage people to do is speak the kind of
> truth that stings like a serpent's tooth, the kind of truth
> that makes your teeth itch, the kind of truth that causes
> some people to lose their minds, up in here, up in here. So
> even when people call your truth a lie, tell it anyway. Tell
> it anyway.
>
> REV. DR. KATIE CANNON, UTS, 1983

The word "seminary" has its roots in the Middle English word for seed plot. I have always loved that image—a garden where theology is studied is a garden where students and ideas—and belief—grow. A seminary in some ways is a place to think, but its important mandate is also to produce active clergy—people who minister to other people, who give succor, who use faith to help other human beings bear hardships, celebrate joys, fight for freedom, and pass through the stages of life.

When I became the first female president of Union Theological Seminary in the City of New York in 2008, I approached the job with that vision of *active* theology. Union was founded on the dockyards of New York City in 1836 by a group of Presbyterian ministers and laypeople who had what for that time was a radical vision for seminary education. Instead of sending future clergy away to the countryside-manor environments of Harvard, Yale, and Princeton to learn about God, they set up tents to teach in the hurly-burly of the city, believing that a rough-and-tumble urban environment provided better fodder for their education.

Students didn't need to be nestled away from the world, the founders thought; they needed to be thrown into the world and forced to wrestle with the unruly and messy demands of God's people in all their wild variety. They were especially concerned that clergy in training needed to grapple with what it meant to preach the Gospel to New York's growing masses of poor people, of immigrants and dockworkers, of the plague-ridden sick and desperately hungry who filled its densely populated neighborhoods. Preaching the Gospel for them meant not just talking about God; it required actively doing the work Jesus had called all Christians to do: Feed the hungry, care for the widow and the orphan, heal the sick, proclaim release to the captive and imprisoned, do justice. They even wrote this mandate right into the preamble of the school's 1836 charter. From the start, it was a seminary "responsive to claims of the world upon the church."

THE UNION I KNEW

Long before I accepted the offer to lead the school, I was familiar with its unique mandate and the remarkable students and faculty Union had produced. During my years at the University of Oklahoma, my reading lists had been packed with the writings of Union professors like Dietrich Bonhoeffer, Paul Tillich, Reinhold Niebuhr, Daniel Day Williams, James Cone, Dorothee Soelle. In my first sociology class at OU, I had also learned about Union's originating role in starting the early-nineteenth-century tenement house movement in America. These houses were constructed by students and clergy from Union who literally built compounds where middle-class families lived side by side with poor families, their money pooled so that everyone lived on their shared resources. These compounds were designed not only to provide mental health service, medical care, education, shelter, and food for all, they were also constructed to break down the walls that divided rich and poor, black and white, old and young, healthy and sick. I remember so well the day my OU sociology professor lectured to us about the radical character of this movement. What he failed to talk about in depth was that it was religious conviction, not just political utopianism, that fueled the movement's fire.

What I later came to appreciate more deeply was that these faith convictions were Calvinist through and through. It was not hard for me to imagine the *Institutes* perched on the bedside table of a Union student and tenement-house resident in New York City. "Religion for what ails you" was alive and well.

When I eventually decided to go to seminary, the pull of my father's alma mater won out, mostly because of its larger scholarship offer, but from the time I started studying at Yale, I was connected to Union. Time after time, my friends and I would take the Metro-North train to New York and get off at 125 Street in East Harlem. We would walk across town to West 121 Street and Broadway to meet up with Union students who had organized buses to take us to protest marches in Washington, D.C. Our first trip was to protest U.S. involvement in the civil war in El Salvador. Still fresh from the plains of Oklahoma, I marveled at the worldliness of Union students: They rode subways and read newspapers I'd never heard of and they had strong theological views on every social issue I could imagine—and some of which had never crossed my mind. A handful of those students became close friends; I cherish these friendships even today, still marveling at their passion for social justice and their nimble, engaged theology. Among these friends were Elizabeth Bounds, Ada Maria Isasi-Diaz, Kelly Brown Douglas, and Dwight Hopkins, all of them Union students at the time, all of them eventually becoming towering figures in American theology.

UNION CALLING

When the presidential search committee at Union first called me in New Haven in July of 2007, I was trying to install an air conditioner in my study's window so that I could work longer in the summer heat. I dropped my screwdriver and left the heavy box hanging halfway out the window as I reached over to answer the phone. The recruiter for the search committee told me she wanted my views on the theological concerns that should occupy the work of Union's next president. I was not prepared for such a call—in fact, I was a bit shaken by the assumption that I had any views worth sharing—so I just blurted out my evolving sense of where Christian seminary education should be headed, all the while hoping the air conditioner wouldn't crash to the ground.

I told her that I had led a faculty seminar at Yale on the role of religious women in global movements for social change that year. To my surprise, it had captured the interest of faculty from across the university. Political scientists, American studies professors, historians, and sociologists, almost all of them secular, showed up to talk about gender, religion, and global social change. It sparked in me a sense for the awakening that was happening in the secular world of the Northeast. Religion mattered. It especially mattered when you were committed to building a more just world.

I described this experience to the recruiter and shared my excitement about what I was seeing. I talked about how enriching it was for me to learn deeply about religions other than my own Christianity. The neoliberal capitalist empire was spiritually bankrupt, I said, and faith was flooding in, from every corner of the world, to fill that void, some seeking a higher good, others simply grasping for power. And I told her that Union, situated at the center of capitalism's empire as well as at the center of so many communities that were faltering under its weight, was better positioned than any other seminary I knew of to bring theology to bear on it all.

"It's in Union's DNA to do this," I said at the end. "To rise to the occasion of this moment in history, all Union has to do is keep being Union."

After the call, I worried that I had been too blunt and disorganized to have made any sense to the people on the other end of the line. I shoved the whole thing to the back of my mind and went back to work on the air conditioner and on the book about theology and trauma that I was trying to finish.

But the call had awakened in me a hunger for Union.

I had just turned forty-eight, was five years divorced, a single mom, a two-year cancer survivor now in good health, and I had spent almost thirty years inside the classrooms of Yale—first as a student, then as a professor. Maybe I could teach at Union? I thought. There I could develop my thoughts on what I sensed was coming, in an environment where those thoughts had enduring traction. When three months later I was called and asked to come to interview for the president's position, I was floored. It hadn't crossed my mind to do such a thing, not because Union wasn't amazing but because until that moment I had never aspired to lead a seminary. Before I agreed to talk to them, I called my father. Having been the president of a small university and the dean of two seminaries, he hesitated.

"I have no doubt that you could do it, but I'm not sure all that stress would be good for you." His protective-father side was, in this case, stronger than his theological-leadership side.

I sheepishly said yes to the interview, thinking that probably nothing

would come of it. I then began to read even more about its history. I
loved the full name of the school. "Union" stood out for its extra emphasis on the mixing of distinct perspectives and people, unified by an
evolving vision of a just, interdependent social order. "Theological"
captured the spiritual and intellectual character of the place, a pre-
eminent educational institution where the brightest minds of each
age came to learn. The "Seminary" idea covered the etymological idea
of nurturing minds, hearts, and souls to lead parishioners through
the messy chaos of life. And "In the City of New York" captured the
vitality of the city that flows through its windows, doors, and hallways.
That Union brings the cares of the world to bear on theology is an inescapable result of the fact that those endlessly complex human cares
reside in the very place where Union lives.

As I read more about Union, I thought a lot about my childhood
in Oklahoma, how being a cowgirl and a Disciples of Christ noncon-
formist somehow aligned me with Union's renegade past. Union's rebel
history—speaking theologically to power, fighting against injustice,
leading the struggle against racism, sexism, and the ravages of poverty,
following Jesus—fit right in with the outlaw faith I had been bred to
believe. As I devoured the specific histories of Union professors, past
and present, I thought of my grandmother and father more than usual.
These Union leaders were their kind of people. Morally and theologically principled, they were driven by energy as fierce as the plains
winds and tough as prairie dirt despite hailing from fields and cities all
over the world.

I became fascinated with a man named Charles Briggs. At the
turn of the twentieth century, he was a Presbyterian biblical scholar at
Union, which was still officially a Presbyterian seminary. Briggs, I read,
was teaching the radical idea that history might be a useful tool in understanding the Bible. Today, his ideas are commonplace in seminaries
everywhere, but back then his position was explosively controversial.

He was brought up on heresy charges by an 1893 General Assembly of the Presbyterian Church, convicted, defrocked, and excommunicated from the Presbyterian Church. The Presbyterian Church also told Union it would essentially be excommunicated, too, if it didn't disavow this proven heretic. Union didn't waver; the Presbyterian Church cut off funding and Union was left scrambling for its life. Fortunately, the liberal moneyed establishment stepped in to save Union, making it even stronger than it had been before the blowup. I cherished such an institutional act of defiance. I was accustomed to my own and my father's acts of civil disobedience, but I also loved it when the Disciples of Christ stood up against the institutional power of church denominations as an antidenominational social movement. The Union I was reading about felt like home, even though it was a couple of thousand miles away from the plains.

And I discovered afresh the backstory of Paul Tillich. Reinhold Niebuhr, still a young professor at Union in the 1930s, knew of this brilliant theologian from Germany who had lost his teaching position because of his opposition to Hitler. He needed to leave Germany urgently. Niebuhr tried to get a position created for Tillich, but there was not enough money to do it. So the faculty all decided to take a pay cut and even pooled money to create a travel fund for Tillich to get out of Germany. Walking the talk, no?

I learned about so many stories like these from the seminary's past. Union graduated the founding leaders of the African National Congress in South Africa and the Three-Self Patriotic Movement in China. The anti-apartheid movement to divest from South Africa started as a student initiative at Union. Myles Horton, the founder of the civil rights training center Highlander Folk School, attended Union as well as Norman Thomas, a Christian socialist and six-time Socialist presidential candidate. The intellectual energy that started the National Council of Churches, the Society of Biblical Literature, the movement for

Clinical Pastoral Education, and the early Peace Corps also bubbled up out of Union's corridors. More recently, the founder of black liberation theology, James Cone, taught at Union for almost fifty years, where he developed liberation theology that fueled the liberation struggles of black people globally. The famous womanist theologians Delores Williams, Katie Cannon, Kelly Brown Douglas, and Jacquelyn Grant all attended Union and generated groundbreaking work on the powerful theological perspective of African American women. Dorothee Soelle, Phyllis Trible, and Beverly Harrison, groundbreaking feminist theological and biblical critics, called Union home. Cornel West, well-known public theologian and prophetic philosopher, called Union home three times during his continued teaching years. The Buddhist teacher and pacifist Thich Nhat Hanh also studied there (our new Buddhist program proudly bears his name). For all of them, "Live what you teach" was never a throwaway line. It defined a way of life.

WHEN THINGS FALL APART

On a blustery February day in 2008—not unlike a typically windy Oklahoma day—I was on campus for my first all-school interview. Around noon, the community was in the James Memorial Chapel for regular daily worship when the service was stopped by an explosive bang, followed by what sounded like boulders bouncing off the roof, shaking the sanctuary's high rafters. I followed as everyone rushed out of the chapel into the seminary's courtyard. There, strewn across the beautifully manicured lawn, lay the shattered remains of what had been the tallest spire on the chapel's tower. Union's steeple had been knocked over by a gust of high wind.

I remember thinking to myself as I looked at the shattered concrete, Thank God no one was hurt. And then quickly reasoned, It's just a steeple. Union can fix that!

I had spent the last twenty-eight years at a well-endowed university where when things crumbled, plans to fix them followed, made by people who, as a student and professor, I didn't know. Other people did the boring work of fixing buildings and raising the money to pay for repairs, whereas I did the important work of learning and teaching about God. The ease with which my professorial past allowed me to brush aside that huge, indeed catastrophic, steeple crash was stunning. A month after it happened, I was offered the position of president of Union, formally president of the faculty, and two weeks later I said yes. I had asked hard, practical questions of the search committee, not just about the crashing-steeple predicament but about the school's academic future, its commitment to rigorous scholarship, its desire to meet twenty-first-century educational challenges, its financial strength, and the answers I received were positive and exciting. The night after I made the decision to accept, I feel asleep with dreams of liberation theology and social justice, not tumbling towers, dancing in my head.

As soon as my appointment was announced, rumors about the falling spire started swirling, and as on any American college or university campus, rumors never failed to escalate into matters of ultimate symbolic significance. To a handful of people at Union, the falling spire predicted that I was going to destroy the seminary, shattering it to pieces. For others, it meant I was going to rebuild Union for the future.

Those discomforting rumblings from others signaled clearly that the community I was soon to join was a far cry from the more genteel world of most seminaries I had known. I would soon learn that you couldn't have a seminary ardently devoted to educating theologically robust, critical-thinking activist pastors and leaders without having, along with it, the ardent desire of that community to question the authority of its own leadership. This was going to be a rough-and-tumble place of God, I remembered thinking as I moved my furniture into my apartment on campus in July 2008, with my daughter's reluctant help.

She was mad about the decision to move. She was eleven and didn't want to leave her dad or friends behind in New Haven. She challenged every step I took to get us there, with all the adolescent fury she could muster. Similarly, for the past twenty years, my authority as a teacher in the classroom had rarely been challenged. Now as a president, I was being questioned before I had even said a word. And then, once I started to speak and lead, the questioning multiplied. In addition to the fundraising and administrative duties I was tasked with, the scholarly and educational challenges were significant and far from simple. Bringing scholarly wisdom to bear on the pressing needs of the world has never been an easy task for Union—but in my mind, there was no higher calling than this one.

"The world needs Union to exist, to remind us all of what theology is really about," I remember the dean of another seminary telling me when news of my appointment spread.

Another seminary president soon added, "If Union ceased to exist, we would have to re-create it. It's the bell tower of Christian conscience everywhere." His words jarred me. That Union would ever cease to exist hadn't even occurred to me.

Little did I know, when I first arrived on campus, how close to nonexistence we were. That falling spire was a harbinger of Union's potential crumbling.

The month after I started, the stock market crash of 2008 hit, dropping the value of our small endowment by almost 30 percent. And on its heels came a series of more devastating reports about the state of religion in America. The Pew Foundation, long known for its polls on religious life in the United States, reported what many of us knew but had refused to fully accept: Participation in religious organizations was falling at a rapid pace. Congregations were shrinking precipitously. Young people were even less interested in religion than their baby-boomer parents had been. Allergy to religion had turned to phobia. Alongside these reports came news from the Association of Theological Schools that these demographic shifts meant that many of North America's historical seminaries would eventually close for lack of students seeking ordination. The churches that had traditionally sent people to seminary were starting to close, and their job prospects were diminishing more and more each passing day. That Union did a good job of attracting social-activist students who weren't typically driven by the desire to pastor huge churches gave me some comfort. They would still come anyway, I hoped, praying our enrollment would not prove me wrong. Happily, my hopes were met—counter to this trend, our enrollment continued to grow.

It wasn't just the numbers that shook me; it was the foreboding sense of doom they conveyed. Seminaries were quickly becoming anachronistic. In an increasingly technological and advanced capitalist society, the idea of a place to think about and to learn to love the divine sounded quaint, if not absurd, especially if it was coupled with the seemingly old-fashioned belief that we are truly called to love our neighbors and our enemies as ourselves. In such a world, places like Union were not just outsiders or crusaders anymore; we were flirting with contemporary cultural irrelevance. I often think back to a pre-Internet age when Paul Tillich and Reinhold Niebuhr were on the nightly news and on the cover of publications like *Time* magazine. Theology seemed urgent and relevant then. And so, too, was Union's influence.

Slowly but surely our society slid into the culture wars that eventually divided the country into two camps, what I call the secular left and the religious right. God ceased to exist among much of the left. On the right, fundamentalists sensed the left's disdain, and some among them covered up their racism and hatred with age-old self-righteous calls to reclaim the Bible and get the nation back to God.

This antagonism between the secular left and the religious right created the perception of a void in the middle, leaving no public acknowledgment of the kind of faith I had grown up with, one fueled by a positive vision of love, justice, and intellectual engagement and a radical belief in God's universal grace. We were there, but the intensity of this divide rendered us invisible. The practical consequences of this were and continue to be devastating to liberal seminaries like Union: We are considered either too religious to be liberal or too liberal to be religious. The left looks at us with suspicion; the right looks at us as bleeding-heart heretics. Repairing the perception is not just a political need, it is a theological and academic one as well. What would it take to bring a progressive theological vision back onto the stage of public debate? The need is urgent, and the cost of the absence of this voice is real. One need only look at our neighbor Columbia University, an aggressively secular, thriving institution. Today, it seems like Columbia builds a new building every month. Union's facilities, in comparison, look like a decrepit, steeple-tumbling monument to religion long past.

As I grappled with this cultural crisis alongside Union's own predicament, I often fixated on a story my grandma Idabel once shared with me.

"When my parents first arrived on our dried-out homestead in Billings," she told me more than once, "my mother, Effie, got very quiet. She got out of the wagon, walked around the scrub grass for a while, and then turned to my father, hands on her hips, and said, 'Charles, it's a bit more than I bargained for.' The two of them stared at each other, the wind whipping up dust around them. She finally shook her head, walked back to the wagon, and lugged out her heavy cast-iron pot to start working on dinner."

In those early years, when I stood in the middle of Union's colossal mess, I often felt like Effie when she got out of the wagon. All a bit more than I had bargained for. Staring at the religious landscape around me—and my own lack of preparation to till it—my ancestral urge to get back on the wagon and go home was strong. For the first time in my life, I seriously questioned whether I had the internal strength the task would demand. I felt a mild sickness in my stomach for days at a time. And try as I might, I searched my pantheon of theologians for wisdom and hope—to no avail. At night when I would take down the usual books from the shelf, my brain felt listless. Theologians had gotten me through McVeigh, divorce, and near death. And now not one of them was rising to aid my mind and spirit. I prayed, like I had so many times before, that one of them would speak to me.

The spire falling during chapel was just a glimpse of our facilities' crisis. We spent two million dollars to fix that most visible and symbolic decay atop our building. That was painful. What hurt even more was what we uncovered when we began to study the whole campus to make sure it wouldn't happen again. Along the way, we found that all of our facades were crumbling, and we received a citation from the New York City Department of Buildings telling us that if we did not secure them quickly, we would have to vacate the property. At the same time, it seemed the wrath of the Devil had visited itself upon the insides of our walls and ceilings. Pipes started bursting; electrical systems went down; plumbing lines broke; whole floors were flooding. And the roof of the residential hall started leaking.

When the buildings were first constructed in 1907, the trustees of Union wanted them to last a hundred years, so they entombed its basic infrastructure in several feet of solid concrete. The good news was that our neo-Gothic fortress lasted a hundred years. The bad news was that we'd slammed into their expiration date and everything was falling apart, all at once, all on time.

If that wasn't bad enough, initial cost estimates for getting the buildings into good working order were one hundred and fifty million dollars. Up to that point in my life, I had never spoken such a gargantuan number, much less imagined that much money as an actual reality. It was more money than Union had raised in its entire history. And unlike law schools and business schools, we had an alumni base of mostly underpaid but devoted pastors and community leaders who gave loyally to the school but never in tens of millions of dollars. We had no idea where to find a cast-iron pot that was valuable enough to start cooking this dinner in.

One evening I was at dinner with friends who had worked as pastors in New York for years. Someone mentioned that it was possible to sell the air above your buildings as if it were real estate. It took me a while to actually not think it a joke. In New York City, people sell the right to develop the air above their homes or buildings? I asked my friend to explain this to me again. In the crowded space of Manhattan, the urge to build was so strong that the city had put in zoning laws that turned every foot of air, up to ten or so stories worth, above every inch of land into a piece of property that could be bought and sold and built out. These feet of air could even be piled up together if they were contiguous, to build taller buildings. It boggled my mind. What a town.

And yet the notion kept nibbling away at me, especially when I thought of that huge price tag. It jumped into my mind like a sneaky, sinful thought. At first, I felt like Judas even considering selling the air above our beautiful, sacred space. And given my devotion to Irigaray and the theology of breathing, I soon considered myself a heretic. Especially selling air to a real estate developer? What was I turning into? The sort of greedy moneymonger I had for so long spoken out against? A compromiser, a leader looking to take the easy way out instead of scrambling to creatively meet our financial needs?

During that same time, I was traveling regularly to Zuccotti Park in lower Manhattan to protest with Union students involved in Occupy Wall Street. We were even holding staff meetings down there, protesting market capitalism's unbridled sinfulness. Ironically, up at Union I began the painful process of figuring out if the market value of our "air" might be our financial—and institutional—salvation. I felt caught. My social justice legs felt unsteady, no matter which way I walked, downtown or uptown. On the heels of Occupy came Union's involvement in Black Lives Matter; our student involvement was so vast that we developed a bail fund and legal service support to back them up. I knew, more than ever, that the world needed Union to keep educating students "concerned about the cares of the world." Struggling religious communities around the world, and in our own city, looked to us for theology expertise and leaders to support them. For Union to crumble would be a grave injustice, one felt not just by its present students but by the generations of future students who would never feel that same fire for justice that burned in Union's heart. But to save her, my commitment to justice was bringing me into contact with people and money that seemed far afield from the ground my justice-seeking legs were used to standing on.

Each step I took to investigate the value of our air rights and the legal requirements of such a transaction made me feel like even more of a traitor to my theological life and upbringing. I tried everything in my power to avoid it. Working with the board, we spent two angst-ridden years looking at every other imaginable solution. Could we raise the money? Given our funder base, no. Should we just sell the campus and close? Absolutely not. Maybe we should dramatically downsize and become a progressive think tank? Again, no. Our mission centered on theology and justice had never been more urgent, and our programs were healthy and growing. Plus, if we weren't around, who would be teaching students about faith and social justice twenty years from now? Or fifty? Or one hundred?

We owed it to the future generations to keep Union going, I kept telling myself. Each option not only failed to address the problem, each carried its own moral ambiguity. Exhausted by these finally futile attempts to find another answer, I faced the harsh truth: There was no pure and perfect path forward. And selling the air rights was the best option we had. So we plunged into the real-estate market and found a buyer for the space above us.

All the while, I couldn't escape memories of Dick Jones figuring out how to sell the space under the land as mineral rights, helping rich people get richer. I knew we wouldn't get rich from selling the air rights—all the money would go to fix pipes and secure stone walls. But his legacy haunted me. It horrified me to be contemplating actions even vaguely resembling his own. And yet, try as I might, I couldn't find a way around our crisis that avoided implicating our justice-heralding school in the sins it so despised. I also knew that Union had always depended on the gains of elite New Yorkers to keep going. After all, a handful of megawealthy families had saved us from our Presbyterian exile and built the school a hundred years ago. We had never been as pure as our protests of others' sins might suggest.

The developer we chose was well known in New York City for building affordable housing, and initially we were going to build apartments that lower-income people could afford to rent. So my theological conscience stopped thrashing me about so much. But before we knew it, the State of New York decided to stop funding such projects in the city and the developers told us that if the project were to move forward, they would need to construct "market-rate condos," which to anyone familiar with New York real estate lingo knew meant condos costing millions. We had solved our own building problem, yes, but on the strict social justice scorecard, we had sold out big time.

THE TOWER OF BABEL

Then, as I should have expected, the protests started. Letter-writing campaigns, sit-ins, teach-ins, community meetings, news articles, social media condemnations. Like the old buildings themselves, the Union community shook mightily in these strong moral winds. And frankly, I couldn't blame the protesters, because I, too, was wrestling with my own righteous demons. In my life, I had always tried to stand on what I thought was the most ethically principled side of issues. To be sure, I was no longer as sanguine about social justice purity as I'd been in my high-minded younger years. Life had mellowed—or jaded—me. I thought often about Niebuhr's eye-opening insistence that Christians had to be more pragmatic about implementing their ideals if they truly wanted to take on the cannier principalities and powers of avarice and totalitarianism. He told progressive Christians that they had to get down in the muck of life if they wanted to change things, and not simply roll over and righteously die when the going got rough. In this case, the mucky, pragmatic facts were undeniably clear: We either had to sell the air rights or close. Neither choice was pure. And to not make a choice was to choose Union's death. Who would benefit from that? No one but the principalities and powers who had long wished us dead.

I suppose that as a symbolic reaction to our plunge into the gray zone, my hair literally started turning gray, more and more with each passing day, each passing protest, each passing decision to build a complicated future. I had to shed the magical thinking that far too many religious and social justice organizations fall prey to when faced with difficult problems. I'd done it in my personal life, particularly with my divorce. Magical thinking is when you imagine that somehow—you don't know quite how—a savior will descend from the clouds and fix things, be it a suddenly different marriage reality (in the case of my divorce) or a billionaire donor who unexpectedly decides to shower you with money.

Churches do it all the time to postpone making theologically complicated, ethical decisions. For example, I've watched mainstream churches avoid deciding where they stand on gay ordination and

same-sex marriage because they think that magically, the reality of
LGBTQ lives will eventually fade and they can keep everyone happy
and their church intact and out of the fray. But by failing to decide,
they end up with empty pews and a weak-kneed theology that fails
to sustain them at all. And sadly, even secular progressive institutions
frequently find themselves waiting for miracles to happen, even though
they logically don't believe in them. Magical thinking can stir creative
ideas and give voice to our firm desire to live in the world as it should
be. But this is simply not the world in which we live. And waiting for
magical answers to ethical dilemmas inevitably fails to advance the
cause of justice. We desire Eden but instead find ourselves on a dry prairie or the vexed terrain of New York real estate. When I was a girl, that
magical person was always Jesus. I would expect him to come out of
the clouds and through a revealing story about God or the touch of his
hand magically make everything all right. Jesus, if you believed in him
and followed his path, was a fantasy savior, the ultimate fixer of all that
plagued his human followers.

As I matured theologically, I realized that Jesus is a miracle worker
but wants no part of magical thinking. The Gospel is right there for us
all day every day—a tough, love-driven example of how to live with
faith and integrity. Yes, Jesus healed people and taught strange truths
about a loving God who was constantly there, calling us to lives of
justice and mercy. But, interestingly, he never heals or leads quite the
way people expect him to. He mostly leaves people with parables that
puzzle more than they reveal. And in the end, he refused to magically
fix the oppressive structures around him, the empire that sought to
silence him. He left that in our hands. He also refused to save his own
life, knowing full well that the way of the world would nail him to
planks of wood and watch him slowly die. Even at the moment of his
own death, he refused to turn God into a magical savior who would,
with a wave of her mighty hand, make everything all right. That was

not, for Jesus, how God worked in the world. It was through the hard, always complicated, persistent presence of love that God worked, be it on the dry plain of a hill outside Jerusalem or in the crumbling world of Union Theological Seminary. For us, the task, then, was to find the path of love and justice as we stumble through the wreckage of life.

A STUDY IN CONTRADICTIONS

As I muddled through Union's financial crisis and grappled with the protests against the board's decision to preserve the seminary, I often wondered what Jesus would really say to me about what I had done and said as I tried to assure Union's future. An article in the *New York Times* about the building project even quoted one of Union's students asking this question of me, implying that if I really followed Jesus, Union wouldn't sell its air to developers.

Jesus was in and of this world, I kept telling myself; he got his hands dirty. He would have understood our work to save the school—and even our compromises. A stereotype of Jesus is that he was all hellfire—uncompromising, rigid in his demands, a borderline anarchist. But the Jesus I have come to rely on was a man driven by knowledge of divine love that led him down streets and across dusty roads, always refusing to meet people's facile and self-interested desires for him to do their bidding. At every turn, he left it in our hands to figure out which street or dusty road we should travel.

Jesus, we all know well, never told people what they wanted to hear. And his actions as a leader seemed extremely erratic. At one moment he's throwing demons to the ground and casting them out; at the next he's sitting down for dinner with friends, talking about harvests and children. At one moment he furiously tosses moneylenders out of the temple; at the next he's asking tax collectors to join him for supper. One day he tells people to leave their families behind and follow him.

The next day he's healing people in their homes, never asking them to leave and take up his mission. And throughout it all, he manages to keep his twelve main followers, and all the many people who joined them, moving in the same direction, marching together, preparing for adversity, sharing troubles, and all the while speaking together the same radical message of God's love.

How did he do all these things at once? How did he hold his multiple callings together? He was a fiery prophet, toppling false gods and denouncing injustice. But he was also a lover, teacher, and friend, gently mending broken bodies and inviting outcasts as well as rich people to sit with him and be fed and taught. And he was an organizer and a builder, making sure there was food to eat, time for rest, calm water for fishing, shelter from storms, a leadership cohort who knew their roles, and most important, a core message about God's love and justice that could steady the unsteady, ground the groundless, and bring wholeness, even to the broken terrain of New York real estate.

But through most of these travails at Union over the buildings, I couldn't find the theological spark to make me live what I could intellectualize about Jesus. Academically and socially, we were thriving and growing, taking the bold step of becoming a more interreligious seminary and speaking out theologically on "the claims of world" that were swirling around us. But when it came to building, no book and no theologian could provide the answers I needed this time. They had gotten me through cancer, molestation, terrorism—but now as the leader of a physically crumbling seminary I couldn't find the theological basis to fight harder, to grow thicker skin, to come up with the morally perfect and financially sound decision. I always felt torn up inside.

During the most intense days of protest, both those on campus and inside my own head, I was oddly determined and utterly lost, both feelings fiercely holding their own. One evening as I was walking from my office back to my apartment, I was shocked to see a big picture of my head pasted on Donald Trump's body (he wasn't yet the president, just a widely despised New York real estate developer) on a poster on a wall in the student center. It was seven thirty and the room was empty. Standing in front of it, I felt crushed by its mockery of me, its dramatic misrepresentation of my commitments, its cruelty (or the cruelty I perceived). As was my policy, I walked away, leaving it up, knowing full well I would be forced to walk by it daily, usually with students around waiting to gauge my reaction. I respected their voices too much to stifle them, even when it hurt this bad.

My first thought was that I hoped my now thirteen-year-old daughter wouldn't see it. She wouldn't understand; it would scare her. My second reaction was despair, a radical sense of loneliness and wearied helplessness in the face of realities far beyond my control. Am I really that horrible? Does someone really despise me that much? What have I become? What have we come to?

DIFFICULT CHOICES

When I got home, I dropped my computer bag by the front door and stood in the evening's falling darkness, looking out my big living room window at the campus surrounding me—its crumbling tower, its chapel, dorms, and classrooms, and the massive shadows cast by the city rising around it, threatening to swallow the campus whole. I loved Union, her passionate mission, her now shoddy form, her striving and creative, if not sometimes harsh, students, her brilliant faculty. I knew without a doubt that I was called to be her leader. This mess of emotions and ethical dilemmas was not something I could walk away from, and yet I didn't know how I could keep mustering the strength it would take to keep standing in the midst of it. It physically hurt. My legs were always bouncing, my jaw always tight.

As was my usual practice, I racked my brain to find the perfect theological book I could pull off the shelf to guide me. Which beloved theologian might calm this inner turmoil? Nothing came. My despair deepened as I felt abandoned even by my own tribe of scholarly inspirers. Did they never have to worry about buildings and contracts? Had I entirely left the planet of theological inspiration?

"Charles, it's a bit more than I bargained for." I heard my great-grandmother say from somewhere in the back of my despairing mind.

"That cool jug was God to me and I never wanted to let go." I heard the voice of Idabel whisper to me from the edge of memory.

Their voices turned me away from the window and sat me down in my favorite chair in front of that Oklahoma big-sky, oil-rig picture. Was the answer there? The theological guidance I needed, coming from two dead Seitz women? And a painting?

I studied the vast reach of its sky and fields, and the haunting metal structure at its center, cool and gray, its pipes plunging deep below the surface. A study in contradictions, it was a beautiful yet horrible portrait of God's world, stunning, huge, grasping, reaching, creating, destroying, surviving, harming, thriving, joyous and greedy, the lopped-off parts and the whole truth, the seen and the unseen, all held together on a canvas edged by a rugged wooden frame. All its messy truths juxtaposed one with the other.

In those colors and forms, I found the theology I needed. I recalled the stories that had brought me here, the women and men who had come before me; all of us, it seemed, were caught up in struggles we didn't create or fully understand and yet were forced to confront; some sought good, others chose violence, most landed somewhere in between. But all of us, generation after generation, stood awestruck before the rugged landscape of our dirty, exquisite existence.

My great-grandmother, sodbuster that she was, knew life on the homestead was far more than she bargained for, but she didn't wait for angels to appear or handsome cowboys to carry her away. She put her hands into the dirt and pulled out life. That's where the life-giving work of faith always happens. In the dirt.

And Idabel, stalwart grandmother that she was, somehow knew that dented old jug meant grace, even in the absence of stained-glass windows and hallowed hymns of praise. God was there, in the hardened dirt, the sweat of unending labor, and the land's eventual harvest. Nothing clean or pure about it. Just the shade of a wagon and a restless horse.

It's one of the many paradoxes of a theological life that the ragged plains and raggedy people of Oklahoma held the key to my New York theological redemption. We are called to pull life out of the rubble, sweaty and exhausted, sinners and saints, none of it pure, every inch of it straining toward meaning, all of it graced. Staring at that painting, I still had no idea if Union would survive this ordeal, but I was utterly convinced that this place deserved every ounce of the collective energy and sweat required to save it.

This vision from God via Oklahoma, if you will, helped me see why theological notions of human sin and God's grace need to play a central role in a theology of institutions. Of my favorite theologians, Calvin was the one who understood this best. He was trying to build a city, Geneva, which could reflect, socially, the goodness of divine grace. Hindsight shows us how he both succeeded and failed, but most remarkably, he saw—as many other theologians did not—that if people are to thrive, they need homes to shelter them, hospitals to heal them, school buildings to learn in, places to work in, all the structures needed to house humanity's endeavors. The work of assuring these buildings exist is profoundly theological. All of this justice work is faith based, in my book.

If you accept that sin is extensive, persistent, systemic, and collective, you are kidding yourself if you think you can get through life, much less build institutional homes, without being tainted by it. Institutions, as collections of this human sin and grace, reflect that. That doesn't mean we don't try to aspire to the ideal; it does mean, however, that we must, by nature, refuse to take shelter in unrealistic plans that let us off the hook from messy decisions. Grace matters in a similar way. It can be institutional; it can take its power from history and collective energy. It gives us courage to take up the daunting task of being a human institution together, knowing that running through everything—getting dirty together and surviving and thriving together—is to experience the ultimate love of God.

JUSTICE: THE SOCIAL LABOR OF HUMANS

Dietrich Bonhoeffer, one of Union's most renowned students, wrote about this theological complexity in human life, and especially in his own life as he wrestled with the rise of national fascism in Hitler's Germany. His theology eventually led to his execution by Hitler:

> God loves human beings. God loves the world. Not an ideal human, but human beings as they are; not an ideal world, but the real world. What we find repulsive in their opposition to God, what we shrink back from with pain and hostility . . . this is for God the ground of unfathomable love.

As Union has always done, guided by "unfathomable love," we faced this issue head-on, and on the other side of our mighty wrestling, we are still as sturdy as ever, mission driven, and growing. We are now in the midst of a complete revitalization of the campus—financed in large part by the air rights sale—and hoping that because of our efforts, it will take another hundred years before a president has to face what I have. That's one hundred more years of teaching about faith and social justice and the always messy, disturbing challenge of being thrown into the world and struggling to minister there.

Standing at the edge of our renovated campus will be the condo building that many will probably never stop magically wishing away. But in a decade or less, I imagine it, too, will become an accepted part of the hallowed space we occupy, standing there as a symbol, at least, of survival. For me, when I visit Union in my retirement someday, it will also be a reminder of Bonhoeffer's notion of our complex human reality. Perhaps some future president will have a big picture of the whole campus, high-rise and all, with the brilliant sky of New York above it and Union's quiet, contemplative courtyard below it to hang on her or his wall, a study in contradictions, a source of hope.

Sometimes still, when I revert to a less mature theological vision of life, I wonder what Jesus would really say to me about what I have done and said over the past decade at Union. Of course, Jesus was in and of this world; he got his hands dirty; he would, I tell myself, have nodded kindly at our work—and even our compromises. Sure, he threw around the carts in the temple and raised hell, but upon the rock of his disciples, a church, vexed as it is, now stands. And it is only because, across the centuries, people built schools committed to teaching his radical vision that Union can lay claim to the radical vision it teaches and will teach to future generations.

What's more, most students at Union will eventually have to wrestle with these issues in the communities they serve: There's no getting around them. And what better way to learn than by doing. Getting it out on the table and grappling with it. Dealing with buildings and keeping institutions going is just one of the overwhelming difficulties facing religious and spiritual leaders committed to social justice today. We are asking the same old questions but from an increasingly weak position. What does it mean to take on the magnitude of concentrated corporate and individual power dominating the world today? If religious leaders are tasked with communicating with and nurturing the spiritual lives of their communities, how are they supposed to do it in a time when most conversations happen not face-to-face but in the unbridled and excessively hostile space of the Internet? How does one preach and pastor in cyberspace? Or in places where no community exists, the traumas of time having fractured them out of existence?

I fear that the hardest thing for progressive religious and spiritual leaders to come by is hope, especially knowing that vast numbers of people in the nation, many of them religious, don't share the social values that overlap with theological ones: basic human equality; the right to health, education, work, shelter, and happiness; and a fundamental desire for collective human flourishing. The playing field and the soil to cultivate and grow theologians, academics, religious leaders, activists, and people with social or world concern is rocky and stubborn and increasingly hostile.

Add to this reality the abiding fact that the planet's surface is heating up, and we have barely begun to imagine, much less address, what that portends, especially for the millions of lives already devastated by climate catastrophes and for the lives of generations to come who may not have that blessed air I talk about breathing. At Union and elsewhere, we are scrambling to find theological wisdom for this crisis, recognizing that for centuries religious thinkers in every tradition just assumed the ongoing existence of a healthy earth. The gap between rich and poor is now bigger than at any point in our history, the number of guns we own outnumbers our people, and the desperate hell of opioid addiction and suicide is far vaster than anyone has yet to measure. And amid it all, the hatred, racism, and violence that has been here since the beginning of the nation continues to thrive, taking ever-new forms, destroying newly emerging communities, exploiting human energy for greed and gain, and refusing, at every turn, the radical notion that all our lives and our planet hold equal, precious value.

What does it mean to teach the sin-grace dance to a new generation of seminary students in such a fractured world? How does the marriage of social justice and theology withstand the pressures of shock-and-awe capitalism and the godless marketplace? I realize each generation tends to think their problems are the worst ever, but it's no exaggeration for me to say that in my lifetime, short as it is, I've never seen the level of massive social collapse we are now witnessing. It's dizzying, horrifying, and profoundly disempowering. And that's why Union's scrappy, restless energy has never been more needed.

When our founders, in 1836, decided to leave behind their rarefied seminary homes nestled in the quiet countryside to set up their classrooms on the docks of New York City, there was a passionate fire burning in them. They realized that to preach a Gospel that speaks to the pain and cares of the world, they needed not to turn away from that world but to jump headlong into its troubles. That's why they started Union, a school perched right in the middle of it and tasked with the mission of engaging all the city's people with a message of love and goodness. Remarkably, almost two hundred years later, that fire still burns in the collective, historic soul of the school.

It burns in me, too. Even so, I still find myself looking for answers to institutional and social questions that I can't find easy theological solutions for. I may never. But there's one story in which I find remarkably contemporary—yet also very old—guidance. It keeps the fires burning and the questions coming. It's the Gospel story; it is and always will be.

CHAPTER 12

Mercy

The power of just mercy is that it belongs to the undeserving. It's when mercy is least expected that it's most
potent—strong enough to break the cycle of victimization
and victimhood, retribution and suffering. It has the power
to heal the psychic harm and injuries that lead to aggres-
sion and violence, abuse of power, mass incarceration.

BRYAN STEVENSON,
JUST MERCY: A STORY OF JUSTICE AND REDEMPTION

The sin/forgiveness/grace progression sounds better in theory than
in practice. It chagrins me to say that. Even after the McVeigh
lesson in how forgiveness can be carved out of sin, I had trouble forgiving my mother for the many things she had done and, really, who
she was. I knew my feelings weren't unique. Most of my female friends
struggle with the same thing. It seems to come with the territory of
being mothers and daughters. I could imagine grace in our relationship, but it took a big imagination to do so. To practice the theological
imagination, to achieve that divine vision that announces grace in the
midst of sin, inevitably requires leaps of mind and heart and soul that
sometimes just . . . don't come.

In Judaism, Islam, and Christianity, the word "mercy" is often used as a synonym for forgiveness. They aren't the same, though, particularly when it comes to human relationships. Forgiveness has a transactional quality to it. A harm happens, the truth of the harm is recognized, and attempts are made to right the wrong, and when a perpetrator asks for it and the victim of harm agrees, then forgiveness is granted, its healing balm embracing both parties. It's hard work to forgive and to be forgiven, especially when harms are centuries old and redress is not offered, as is the case with so many of the harms inflicted and suffered in history.

Mercy is different. In common parlance, people "throw themselves at the mercy of the court," meaning even though the court's guilty verdict may stand, the person requests that the sentence be lifted or, at the very least, lessened, simply because the judge decides to do so, usually out of some humanitarian impulse. This captures what Bryan Stevenson says about mercy. It is most potent when it is least expected and when it falls upon the undeserving. To have mercy upon someone is to simply release him or her from punishment. Of course, in our court system, mercy is granted by people with more power than those who are forced to ask for it. In the broader culture, too, mercy is most often associated with what the powerful decide to grant the powerless.

As it is theologically understood, mercy is different from its secular interpretation. God's mercy falls upon us, releasing us from judgment, even when our sin remains. Everyone gets it, even when we haven't thrown ourselves at the feet of a Divine judge. It just is. In this regard, Divine mercy toward humanity's sins is a one-way street. God grants us mercy despite the absence of any human merit. But when knowledge of this mercy is reflected in human lives, it flows in all directions. It occurs whenever, against all odds, human beings choose compassion over punishment. Compassion is the root of mercy. Compassion is not something you have to earn or deserve—if that were the case, there would be no lasting compassion to speak of, just momentary flourishes of love feelings. Compassion flows from a deep recognition of our shared brokenness and our shared divinity. Compassion's urge to heal is why, theologically, mercy and justice are always talked about together. Mercy grants freedom from the bondage of harms. Justice is the struggle to make sure those harms stop.

A MOTHER'S MERCY

When it came to my relationship with my mother, it was not forgiveness that I needed to summon. The only hope for repair was mercy. It was that bad.

I remember one visit, when she was in her early seventies, when we actually talked about mercy. My parents had just retired to a cabin on Lake Fort Gibson in eastern Oklahoma. It was on a small parcel in an old fishing camp that my aunt Sissy left to my mother, and over the years, she and my father had turned it into their haven. I had come to spend my usual July week with them.

Before retiring, my mother had worked for almost twenty years as a marriage and family counselor and a spiritual director. Her job had taught her a few things about herself, giving her slivers of insight into flaws she hadn't seen in her younger years: her vanity, the quickness of her temper, her repressed anger at her own mother's inability to be a mother to her, and her frustrations at becoming a mother so early in her life. She even managed to apologize once for being so mean to me as a child. She admitted that she had seen me as a ball and chain around her ankle and not as a child who desperately needed her love. As she succinctly put it, "You stole my youth from me." Even as she said this, her confession sounded like blame.

Sadly, seeing these things about herself didn't amount to changing them. The older she got, the more proudly she owned them, including being increasingly angered by the mere presence of me in her life. The fact that she now understood herself better but didn't change her behaviors made it all the harder for me to bear her hurtful rages when they came. And they were coming more and more, manifestations of her deep-seated unhappiness. But, looking back, I realized she had always been prone to fits of anger. I had simply thought they were part of growing up until I saw that my friends' mothers did not all act that way.

The most recent of those rages had happened only two months earlier. She seemed to have forgotten it by July, but I was still smarting from her lashing. I had considered not coming, but I wanted to see my dad. It had been one of her worst blowups ever. But it was also just one more blowup in a long line of them that had marked her relationship with me from the start. When I lost her watch, it took the form of pretending as if I didn't exist—a terrible thing to do to a child who is trying to figure out what it means to exist in the first place. Over the years, the fits had slowly escalated, coming out in sudden explosions of anger and violent verbal attacks.

This time, Charis and I had flown into Oklahoma City from New York on a Friday morning in early May 2011 so that on Saturday I could receive an honorary doctorate from the University of Oklahoma during their spring graduation ceremony. We were staying with Kindy and her family, and my mom and dad had driven down from the lake cabin to be part of the festivities. That Friday afternoon I went shopping for a dress to wear. A childhood friend of mine who owned a small clothing store nearby had already picked one out for me—we'd talked about it for months. It was a big occasion, being honored by my own and my whole family's school, and my sisters and Charis and all the Joneses in Oklahoma were excited to be a part of it.

When I returned from shopping later in the afternoon, I walked into Kindy's family room eager to show everyone what I'd found. Charis, my nephew Jess, and my mother were sitting there watching TV, and Jess switched it off when I came in. I pulled out the dress, a fancy black-and-white linen thing, and held it up, swirling around the room. Just as Charis was jumping up to tell me how beautiful it was, my mother, sitting on the couch, exploded.

"What nerve you have, going off shopping for yourself," she said. "You act like you're so important, little miss smarty-pants, but I know who you really are. You're a spoiled brat, that's who you are. Always have been. Needy, needy, needy. Always wanting something. Me, me, me, all the time. A self-centered little bitch who can only think of dresses, dresses, dresses on the day before HER BIG DAY."

Her fury and sarcasm startled us.

"You're a terrible mother, too," she continued. "I can't believe you let your daughter miss school just because you were getting some stuck-up academic award. You think you're smarter than everyone, don't you? I know you do. Your selfishness is shocking, Serene, utterly shocking and shameful, and it is going to destroy your daughter just like it did me. She'd be better off without you." She stopped as suddenly as she started.

Jess, Charis, and I stood frozen in place. No one had seen it coming or had any idea what provoked it. My shock at her outburst made me speechless. Had she really just said those things? The worst part was about my daughter. How could she say that? In front of Charis?

I had long ago given up fighting back when she attacked me. It never helped matters, only made them worse. This time, too, I held back. Stood silent before her. Our eyes locked. Her, furious. Me, crushed and confused, just like I'd been when I was five and she beat me with a brush for coming home from kindergarten happy, or when I was ten and she ripped up my A+ essay because it was too smart for someone my age, or when on my wedding day she'd told me I was lucky to find a man as nice as Shepard to put up with me. Or when she pinched me, pulled my hair, hissed at me, dug her fingernails into my arms, or "accidentally" stepped hard on my bare feet.

Jess, who was then eighteen, broke the spell. "Wow, Grandmom. What was that about?"

My mother found a magazine and sat down to read, as if nothing had happened.

I looked at him and shrugged my shoulders, years of therapy paying off. "Ya got me." I then smiled at him and Charis and remembered my grandma, the woman who loved me. "Don't you think it's time for a Coke?"

BEGGING FOR MERCY

Two months had passed but my nerves were still on edge with my mother, as they had been throughout most of my childhood. The two of us were sipping coffee on her patio as the sun rose over the lake. In these early-morning talks, she confessed things to me that my father and sisters rarely heard. It was another way of making me carry her burdens.

"I'm not a very forgiving person, sweet girl, you know," she said. I did.

I didn't know what early-morning thought process had provoked this particular confession, although I could think of many events just in the last several days. She was always mad at someone: the newspaper boy who was late, the next-door neighbors for not mowing their lawn, the minister for his boring sermon, the president of the United States, my father, and, of course, me, her eternally wicked ball and chain. I kept these thoughts to myself in order to see where she was going.

She continued. "My grudges last for years. Once someone does something I don't like, I get mad and it grows stronger over time. I never forget when someone wrongs me, and I don't forgive them. Frankly, I want to hurt them, make sure they get the punishment they deserve."

"Punishment?" I already knew her answer.

She smiled. "I'm still furious at that girl, what was her name . . . Nancy, I think, who blocked you from joining my sorority when you started college. And that awful boss at the grocery store, Mrs. Johnson, who wouldn't let you off work for your senior prom, especially after I bought you that beautiful dress. I wanted to just smack 'em. Make them pay."

"Jeez, Mom. That's kind of extreme, isn't it? And besides, that was years ago. I've completely forgotten them both." I couldn't help but wonder how many of her smacks at me she remembered.

"I haven't," she answered.

"That's a lot to carry, isn't it?"

She took another sip of coffee. "Not really. It's how I keep track of my life. I have an internal history book of wrongs and deserved paybacks."

I nodded, recalling another of the more chilling wrongs she believed she'd suffered and the smack that followed. "Do you have on your list of wrongs the time you told Charis she couldn't go swimming in her bikini and you slapped her when she sassed you back?" It was a sore point with me, her enraged reactions to my then seven-year-old daughter who was clearly acting out because of the divorce. Any reasonable therapist or parent could have seen it.

"Yes, it's still there. I'm sorry about it, dear, but it's true. She's a handful, that child."

That old image of Charis as a sassy floozy had never faded in her head. It wasn't even worth arguing about.

"Are you on the bad-people-who-deserve-punishment list, Mom?"

"Many times over, my dear. You'd be shocked." She smiled, rocking back in her lawn chair.

"With no mercy, ever?" I probed.

"No. If I had mercy for other people . . . or myself, I would have to change the list in my head, and if I did that, I'd lose track of my past."

That was her to a tee. A relentless counter of sins and distributor of punishments. So many of them of her own making.

I envisioned the clutter of old sins that filled her head and figured the next stage in our talk was going to entail an actual list of her grievances about me. I got up to get more coffee, ending the conversation before it took an even nastier turn.

Later that same week, we were alone in the kitchen making a salad for dinner. I'd been peeved at her since that morning's conversation about my daughter and had finally decided to push it one step further, to see how far she really carried things.

"Do you think God keeps a list like yours, too? With no mercy, ever?"

She paused. "Yes, I guess I do." She handed me the lettuce to chop. "Terrifying thought, isn't it? But true." She dumped sliced carrots in the bowl and then drifted away into her own world of thoughts. This was a woman who for years had professionally counseled couples and helped families? I shook my head and chopped the lettuce.

Forgiveness, as I've experienced it, can happen over time, as past wrongs are repaired or as they fade in importance and memory, the hurt slipping away with the years. Eventually, wrongs either heal or become simply irrelevant and forgotten. Clearly, time had healed nothing for her.

In my theological imagination, I also believed that God, rather than keeping lists, is so powerfully loving that Divine Love washed away all sins, even the most incomprehensible ones like McVeigh's or painful, abusive ones like Dick Jones's and like my mother's—even when the victims of these sins never heal or forget. When viewed through the eyes of Divine Love, everyone and everything is ultimately beloved and forgiven. No final list of sins is kept. That's how believing in divine mercy toward the world helped me experience mercy in relation to others. But it's so, so hard to live cognizant of this divine reality.

This isn't a Pollyanna-ish view that made it okay to do harmful things. Divine Love is also the measure of the quality of our living days. It bids us to seek justice, because the compassion that mercy cultivates in our hearts requires us to make the world a better place, to heal wounds and fix oppressive realities. Compassion makes the harms of the world intolerable to you because you know, in God's mercy, hatred and greed are lies and should be opposed. That rage against any form of oppression comes to you not as a mere principle of justice that you adhere to intellectually. It is nurtured in your heart, your full being, your soul. You simply cannot live without compassion. In this sense, justice is the child that mercy births.

I now see that when it came to my mother, I simply could not live what I believed. I had no capacity for mercy toward her, unable to imagine why her view of me and of her life was so negative and punishing. My own inability to let go of her gross obsession with my imagined wrongs was due partly, I knew, to the fact that she kept adding new grievances to the list.

So little had changed between us over the past fifty years. When there is no change in the behaviors that produce harm, it's almost impossible for people to actually forgive one another. Theologically, that change of heart is called repentance. It literally means to "turn around" or "to see and do things differently." Without such a shift, forgiveness is virtually inconceivable. That's why, in human relations, mercy is the only way forward. It allows you to let go of the harm, even in the absence of repentance, and, in compassion, move forward with love.

Over the next several years of her retirement at the lake house, she seemed to soften in some ways. She laughed more and took longer naps. The natural world surrounding her worked its magic, grounding her in the sights, sounds, and tactile feel of trees, animals, earth, sky, and water where nothing was right or wrong; it just was. She planted roses and a vegetable garden and said she didn't care if they flowered or bore fruit. She just loved digging and planting, tending and watching. One summer at the lake house, she actually apologized, sincerely and without blame, to me for not being a kinder mother. Wary but yearning, I hugged her and felt my own heart begin to thaw as forgiveness started its minuscule but miraculous work, sparked by that single, short-lived moment of repentance.

My own incapacity to imagine the shape of her interior world had always blocked me from really seeing her. If I had truly seen through the eyes of compassion, I would have remembered her consuming grief over her brother's suicide ten years earlier. A gentle, loving man, he was her only sibling and an alcoholic. He shot himself in the head one night in an alcoholic blur, in the lake cabin, while my parents were gone. I would have also recalled her never-present alcoholic father. Her childlike mother whose own mother's death haunted her. The self-absorbed vanity imposed by her uncanny beauty. Her stunted childhood. None of these were things she could control.

I realize now that the most difficult forgiveness comes when we try to forgive those we love—or want to love—the most. Forgiving McVeigh was ultimately easier than forgiving my mother. I do not want to hurt any victims of McVeigh's bombing by acknowledging this sin of mine. I am ashamed of it, but I admit it. I am not sure if my mother ever truly loved me in the profound, cosmic sense of the word. In turn, after I grew out of my adolescent need for love, I never achieved the same love and understanding for her that I have always held for my dad.

And yet I always wanted to love her—so desperately, so needily, so fundamentally. We want to love our mothers; it's both a cultural expectation and a genetic impulse or direction. Yet something in me— self-preservation?—resisted mightily. Something told me it would be dishonest to love someone who had so abused me for years. The harshness of that reality stunned me. But I also realized that faking love for this grudge-holding, twisted-up woman felt impossible. What's worse, I knew she would never have the same longing to love me that I had to love her. She didn't feel that divine spark of mercy; she wasn't moved by that cosmic need. Apparently the same held true for me when it came to forgiving her.

Six years later, my mother died without my having come to love her with the depth and power that I wanted to love her with. At the end, I felt the same anger at her that I had felt the day in Kindy's family room. Even as she was dying, she cursed my daughter and told me I needed to lose weight, that I was a Yankee elitist, and that I was going to hell for not visiting her more often. But these attacks, old as they were, paled in comparison to the final act of vengeful confession she threw at me during the final months of her life.

WEAPONIZED CONFESSION

At the same time as I was diagnosed with cancer in 2005, my mother began to lose her vision. Six years later, she was told she had an irreversible, terminal disorder called progressive supranuclearpalsy (PSP). Over the next four years, she slowly lost the ability to walk, to care for herself, to swallow, and to talk with ease. In the fall of 2015, I had flown in from New York to see her and had taken her, now age seventy-seven, in her wheelchair to her favorite local chain restaurant for lunch. I expected her usual begrudging questions about what I was up to, but before the waitress could even fill our water glasses, she spewed out this final confession to me, the thing she must have been thinking about all those years ago when she talked about unforgivable wrongs.

"Serene, I think this illness is God punishing me." She reached out to grab my hand across the table, her weak fingers still able to claw at mine.

I sighed and began my usual mantra. "Mom, I don't believe God works like that. You just got sick, and we don't even know why you got this illness."

She vehemently shook her head, piquing my interest.

"Okay. As you say. But, seriously, why would God punish you like this?"

"I had an affair." She struggled with the words.

I sat back in the booth. I hadn't seen that one coming and imagined immediately how much it would crush my father if he found out. He had just turned eighty and still took pleasure in telling my mother how much he adored her, like he was a teenager falling in love with her for the first time over and over again.

The thought of my mother having a random one-night stand with some stranger completely creeped me out. But then my own life had hardly been perfect in this regard. It certainly didn't deserve a death sentence. I chuckled.

"Mom, if God killed people for having flings, half the people in this restaurant would fall out of their chairs dead on the floor right now. Me included. Come on." But I was curious. "So who was it with?"

"Burt."

Shock waves rolled through me.

When Kindy and I had left home for college in the late seventies, leaving my sister Verity, still in high school, alone at home with her, my mother had declared her new independence by, of all things, learning how to fly. The whole family was surprised, and we watched with unaccustomed wonder over the next decade as she soared into the skies above Enid, making lazy eights and pulling out of downward spirals. She got her pilot's license and flew as far as Dallas and Kansas City. It was the happiest I had ever seen her. She woke in the morning full of energy, and talked constantly about cloud formations, wind currents, and the cowboy culture of Okie pilots. She'd come home late in the evening filled with stories of her day's adventures.

Burt was a friend from the airport, a fellow pilot, a man who practically became part of the family.

"Mom! Burt? Oh my God." I instinctively tried to pull away from her hand, but she held on tighter and nodded. "How long did this last?" I prayed she would say it was just a one-night stand. He wasn't handsome or smart or interesting, just a regular, likable guy. Not that those things mattered, I kidded myself.

"Seven years."

She then spewed out an endless stream of details about how much she had loved him and how they had talked about getting married. She said they would have, but he didn't want to hurt his wife. She told me intimate details of their encounters on rural landing strips across Oklahoma and at the lake house. I sat in stunned disbelief, too shocked to tell her to stop. She kept going, the details of her deceit pouring out like a criminal desperate to finally confess her crimes. She added only as a short aside that my father never had a clue.

"Were there others?" I had to ask.

She shrugged and looked away. "The only one I ever loved was Burt." It was hardly an answer.

"Are you still in contact?" I couldn't bear the thought that it might still be happening.

"We used to write letters and email now and then." Later, we would find their love letters in her personal files. "I want to see him one more time, but I'm so sick and fat that I think he would be repulsed by me. I don't want him to remember me this way."

I yearned for her to show some kind of remorse, to tell me it was all a big mistake and it was over forever. But all she could do was share purely vain reasons for not seeing him one more time.

"So this is why you think God is punishing you?" If I had believed in a punishing God, she was definitely on the list.

"Yes. But mostly God hates me because I'm not sorry I did it."

"You're not sorry at all?" Surely there was some seed of regret in her somewhere.

"No. In fact, I planned it. When I was seventeen, I snuck into the movie theater to watch *The End of the Affair*. Deborah Kerr was beautiful and dramatic and so exquisitely tormented by her betrayal. I knew then that when I got married, I wanted to be her. To be that interesting. I even craved her torment."

Who could have imagined this already horrid conversation could get any worse? Our food arrived, and we fell silent as she struggled to raise small bits of pasta to her mouth.

I played with my chicken, vaguely recalling Graham Greene's 1951 novel turned movie, *The End of the Affair*. Its main female character— who has the affair—is a beautiful, deeply religious wife who is so consumed by guilt about her infidelity that she eventually dies from exposure to the damp cold of London. Her name was Sarah, my mother's name.

Was my mother still playing Deborah Kerr's character, even as she was dying? I couldn't decide which was worse. That my mother had planned her affair since she was a teenager? Or that she craved its torment? Or, worst of all, that she had based her life—and her deceit—on a Hollywood movie? Was this the story that filled her imagination and inspired her all-consuming secret life? Did a movie, of all things, spawn her view of a punishing God?

She gave up on the pasta and began, haltingly, to plead with me not to tell my sisters or my father. I agreed, in turn asking her, "Please, please, please, do not tell Dad." Please God, I prayed, let her spare him this betrayal. To protect him, I willingly accepted my own role in her lie. Indeed, I begged my way into it.

Our agreement to keep it secret held for only a few months, during which time I broke my promise and told my sisters everything, refusing to let her confession torment me in isolation. But when it came to my father, my sisters agreed that it was best if he didn't know. When he spoke of her illness and the near end of their almost sixty years of marriage, he wept, still so innocent, telling us over and over again how he couldn't bear the thought of losing his beautiful Sarah, the rare and perfect love of his life.

Despite my pleas, she eventually told Dad everything. Everything. And as the PSP began its slow creep through her brain, she began compulsively telling anyone who would listen: the nursing care staff, her doctors, old high school friends, visitors from church, the minister. Her affair quickly became Oklahoma City's talk of the town. I'm sure if she was still around, she'd be happy I was writing about it now. But no matter whom she told, what was most painful of all was her relentless insistence on telling my father, day after day, as he kept caring for her, that she never loved him. It was only Burt.

My family will never know how much of her story was the invention of PSP-related dementia and how much was true. The love letters we found in her desk stopped us from dismissing it altogether, along with her constant recounting of the affair's sordid details, always consistent, always disturbing.

To say my father was devastated is to vastly understate its effect on him. For the first time in my life, he fell silent. Deeply silent. Up until the end. My sisters and I tried to convince him that our mother didn't know what she was saying, that she had not married Burt but stayed with my father, proving she really loved him best, that she was just furious that she was dying and lashing out at him, her closest companion. Nothing worked. He would just listen in numbed silence, waiting impatiently for us to stop our manic attempts to dull his pain. Then he would tread over to her room in hospice care and spend the day sitting with her, compassionately so. I'd never witnessed a human being enact mercy of this magnitude toward someone who had unrepentantly harmed him and kept doing so. Who knows what all was rumbling around in his soul? What his actions conveyed was mercy—compassion on steroids.

On the Saturday after Easter in 2016, my mother died with my father by her side in the nursing home. We knew it was coming. My sisters and I had been with her for the previous six days, sleeping in her room at night and during the day reading her scripture, especially her treasured Psalms, and playing her music, most of it old-school gospel hymns she had first learned in Methodist Sunday school. "How Great Thou Art" was her favorite. I kept waiting, even though she could no longer speak, for some sign, no matter how small, that she was sorry, not just about the affair but for her abusive treatment of me. That she was experiencing some semblance of mercy, my father's mercy, and even more, the divine mercy that she did not deserve but nonetheless received.

My sisters and I had momentarily left to get breakfast when her heart finally stopped beating. That sign I was looking for never came.

It turned to me, as the oldest, to give the eulogy. The root of the word is *logos*, the Greek word for "word." *Eu-* is a prefix meaning "good." A eulogy technically is the good words we speak about someone who has died. We summon memories, recall their inspiration, blend kind jabs with profound reflections.

I cringed at being chosen to speak these good words at my mother's memorial service. A good word. I had many, I realized. But for each good one, two or three bad ones came to mind. Self-absorbed. Obsessed with weight. Prone to ditziness. Emotionally infantile. Vindictive. A liar. And unspeakably cruel.

But the most damning thing I wanted to say—but could not say in church—was that she never approximated, let alone embraced, the reality of God's mercy—not for God or for others or for herself. She spoke about God, yes; she went to church; she supported my father's work unquestionably; and she'd even pieced together her own childish version of a controlling, punishing God. But throughout it all, she never experienced unmerited divine love; she got stuck in the wicked part of the sin-grace dance. It wasn't just that she didn't forgive; it was that she felt no impulse to forgive and saw no reason to be forgiven. Indeed, she seemed to relish the agony of her own alienation from God. The more I had grown aware of that reality over the years, the more I could almost physically see it: Sin was like the glue or honey in which she was perpetually stuck. It dragged her movement; it slowed her smile; it weighted her spirit; it restrained her generosity, the giving of her "self."

She was never able to get outside of herself to love. To be loved. To accept her own brokenness and to accept others' broken lives as well. Stuck inside the cruel world of just deserts, she failed to reach beyond her own wounds to feel the healing power of compassion for others' wounds.

Most people never can. We live in a nation governed by a merciless thirst for revenge. That blood thirst executed McVeigh. And it's that same corrupted spiritual vein that runs through our criminal justice system and economic policies that punish people for being poor or black or undocumented or mentally ill. Dividing the world into the good and the bad, the deserving and the undeserved, the well-heeled and the disinherited, we live mercilessly.

I included myself in this culture, especially when I reckon with my lifelong inability to get out of myself enough to show mercy toward her.

Caught in the web of my own hurt, I never had the courage it would have taken to act mercifully toward her. I didn't have the theological bearing. Despite my life's commitment to teaching the virtues of social justice, when it came to my own mother, I lacked the spirit of mercy that makes the work of justice also the work of compassion. If I couldn't practice mercy toward her, I had to wonder whether I could practice it anywhere else. I saw my father, who if I am being honest, was most hurt by knowing her actions, treat her with mercy and love as she lay dying. It made me feel inadequate, and as a pastor, a fraud.

At her funeral, I complied with the protocol of remembrance and offered an elegant reflection on her life. A good mother. Loving wife. Woman of faith. Servant of the community. Pilot, therapist, and spiritual director. And in good form, I reminded everyone that she was now, as she had always been, held in the loving grasp of God's grace and mercy. We all wept. She was buried with her brother on one side, an empty plot for my father on the other. After the funeral, Kindy hosted a gathering at her home. Everyone drank too much and told funny stories about her passing gas and the weird-looking stretch pants she wore that made her butt look so enormous and her complete inability to tell a joke well. They were good memories. Real ones.

THE SECOND EULOGY

On my flight back to New York the day after, I stared out the window at the Oklahoma terrain for as long as I could after takeoff. Its red dirt. That endless blue expanse above it. Those checkerboard stretches of wheat fields below. I had a powerful sense of floating between the heavens and the earth, between the divine and Oklahoma and all it meant to me. The truths and the lies it had taught me. And all the unresolved pain left hanging in that space between sky and dirt.

About a week after the funeral, back in my Union apartment, I pulled up the eulogy that the church had published online and began to write another version. A second eulogy.

I had been wrestling with the funeral, feeling like I'd somehow failed to speak the full truth about sin and grace, about mercy and justice. I recalled how I'd felt the summer I discovered that the hard verses in Woody Guthrie's song had been lopped off by Sunday school teachers who thought them too negative. I grappled with all the stories my family had never told about our past, huge pieces of violence cut out and forgotten. I couldn't leave her story with its own hard parts lopped off. I could feel in my bones that deep connection between justice and mercy. Until the truth of injustice is revealed, mercy has nothing to land on, to hold and mend.

That didn't mean I wanted to cut out any of the good parts. They were true. But between the lines was another story that needed telling, verses that needed adding, truths that were still tearing up my family with tornado force. I felt the need to do it for them, yes, but also for my mother's sake and for my own. The cosmos, I felt, needed to hear these truths so that both her good and bad parts could be named and together held in the grasp of God's mercy.

That morning, it was like a dam in me broke and that second eulogy came tumbling forth with torrential force.

When I finished, I sent it to my family with this cover email.

Dear Dad, Kindy, and Verity,

I've been reading over Mom's eulogy, and for my own sake, there were some things I needed to say that I didn't say at the funeral. So here it is. None of the good things are diminished. But the broken parts of her are named more honestly. I could have said more. But I wanted this version to still have the form of a "public eulogy." Read it if you want. Throw it away if you choose. Share it with your kids if you think you need to. I did it for the record of my own heart.

May we one day live in a world and a church where words such as these can actually be spoken out loud to all—and treasured. It affirms her and us all, ultimately.

My second eulogy was not as long as it could have been, or as telling. I pretended as if it were something I would actually preach in church, although I thought I never would, at least about my mother. But the form of an actual spoken eulogy stayed with me. It was written to be heard.

It's not hard to imagine all the good things I said. They are standard fare when a mother leaves the world of her children. But the other parts were more truthful—and ultimately merciful.

She grew up too fast as a child—really, she never had a childhood, nor was she mothered as she should have been. She was left alone to fight her way forward in a world where women were not yet allowed to fight, much less to unfold their wings and fly. She had to wait until she was forty for that, when she learned to actually fly. It was brilliant to watch her take to the skies, literally. But, even then, her flying itself was captive to her own unhealed wounds, and she finally could not escape them, and she sadly left it to our family to bear the heaviness of her wings.

She was too beautiful for her own good; people liked her too easily for her to learn what it meant to earn it, and because of that it was hard for her to trust what their "liking her" really meant. It also made it impossible for her to feel compassion for others who weren't, like her, beautiful. The privilege of her beauty stopped her from claiming the joy compassion brings.

There were mother-things she never taught her daughters to do: put on makeup, do our hair, shave our legs, go shopping for clothes, cook, clean. She hated these things. This failure may have to do with the fact that looking beautiful was so effortless for her, she wished it to be equally easy for us. But it wasn't. She was also probably relieved, in her vanity, that on this score, we couldn't compete. It may also have been that long before feminism was on the scene, our mother knew these things didn't matter because they mattered too much.

Those who knew her well, knew she wrestled with demons, including her brother Sam Jones's alcoholism and eventual suicide. She also wrestled with imaginary demons that existed only in her embittered mind. That's how she saw me, a demon daughter whose simple childhood needs were threats to the freedom she wanted so desperately but never had. Her torment of me stayed strong till the end.

Her mightiest demon, of course, was the one that drove her into an affair that she hid for years and then used as a weapon against us. To this day those of us who know about it can't get our minds around it, particularly her sustained lying and her lack of regret. Perhaps her lost childhood was what she sought to find in her affair? Perhaps only her late-in-life disease made her hurt us, again and again, with its telling? We are left not knowing.

All of this rests partly in the fact that our mother wasn't good at forgiveness, toward anyone, but especially forgiveness for her own flawed humanness. Was it because she worked so hard at appearing "perfectly loving" all day long that when she came home at night, she had little real love left for herself or her closest loves?

The most cursed thing of all is that she was struck down, too early in her life, by an affliction that twisted her up inside and outside, and the last years were nightmarish. PSP slowly pulled her into its shadowy cave, and it finally killed her, there, alone in its shadows. Each day, our father cared for her, fed her, tended to her, and experienced her meanness grow as the disease pulled her in. She did not go gently into that good night. Nor did she allow us to be "gently" beside her in those shadows.

But that's not the last word about her. I have one more word to add to this list of her sins and graces.

Our mother fancied herself the mystic in the family. As one friend said, she was a spiritual director before it was cool. Her bedroom and office were filled with prayer beads and poems by Emily Dickinson. She knitted prayer shawls for us girls, hoping we'd wear them and feel her praying for us. There were always candles burning, oils smelling, feathers, trinkets hanging, and sweet gospel music filling the sacred spaces she created wherever she went, her altars. She even became an oblate working with religious sisters in a nearby convent, seeking silent retreat and a life of contemplative prayer. Maybe seeking truth, too; something that had, before then, evaded her.

What did this mean in terms of her faith? Well, she was not an orderly theologian, that's for sure. She believed that spirits lived in the woods around the lake house, that our life-force energy never died, that angels were around us all the time and the dead sometimes speak to us, that some people had the gift of second sight, like herself. She believed that time itself was a cycle that circled back on itself, and that people had destinies and callings that were divinely planned, hers especially.

But as with all of us, believing her own most cherished beliefs was hard for her, and in the end, I don't know which of these beliefs managed to hold steady inside her. I do know that she stopped believing in mercy, either human or divine. Maybe she never fully accepted it because she never experienced solid, anchored love as a child. That hardness of her unforgiving soul left her frightened and furious to the end.

More than any place in the world, our mother loved our family cabin, a home she named Anchor Point. She wanted it to be a place where friends and family could experience safe harbor.

What that safe harbor meant was tables full of food, lots of laughter, dancing and singing, arguing politics, big ideas and any silly thing you could think to talk about, always with intensity and passion. Yes, we often all drank too much and, at times, fought too much to measure up to our "anchoring" name, but, in the end, the place itself seemed able to hold tenderly that part of our family, too. Our brokenness.

It also meant before dinner, saying prayers where everyone had to share what they were most thankful for and sing "Amen" with gusto. The singing was joyful, yes, but also, perhaps, it was a collective plea for forgiveness, for the sins and secrets we all carried, especially our mother.

Anchor Point also meant watching eagles perch on the lake house tree, beholding the sunset, brilliant and broad, and a night sky scattered with endless stars. But this part, too, is hard to fathom. Under that sky, for the first time in her life, our mother began to heal. With her hands in the soil, her deepest lifelong wounds began to mend. But just as the healing began, she became a desperate lover to the disease that would kill her. The same stars of Anchor Point were a witness to both.

I end with one more image of Anchor Point. I remember all of us Jones girls, on late summer afternoons, lying in the middle of that vast, vast Fort Gibson Lake, on big blue foam floaters, mindlessly chatting and dozing, the water holding us up, rocking us, the sun warming our skin. As we floated there, each of us would hold on to a ski rope that, strung out across the water's surface, kept us tethered to the boat, where my dad would sit, in the shade, listening to the mayhem of our chatter and laughter.

On April 2, 2016, at around 9:00 a.m., her hand still clenched, struggling to hold on to that rope, our mother took her last breath and was finally pulled free from that tether to this life.

Buoyed now by the grace of God, she is at rest, dozing, and yes, healed, an eagle circling overhead, waves of love rocking her, gently, amidst the endless blue of sky and water.

As I wrote those last words, for the first time in my life with her I felt the grip of my own anger start to lessen its hold on me and my aspirations for a theological life. I felt mercy. Mercy toward her, toward my family, myself, and mercy toward all the cruel lies and divisions that damage and define our culture. It was a vast, all-encompassing experience of compassion for my mother, my people, all people, all life, and the universe.

It was then I remembered it. Something always there but never really seen.

On a plank of old driftwood nailed to an aging scrub oak tree outside the cabin, she had burned the words ANCHOR POINT. The whole thing looked awkward, crosslike.

Why this name? So others could find safety there? No, it was what she herself was looking for. An anchor that could hold her existence steady when nothing else inside her was able to provide enough weight. Lacking that, she had desperately tied herself to the impermanent pleasures of status, grudges, beauty, imaginary lists, strange gods, lake houses, and the power of secrets.

Could it be that by naming that sacred place Anchor Point, she at least glimpsed the very thing she never allowed herself to receive?

Perhaps it should have simply said Mercy Point. That truth she sought and thought she'd lost, although it never lost her. The immovable, unearned, and never relinquished love of God.

In the Hebrew Bible, it is written that above the Ark of the Covenant, there is a throne formed by the wide-spread wings of two cherubim who stand facing each other, on each side. A golden shield covers it. According to scripture, upon this throne sits God, Yahweh, the ultimate judge of all that is. God, hidden but present, meets humanity. On the Day of Atonement, it is written that the high priest approaches the throne and sprinkles upon the golden shield blood from a sacrificed animal. In that blood, humanity is brought before God, and all of history's brokenness and sin is revealed. Then, from the throne of God almighty, divine mercy is bestowed.

It's a powerful ritual image, apocalyptic in its magnitude and furious wonder. And like so many of our most sacred rituals, its truth has been twisted over time, its symbolism distorted to fit our desires. But, oddly, American rock music has redeemed the image for me. Nick Cave, and later Johnny Cash in a cover, provided me with a song, "The Mercy Seat," that I think I listen to more than any other. Whenever I play it, I think of my mother, of America, of Jesus, of all that is merciful and unmerciful, hated and forgiven.

I grieve that my mother never managed to stop playing the punishment game. She carried it with her to the grave. Never knowing the full pleasures of a merciful life and of God's mercy. As for me, I catch glimpses of that mercy in my gently growing compassion for the woman who raised me, hurt me, and in her own contorted way, tried to love me. I also catch sight of the true mercy seat at Union, in those moments when the most zealous social justice activists realize that without mercy, justice is lifeless. Practicing compassion is a harder task, in fact, than our ostensible quest to right the scales of life. Justice follows mercy's lead. I exacted justice on my mother with my second eulogy and mercy grew out of it. I went into it thinking I was going to condemn her; I ended up feeling mercy for her and for myself—and, as it tends to happen, for this planet and its people. Mercy, forgiveness, grace—all these theological concepts become habits. The habit of theology, I believe, is what our world most lacks today.

CHAPTER 13

Love

> I could say grace was a woman with time on her hands, or
> a white buffalo escaped from memory. But in that dingy
> light it was the promise of balance. We once again under-
> stood the talk of animals, and spring was lean and hungry
> with the hope of children and corn.
>
> JOY HARJO, "GRACE"

Forgiveness is the pivot that moves you from sin toward grace; it's that turn of the heart that requires you to face harms, transgressions, and hurts and allows you to move forward to grace. Mercy is the whole process of becoming permanently forgiving, of living in a mode of divine knowing and presence. Sometimes, unfortunately, life moves us the other way, pivoting us away from grace and leaving us standing bereft in the desolate land of sin.

My father, at age eighty, learned this hard truth the day he heard of my mother's infidelity. He forgave her for her lie and never felt she should be punished for it or willed her any harm. He forgave her because he lived with the constant knowledge of mercy. He knew she was a haunted woman. But he could not reconcile what she had done to him with his larger vision of God and the ultimate meaning of human life. It was as if her betrayal threw a huge boulder into the middle of his core belief system, shattering his sense of the divine and all the theological truths he thought he held. He lost hope; he felt despair with a depth and anguish he had never experienced in all his years of faithful living.

Watching this happen to him reminded me of the trauma patients I have worked with as a pastor. When a person's world is violently exploded by an event that exceeds his or her capacity to make sense of it—usually because it doesn't make sense or couldn't have been foreseen or stopped—ordinary thought processes freeze up. Everything stops making sense. We suddenly feel powerless, disconnected from others, and easily startled by or afraid of the next anticipated blow. It's a hellish place to be stuck. I also know from my pastoral work on trauma—and from my own life—that the only way forward, if one is lucky enough to find it, is a painfully slow process. One must piece one's world back together in such a way that the trauma is named and included in the reconstruction of your life story.

There's a theological word for this process that I've found more apt for my father's experience than forgiveness, or even mercy, because mercy comes regardless of actual healing. The word is "reconciliation," which names the process of bringing together things that are in opposition so that they somehow align with each other. And reconciliation requires, I believe, a new vision of love, one that Luce Irigaray proposes in her difficult but groundbreaking book *The Way of Love*. In fact, Irigaray imagines an entirely new form of loving based on a simple turn of phrase. "I love you" becomes "I love to you." My father would have to learn to let go of my mother, reconcile with her failings and transgressions, and stop loving her and instead send his love to her. Perhaps an impossible task.

Irigaray wrote:

> "I love to you" is more unusual than "I love you," but respects
> the two more: I love to who you are, to what you do, without
> reducing you to an object of my love.

This premise, the de-objectification of every human being, even
the romantically beloved, turns into a divine beholding of one another
and of life. We share this air, this planet, this life and cherish one another for the sharing. This, as I would come to see it as I helped my father
see it, was as much a political statement as a romantic one.

For a long time, my sisters and I feared such a reconciliation of
love—in part emotional, psychological, and theological—was beyond
our father's reach. While she was still alive, my mother pounded him
into the ground with the details of her infidelity. She never let up. Over
and over again, she told him their love was a lie, she had never loved
him, she wished she had married Burt, how Burt was so much more of
a man than him, and that her whole life with him had been miserable.
She constantly pointed out flaws of his we knew were true; he could be
overly opinionated and argumentative, extremely bossy, and easily angered when challenged or ignored.

But she also made up flaws that were flat-out lies: that he had had
many affairs (he hadn't), that he never loved her (he did), that it was
his fault she was sick (impossible), and that he was happy she was dying
so he could be with other women (unimaginable). He became the scape-
goat for every ounce of rage stored up inside her, and it flowed out of
her toward him with a fury I had never before witnessed in anyone.
Those gross scenes from *The Exorcist* come to mind. She spewed hatred.

We all knew that the PSP was warping her mind, but it was still
hard not to feel her attacks were calculated to hurt him, or even to

destroy him. To my father's credit, he visited her and cared for her every day during those last terrible months. He rarely talked about what was happening to her and to him, at least until she died.

He waited until then to fall apart.

The way he unraveled was so utterly in keeping with his style. He didn't cry, at least not much. He didn't rant and rave or throw things. He just talked . . . a lot. His ever-churning mind, usually spent parsing out the meaning of the universe, began instinctually searching for an underlying reason for her betrayal. He tried to philosophize himself through it; problem-solve it; calculate its probable causes and effects. He racked his brain for answers, coming up with one theory after another, all of them aimed at bringing order to the cosmic disorder he felt. He blamed her. He blamed himself. He blamed her parents; her brother, Sam; our promiscuous culture; the church; the disease. But no theory ever held for long, and he inevitably returned to the same litany of possible reasons, always arriving at the same failed ending.

Most of the time, my sisters and I listened patiently to his repeating list of whys. And we made sure he got counseling, which helped a little. But it couldn't address his intellectual bewilderment and, most painfully, his loneliness. When he looked over at her empty chair in the living room where they had watched the nightly news together, he found no peace in remembering her lovingly. All he saw was viciousness and hurt.

From the outside, it is impossible to know the intricacies of any couple's relationship. I'm sure there was much about their life together that I didn't know and never will or want to. What I did know was that the man who had been the anchor point for my life became unmoored and traumatized.

And the most gut-wrenching part of his suffering was his complete inability to find solace or meaning in that sturdy sin-forgiveness-grace theology he had always lived and taught us to live. He had taught me the trick, really, beginning that day on the street corner when the spittle of those racist men sprayed across us. We are saints and sinners, flawed and graced, the extremes always mingling in us, one asserting only for the other to fight back. He had taught me to accept that tension, but, more important, he had taught me to forgive perpetually, both myself and others. He had taught me the life of mercy, the way to it, the satisfaction of it. After the McVeigh years, I realized he had been trying to teach me this lesson not just so I could step back and forth from sin to grace, but so I would not get stuck in my mother's own static existence.

And along the way, I had depended not so much on his certainty as his assuredness. He did not preach certainty, nor did he ever once tell me he was certain about any theological tenet, let alone the existence of God. Assuredness, as I understand it, is a state of mind marked by trust and confidence in what you know, even when it cannot be factually proven. Certainty, in contrast, is anchored in the proven and the factual. The difference in real life—life alongside this man—was even more revealing. Certainty would have made him unapproachable, superior; assuredness made him wholly accessible. Certainty would have made him intellectually rigid; assuredness kept him honest and agile. Certainty would have closed his mind; assuredness gave him the confidence needed for openness.

But now my sisters and I found him both uncertain and unassured. What he had known and believed to be true had been obliterated by that supposed truth itself; his manner—all his assuredness—went out the window with it.

I sat on my family's old leather couch the Thanksgiving following my mother's death and tried to describe to him the lecture on "Revolutionary Love" I had just delivered as president of the American Academy of Religion. Much of its argument came from ideas in Baldwin's *The Fire Next Time* and Irigaray's *The Way of Love*. I'd worked hard on it, and it was a big deal to have shared it with thousands of theologians and religion scholars. My younger dad would have been eager to hear about it, proud of my accomplishment and ready to argue the lecture's finer points. You'd feel the electric buzz of theology run through him once he got started. But I soon realized that he wasn't hearing a word I said. He just stared out the window.

"I just don't know why she lied to me for so long," he said when I finally stopped talking. Implicit in his evading a direct comment on my speech was his recognition that I was trying to engage him and maybe even edify him; implicit in his statement was a rejection of engagement or edification of any theological sort.

Later that day, I asked him bluntly if he still believed in God. I was trying to spark something in him, anything really, and I'd decided it required asking a question I didn't really want to hear the answer to. But the answer, if you could call it that, came anyway.

"Honey, I just don't have the energy to think about that. When I try to, nothing comes." He couldn't even bring himself to say the words "God" or "believe." Just "that."

How could the assuredness of belief in the divine succumb in one fell swoop to utter theological lethargy?

On the phone a few weeks later, I told him that even if he couldn't think about God anymore, I knew God loved him, and that I would believe for him. It sounded hokey, but I meant it. "Dad, you always told us that faith is a community thing, and when people go through periods of crushing doubt, they can be carried along by the faith of people whose assurance is strong."

"I guess I did say that. Well, if you want to do that for me, that's nice. I appreciate your concern," he responded woodenly.

I was crestfallen. How could this man who had so long walked in grace grow so suddenly cold to any notion of the divine or grace or the power of community and love?

THE WAY FORWARD

I called my sisters often during this period. They were struggling, too, with his complete disinterest in his whole life's work. We began to see a pattern emerging among all of us: Our mother's betrayal had triggered his crumbling theology; his crisis, in turn, was triggering our own questioning of faith; we depended on him as much as he had on her. The whole social network—our little family community—that held faith together was falling apart. It reminded me of what I already knew, namely that faith is a social act and lives inside our social webs of meaning. Far from the monastic vision of saints beholding God in a cave or alone on a hilltop, faith is about both God and community. Belief lives in the in-between space of our relationships, our connective tissue. When that tissue tears, the whole group feels the rip.

This was true even for the small community of two that made up my parents' relationship. For my dad, his faith didn't necessarily grow out of his relationship with his wife, but it surreptitiously depended on it. She ordered his earthly life—her beauty consoled him; her social graciousness made his hardheaded intellect easier for others to manage; her apparent patience with his intensity calmed him. So the leap from the earthly to the divine was easier for him because of her: she was like a step stool to the heavens, always under his feet.

She was also more than that. I had begun to see what I had missed all these years. My father's seemingly bold imagination had early on in his life been captivated by and held captive by his adoration of my mother. She so suffused it, conquered it, dominated it that his imagination of her fed his theological imagination more than he himself could admit. His consuming desire for my mother had seeped into his own love for God, my father's own earthly desires entangled with divine ones.

As a theologian, I have read countless male theologians over the years who, when they describe their love of God, sound more like swooning schoolkids than rational adults. I have also seen, on the flip side, how many of our Western images of God's love for humanity looks more like an obsessive male lover seeking to control and consume his beloved than it does a divine, unselfish power for good. My father wasn't exactly like that; before their final meltdown, my mother and father's relationship wasn't abusive. And the God he'd taught me to believe in wasn't, either. But the overlapping of divine and human desires in his theological imagination was indisputable, particularly now that he'd lost it. That this beautiful woman loved him helped him to believe that God loved him, too. And, in turn, his love for my mother helped him grasp the quality of his own desire for the divine.

So when my mother's aggressive admissions brought him to his knees, he no longer could even reach back up for God.

Sin rolls that way—it seeps into a person then spreads, bacteria-like, to the people in our webs of relationships. My mother's inability to overcome her anger and deceit kept her sin's contagion festering among us. It was really only a matter of time before it knocked out all our knees, especially since our knight of faith had dissolved into a trembling puddle of doubts. We were no different from him in our need for his faith to keep the in-betweenness of our own beliefs going.

"You can't do this to us!" I remember shouting at him the Christmas following that awful Thanksgiving, after I'd failed miserably to convince him to attend church on Christmas Eve. I couldn't miss the painful irony that here I was trying to get him to go to church instead of him, as he had for years, checking to see whether I made regular time for worship.

He looked at me, confused. "I'm not doing anything to you," he said, unaffected.

"You're hurting us."

He looked even more baffled. I felt a sudden shot of guilt inside.

How could I be blaming an eighty-year-old man for feeling weak, hurt, uninspired? It was my turn, wasn't it, in the relative prime of adulthood, to make the transition from daughter to leader? It was our turn, my sisters and I, at last to take his lessons apart from him, to live as he lived but not to need him to live that way, wasn't it?

"Serene, I'm not trying to hurt you at all. I just can't make sense of this in my mind," he said. "After all these years I thought your mother and I had one kind of relationship and she was living another kind of life. I just can't reconcile that with what I thought was true."

A full year out from her confession, he had stopped churning out reasons for her betrayal. He had also stopped writing and reading theology. Or any books, really. He stopped seeing friends. He withdrew from his church and dropped out of conversations with the former theology students and colleagues he'd stay in touch with over the years.

His life slowly became graceless. That was the most extraordinary thing to me: the utter and total absence of grace in his life.

It's no secret. There are traumas too great to overcome. Breaches of trust too deep and profound to ever be reconciled. At least by us mortals.

That's when the trick he taught me as a child kicked in, almost reflexively. He had lost God. Yes. But I knew—I felt it in the marrow of my bones—God had not lost him.

Now close to three years after her death, my father talks less and less about my mother, and he occasionally admits that he misses the theological passion he once held. At least that's a start. I've stopped trying to spark it in him, finally realizing that it was more about my need for his faith than his own.

But amidst his faith's lingering fog, other strong signs of life are stirring. He has started going online to write penetrating reflections on the implosion of American democracy as he sees it. His theological story may have been lopped off at the knees, but he is "damn sure" not going to lose his political theology, he said, and his passionate love for America and the promises he believed it once held.

When I read his essays, I am often reminded of the populism that ran through my Okie grandparents' faith. Their fierce critique of unworthy authorities is vividly alive in his words. He has harsh words for our nation's failed leaders. He writes a lot about the spiritual vacuity of current-day America, where personal greed and communal hatred seem to have been painted over values like neighbor love and the public good.

But more than these critiques, I'm moved and inspired by the image of America his writings conjure up. Like his Disciples forebears, his America is a vast nation of people, ordinary folks, Democrats, Republicans, and everyone else, struggling to make healthy lives for their families—scrappy, endlessly different, and basically good-willed, if not a bit misguided, like we all are. (He always adds this little "sin" reminder, lest anyone comes off looking too pure or perfect.)

We also have more honest conversations about our own little piece of America, our family history, especially the formerly lopped-off parts. When I recently uncovered the full story of the lynching of Laura Nelson and her son in Okemah in 1911, I asked him if he wanted to hear it. He nodded and began to listen with his head in hands.

"They hanged this young mother, Laura, and her child from that bridge where Grandpa used to go fishing," I told him. "I found a postcard from back then that shows the whole town of Okemah photographed on that bridge above their murdered bodies, everyone smiling for the camera like it's the Fourth of July."

I pulled out the now faded postcard to show him. He held it for a moment and then gave it back to me, as if its horror might rub off on him if he held it longer.

I kept going.

"Dad, Woody Guthrie's dad helped rally the lynching mob. I find it impossible to imagine that Grandpa's dad and maybe even Grandpa, as a young kid, weren't up there on that bridge. You can see there are women holding babies in one arm, waving at the camera with the other. Kids everywhere. I can even imagine your own grandpa in that murderous lynch mob, dragging Laura and her son through town, all self-righteous and drunk with violence, pretending like what they were doing was God's will."

There was more I could have told him, but I stopped.

"You're probably right, Serene. God, it's awful. My own family." He curled over in his seat for a second.

He looked up. "You know, my father never admitted he was Cherokee until he figured out a way to make money off it. We're no better than the worst of them."

"I know. This is where we come from." I almost choked on my words.

He finally sat up straight in his maroon La-Z-Boy recliner and something clicked, his eyes regaining that familiar political fury. "Yes, it is."

He said, "In the 1930s in Oklahoma, you couldn't find any Southern Baptist worth his salt who didn't believe in our collective right to education, work, shelter, food, and health. What the hell has happened to them?"

This spring, Union's beloved professor James Hal Cone passed away after fifty years of teaching and living on Union's campus. He and my father were the same age. No one ever called Cone an easy person, but at his memorial service, the theological love that he cultivated in generations of students flowed out through the crowd of thousands gathered in Riverside Church. Capturing that energy, the students made signs saying REST IN POWER, DR. CONE. REST IN POWER. The energy in the church felt like a force of nature. Powerful, questing, demanding love.

He will be forever known as the father of black liberation theology because of his theological writings and teachings and his own deep theological commitment to spiritually and politically empowering victims around the world. He also inspired black liberation by lifting up the hope embedded in the often-silenced faith of the oppressed. He saw with an eagle's eye the truth that even in the midst of horrendous evil, love insinuates its way forward in ways strong and resilient, never defeated.

In his book *The Cross and the Lynching Tree*, he tells the story of his parents' Christian faith and how when they imagined Jesus hanging on the cross, they saw alongside him the thousands of lynched black bodies that had hanged on trees in their own communities. By my calculation, they were born and made their impoverished path forward in Arkansas around the same time Dick and Idabel were born in Oklahoma, setting Dick on a path that put the lynching rope in his community's hands and a wealthy judge's gavel in his own. For Cone, the identification of Jesus's cross with the violence of white supremacy gave his community courage. If Jesus underwent their plight, then God really understood their suffering at the hands of hateful power and God was with them, loving them even as they stood in that place of evil and death. And from that faith unfurled bonds of love that sustained and empowered the generations that followed.

Cone thought, as did (and perhaps will again) my father, that theology actually matters to people, as we struggle to move our individual and national lives forward. Theology helps us capture those rare glimpses of truths that make a world of difference if we grasp them. How do we say no to evil if we do not believe in the possibility, indeed the reality, of good? How do we resist the corrupting power of greed if we have no spiritual sense that generosity and justice are ultimately more important? How do we conquer hate if we have no love? Or capacity for mercy? How do we learn to breathe together if we don't accept the connecting power of breath and spirit that flows in and through us? How do we ask for or receive forgiveness if we have no sense of sin? How do we know grace if our imaginations have rendered our world graceless?

Cone's thinking, I realized, related to Irigaray's idea of learning to love beyond love. Irigaray's fundamental concern in *The Way of Love* is the difference between subject-object relationships and subject-subject relationships. Our current languages and cultures, especially those of the West, are subject-object oriented. So, too, was my father's relationship with my mother. She was his object; everything and everyone, including my father, were her objects. Neither of them achieved a theology beyond the visible, the patterned nature of human relationships and sight. Frankly, though, I can't say I know anyone who has. It's a vision our world has yet to grasp, yet grasp for it we must. In Irigaray's estimation, our present languages are riddled with masculine forms that prefer the naming and taming of the other. It turns the other into a project, a thing—even God or the divine. In Cone's theology, that othering is what white people do to black people, horrifying sin of our nation's own despicable making.

GOD IS LOVE

One of my father's favorite quotes to describe God came from Karl Barth. I can't say I have it memorized, but when I read it I can almost close my eyes and hear my father say it:

> God, the pure limit and pure beginning of all that we are, have, and do, standing over in infinite qualitative difference to us and all that is human, nowhere and never identical with that which we call God, experience, surmise, and pray to as God, the unconditioned Halt as opposed to all human rest, the yes in our no and the no in our yes, the first and last and as such

unknown, but nowhere and never a magnitude amongst others
in the medium known to us . . . that is the living God.

In 2018, on a hot July afternoon in New York City, I called my father
and read that quote from Barth again. And then I took the gamble of
having one last conversation with him before putting the final period
of this book in place. I got straight to the point.

"Dad, do you still not believe in God? It's kind of a downer way
to end my book," I joked, trying to cajole some humorous insight out
of him.

His immediate seriousness surprised me.

"Serene, it's not that I don't have any faith; it's just that I've put
thinking about it aside for a while. You know, I spent my whole life
thinking about God." Like he was telling me something I didn't know?
Thank God he couldn't see my eyes roll.

"So when you put the thinking aside, what's left?" I pushed him.

"There's no getting around politics. You know that. As for formal
theology, it's just not on the surface of my mind anymore." I could tell
my question was tiring him.

"So what can you say?" I gave it another shot.

He coughed a couple of times as he thought.

"We find our ultimate destiny in God, daughter dear. I still know
that." What an unusual soul he was, that he would answer me this way.

"Would you call that ultimate destiny love?" I wondered what he'd
think when he saw in this book how close I had come, time and again,
to saying God is love. Or mercy. Or justice. Or breath. I'd come so
close, I'd remind him, but not quite.

"Well, yes, God is love, but not love as we know it. God's love is
God's." I grimaced at his mention of "love as we know it," immediately
thinking of his love betrayed.

I quickly pushed him again. "How's that different from saying, let's see, 'God's love is the biggest love ever'? Bigger than any love we ever experience. Does that work?"

"Not quite. 'Biggest,' as an adjective, still suggests that God's love can be defined by human metrics of size and shape. It also suggests God is an entity that has attributes, like people do. But God isn't one more person or entity among others. God is God. Existing beyond all the words and ideas we pile on God—even beyond the word 'existing.' Look at all the different images and theories of God we've conjured up over time. These Gods always look like us, whoever we may be. It's horrible to see wrongs perpetrated by people who project their own image onto God—and turn themselves into mini-gods in the process. Even the good ones. And come on, Serene, honestly, we don't even fully know ourselves. Most of the time, we are utter fools. Products of the lies of our upbringing. I'm living proof of those lies! How can we, fools that we are, pretend to know ultimate reality?" He stopped to catch his breath.

I thought of the medieval theologian Thomas Aquinas's rumored last words, after years of writing theology, that it was "all straw."

"So do you think we can't know anything about God's love?" His estimation of my book was shriveling up in my mind as I listened.

He paused.

"No. We can say one thing. God comes to us, even though we can't reach God."

"And?" I waited.

"That's love. It's all we can say. We can only call it love."

Then he stopped and let out a long Jones sigh, as if to say it was now time to rest.

In his sigh, I heard echoes of Idabel's sigh, under the cool shade of the wagon. And my own daughter's sighs, as her body fell into restful sleep. The sigh of humanity, of confusion, of surrender, of grace, of a person relieved to have her burdens lifted by a reality beyond reality and yet as close as the breath we breathe. Love has become a trifling word, but it still, as a theological concept, has the power to redeem if we can grasp that it exists within and yet comes from beyond desire, language, need, and want. That is the simple reason, really, why we call that love "grace."

ACKNOWLEDGMENTS

I am thankful for the insight and expertise of Greg Jordan, who worked with me on this book from start to finish. To have a writing partner who really gets it is uncommon. I especially appreciate the patient support of Viking's president and my editor, Brian Tart, and my literary agent, Gloria Loomis, who saw potential before I did.

I am also grateful for my colleagues, friends, and students at Union Theological Seminary who supported this book and patiently abided my periodic absence. The Union community gives me the verve it takes to keep theology honest and politics real. I wrote this book for Union—my home and my constant inspiration.

I write about the Christian Church (Disciples of Christ) churches I grew up in, the denomination of which I am still a proud member. I stand on the shoulders of generations of these folks. I draw strength from enduring connections to the faculty and students of Tamil Nadu Theological Seminary in Madurai, South India. This book tells the story of the bombing of the Murrah Building in Oklahoma City; to the people of that big plains town, I am awed by your resilience and hope. I am moved by the witness of those who held vigil outside the Terre Haute prison where Timothy McVeigh was killed by lethal injection, and for many others who continue working to end the death penalty and the death march of mass incarceration and mass deportation.

Early in this book it was easy to name the handful of "great men" theologians who influenced my younger years because I was not yet exposed to the remarkable power of the theologians who now fill my life and my bookshelves with their theological truth telling. The Constructive Theology Workgroup traveled with me as some of these stories unfolded. There is a long list of womanist, feminist, black, mujerista, Latinx, queer, trans, socialist, anti-imperialist, environmentalist, disability rights activist, anti-racist, liberationist, and just downright wise and courageous theologians whose brilliant works are changing the landscape of theology. This book only scratches the surface of their growing, voluminous power. I also have learned from and been humbled by colleagues who are humanist, atheist, agnostic, spiritual, and also Buddhist, Muslim, Jewish, Hindu, and indigenous religionist. This book is not nearly as interreligiously engaged and as knowledgeable as I, as a Christian, am struggling to become. Maybe that's the next book.

As I was finishing this book, I learned that the story of Laura and L. D. Nelson, who were lynched in Okemah, Oklahoma, on May 24, 1911, is told in full (or as fully as can be known) at the Legacy Museum and the National Memorial for Peace and Justice in Montgomery, Alabama, along with the stories of four thousand victims of lynching. For this important monument to the terror and truth of our nation's white supremacist past and its continued presence, I am grateful for the work of Brian Stevenson and others, and I am deeply heartened by the future it opens to us through its honesty about this country's catastrophic history.

I am grateful beyond measure to Fred Davie and Kelly Brown Douglas, who were always ready to read these pages and who kept me going, especially when I was writing about hard, tough truths. They embody the grace of friendship—sustaining, joyful, and strong. Elizabeth Dillion, Farah Griffin, Joanne Silver, Erika Schwartz, and Betty Sue Flowers kept my body/mind/heart/breath in some semblance of balance, which kept me healthy and writing. My gratitude also goes to Krista Tippett, loving friend, side-by-side writing companion, and, most important, an Okie girlfriend. I am thankful, too, for Bill Moyers, another fellow Okie, and for Judith Moyers, for their always encouraging support of me, this book, and Union. Michelle Alexander, my greatly admired friend/writer/activist inspired me throughout my writing and even read this book while it was in progress.

As for my immediate Jones family, not only did they give me permission to spill the beautiful and awful truths of our family history all over the pages of this book, they actively supported me in doing so. They also read it and, even then, still delighted in it! I'm thankful to Shepard Parsons and Karen Klein for their kind *yes* to the book. My mother, Sarah Jane Jones, would have also appreciated these pages, I think, if she were still living, not just despite but because of the difficult stories it tells about her. My wild, indomitable sisters, Kindanne Carole Jones and Verity Augusta Jones, and my cousin, Krista Marie Jones, are the pillars of strength upon which this book stands. Not only did we live through these stories together, we held each other up through them more than once. My daughter, Charis—whose name means "grace"—is the light that keeps shining. She is the joy that fuels it all. I am also grateful to Gary Zarr, my writing companion who, among many things, kept me from falling into sugary platitudes about faith. He is grace to me. Without this close circle of my family, my own search for meaning in a fractured world would have been a lonely, unproductive chore. We are more of each other than we are of ourselves. That said, each one of them would tell these stories differently and probably better. This version, flaws and all, is mine alone.

My greatest debt of gratitude goes to my father, Joe Robert Jones, who continues to inspire me every day. Without his lifelong passion for teaching and writing theology, his social conscience and activism, his moral courage, his brilliant mind, and his abiding love for his three "daughters dear," this book on grace quite simply would not be.

BIBLIOGRAPHY

A Reader's Guide

For readers who found the theologians referenced in this book compelling, please read them yourself. They may change your life, as they did mine. I offer this list not as a full bibliography of the book, but as a general guide to aid your own reading and reflection.

James Baldwin, *The Fire Next Time* (New York: Vintage, 1992).

Karl Barth, *The Epistle to the Romans* (Oxford: Oxford University Press, 1968).

Karl Barth's *Church Dogmatics* consists of fourteen volumes published from 1932 to 1967. See especially, *Volume II. 1: The Doctrine of God* (London: T & T Clark, 1980), and *Volume IV. 1–3: The Doctrine of Reconciliation* (London: T & T Clark, 1961, 1967, 1968).

Dietrich Bonhoeffer, *The Cost of Discipleship* (London: SCM Press, 2011).

John Calvin, *Institutes of the Christian Religion*, edited by John T. McNeill, translated by Ford Lewis Battles (Louisville, KY: Westminster John Knox Press, 1960).

Katie Geneva Cannon, *Katie's Canon: Womanism and the Soul of the Black Community* (London: Continuum International Publishing Group, 1996).

James Cone, *The Cross and the Lynching Tree* (Maryknoll, NY: Orbis Books, 2011).

Kelly Brown Douglas, *Stand Your Ground: Black Bodies and the Justice of God* (Maryknoll, NY: Orbis Books, 2015).

Woody Guthrie, *Bound for Glory: The Hard-Driving, Truth-Telling Autobiography of America's Great Poet-Folk Singer* (New York: Plume, 1983).

Gustavo Gutiérrez, *A Theology of Liberation: History, Politics, and Salvation*, translated by Caridad Inda and John Eagleson (Maryknoll, NY: Orbis Books, 1988).

Robert T. Handy, *A History of Union Theological Seminary in New York* (New York: Columbia University Press, 2012).

Joy Harjo, *How We Became Human: New and Selected Poems 1975–2002* (New York: W. W. Norton and Company, 2002).

Luce Irigaray, *The Way of Love* (London: Continuum, 2002).

Luce Irigaray, *Speculum of the Other Woman*, translated by Gillian C. Gill (Ithaca, NY: Cornell University Press, 1985).

Joe R. Jones, *A Grammar of Christian Faith: Systematic Explorations in Christian Life and Doctrine* (Lanham, MD: Rowman and Littlefield Publishers, 2002).

Søren Kierkegaard, *The Sickness Unto Death: A Christian Psychological Exposition of Upbuilding and Awakening,* translated and edited by Howard V. Hong and Edna H. Hong (Princeton, NJ: Princeton University Press, 2013).

Toni Morrison, *Sula* (New York: Knopf, 1976).

Toni Morrison, *Paradise* (New York: Vintage International, 2014).

Reinhold Niebuhr, *The Children of Light and the Children of Darkness: A Vindication of Democracy and a Critique of Its Traditional Defense* (Chicago: University of Chicago Press, 2011).

Dorothee Soelle, *Suffering* (Minneapolis, MN: Fortress Press, 1984).

St. John of the Cross, *Dark Night of the Soul,* translated by E. Allison Peers (Radford, VA: Dover Publications, 2012).

St. Teresa of Ávila, *The Way of Perfection,* translated by Kieran Kavanaugh (Washington, DC: ICS Publications, 2000).

Howard Thurman, *Essential Writings* (Maryknoll, NY: Orbis Books, 2006).

Paul Tillich, *The Courage to Be* (New York: Yale University Press, 1963).